Gender and Lifelong Learning

Lifelong learning is a key feature of the educational landscape today. This important book breaks new ground in examining issues of gender in relation to lifelong learning. Drawing on policy analysis and research in the UK, European and global arenas, *Gender and Lifelong Learning* demonstrates the ways in which patterns of access to, participation in, and outcomes of lifelong learning reflect gender divisions and power relations.

The scope of the book is wide-ranging. Divided into three parts, the discussion encompasses school, adult, community, further and higher education. The issues covered include gendered subject 'choices', reasons for non-participation and pedagogies of lifelong learning. There are also fascinating chapters that explore the widening of participation, the experiences of disabled students, and the visibility/invisibility of black women in higher education. Utilising many different theoretical and methodological approaches, the book offers a range of critical feminist engagements to make visible, understand and critique gender inequalities in lifelong learning.

A key theme throughout the book is a critique of neo-liberalism and of the dominance of economic rationales in shaping the concept of lifelong learning. Yet the book offers not only criticism of current policies and practices, but also alternative visions, different possibilities and new ways of conceptualising and doing lifelong learning that might better reflect social justice concerns. It also includes many ideas and suggestions that can be practically drawn upon, and the concluding chapter ends with a summary of key implications for both policy-makers and practitioners.

Carole Leathwood is Reader in Education at the Institute for Policy Studies in Education, London Metropolitan University.

Becky Francis is Professor of Education at Roehampton University.

Gender and Lifelong Learning

Critical feminist engagements

Edited by
Carole Leathwood and
Becky Francis

LONDON AND NEW YORK

First published 2006 by Routledge
2 Park Square, Milton Park, Abingdon, Oxon, OX14 4RN

Simultaneously published in the USA and Canada
by Taylor & Francis Inc
270 Madison Ave, New York NY 10016

*Routledge is an imprint of the Taylor & Francis Group, an informa
business*

Transferred to Digital Printing 2007

Typeset in Bembo by RefineCatch Limited, Bungay, Suffolk

British Library Cataloguing in Publication Data
A catalogue record for this book is available from the British Library

Library of Congress Cataloging-in-Publication Data
Leathwood, Carole.
Gender and lifelong learning : critical feminist engagements /
Carole Leathwood and Becky Francis.
p. cm.
1. Sex differences in education—Great Britain. 2. Adult education—
Great Britain. 3. Feminism and education. I. Francis, Becky. II. Title.
LC212.93.G7L43 2006
374.0082—dc22
2006006452

ISBN10: 0–415–37484–7 (hbk)
ISBN10: 0–415–37485–5 (pbk)
ISBN10: 0–203–96953–7 (ebk)

ISBN13: 978–0–415–37484–2 (hbk)
ISBN13: 978–0–415–37485–9 (pbk)
ISBN13: 978–0–203–96953–3 (ebk)

Contents

List of illustrations

Figures

Tables

Contributors

Louise Archer is Reader in Education Policy in the Department of Education and Professional Studies, King's College London. Her research interests centre around identities and inequalities of 'race', gender and social class in relation to compulsory and post-compulsory education. She is the author of *Race, Masculinity and Schooling: Muslim Boys and Education* (2003, Open University Press) and is co-author of *Higher Education and Social Class: Issues of Exclusion and Inclusion* (2003, Routledge). She is currently completing a book with Becky Francis on *Understanding Minority Ethnic Achievement* (forthcoming, Routledge).

Jill Blackmore is Professor of Education in the Faculty of Education, Deakin University, Australia. Her research interests include feminist approaches to globalisation and education policy, administrative and organisational theory, educational leadership and reform, organisational change and innovation, teachers' and academics' work, and all their policy implications. Previous publications are *Troubling Women: Feminism, Leadership and Educational Change* (1999, Open University Press). Her forthcoming book with Judyth Sachs is *Performing and Reforming Leaders: Gender, Educational Restructuring and Organisational Change* (SUNY).

Jacky Brine is Professor of Education at the University of the West of England, Bristol, where she is Director of the Lifelong Learning Research Group. She has published widely in journals on the broad theme of EU education, training and related social policy where she focuses primarily on analysis of gender and social class. She is the author of two monographs: *Under-educating Women: Globalising Inequality* (1999, Open University Press) and *The European Social Fund and the EU: Flexibility, Growth, Stability* (2002, Continuum). More recently, her published work also includes, within the context of lifelong learning and policy, a focus on the relationship between compulsory and post-compulsory learning.

Penny Jane Burke is Senior Lecturer in Education in the School of Educational Foundations and Policy Studies. She is the course leader of the MA in Higher and Professional Education and the Programme Director of the Graduate Diploma in Professional Studies. As a sociologist of gender and education, she is currently directing an ESRC-funded research project on masculinities and widening educational participation. This project aims to contribute to sociological understandings of how different formations of masculinity impact on educational access, participation and experience in the wider context of changing policies and practices of widening participation. Her publications include *Accessing Education: Effectively Widening Participation* (2002, Trentham Books) and she is currently writing *Reconceptualizing Lifelong Learning*, to be co-authored with Sue Jackson and published by Routledge.

Helen Colley is Senior Research Fellow at the Education and Social Research Institute, Manchester Metropolitan University, and a Fellow of the National Institute of Careers Education and Counselling. She researches from a critical feminist standpoint, with key interests in the interaction of class and gender in post-compulsory education, guidance and mentoring. Her book, *Mentoring for Social Inclusion*, (2003, RoutledgeFalmer), presents a ground-breaking analysis of mentoring as a form of emotional labour. She has continued to develop this theme in researching learning cultures in further education, within the ESRC's Teaching and Learning Research Programme. She acts as an expert for the Youth Research Partnership of the European Commission and the Council of Europe, for whom she is currently editing a book on social inclusion.

Becky Francis is Professor of Education at Roehampton University. Her research interests include education and subjectivity, feminist theory, and gender and achievement, and she has published widely in these areas. Her recent authored books include *Reassessing Gender and Achievement* (with Christine Skelton, 2005, Routledge); and *Boys, Girls and Achievement: Addressing the Classroom Issues* (2000, RoutledgeFalmer). She is editor of *Gender and Education* international journal (with Christine Skelton), and has co-edited several readers concerning issues of theory and practice in gender and education, including the *Sage Handbook of Gender and Education*.

Barbara Kamler is Professor of Education at Deakin University, Australia, and Convenor of the Quality Learning Research Priority Area. Her research focuses on writing across the lifespan, critical literacies, cross-generational pedagogies and cultural narratives of ageing. Her passion for teaching writing has taken many forms during her career, most recently in mentoring programmes for doctoral and early career researchers to publish from their PhDs. Her books include *Relocating the Personal: A Critical Writing Pedagogy* (2001, SUNY) and *Helping Doctoral Students Write: Pedagogies for Supervision* (2006, Routledge, co-authored with Pat Thomson).

Carole Leathwood is Reader in Education in the Institute for Policy Studies in Education, London Metropolitan University. She specialises in research in post-compulsory education, drawing upon critical feminist and sociological theoretical frameworks. She has a particular interest in issues of gender, 'race' and class, including working-class access to higher education, gender and new managerialism in further education, and critical analyses of educational policy, and has published widely in these areas. She is the Ireland/Britain Editor of *Women's Studies International Forum* and an Associate Editor for *Gender, Work and Organisation*.

Heidi Safia Mirza is Professor of Equality Studies at the Institute of Education, University of London. She is known internationally for her work on ethnicity, gender and identity in education with best-selling books such as *Young, Female, and Black*, and *Black British Feminism*. As a member of the Labour Government's Schools' Standards Task Force she helped shape many initiatives to do with raising standards in education for black and minority ethnic pupils. She has established the Runnymede Collection at Middlesex, a unique race-relations archive and library documenting the late twentieth-century civil rights struggle for a multicultural Britain. Her most recent book, co-authored with Reena Bhavnani and Veena Meetoo, is *Tackling the Roots of Racism: Lessons for Success* (Policy Press).

Shahrzad Mojab teaches in the Department of Adult Education and Counselling Psychology at OISE/UT and is the Director of the Women and Gender Studies Institute, University of Toronto. Her areas of research and teaching are: critical and feminist pedagogy; immigrant women and skilling; women, state, globalisation and citizenship; women, war, violence and learning; and comparative analysis of lifelong learning theory and practice. She is the editor of *Women of a Non-State Nation: The Kurds* (2001, 2003), co-editor with Himani Bannerji and Judy Whitehead *Of Property and Propriety: The Role of Gender and Class in Imperialism and Nationalism*; and co-editor with Nahla Abdo of *Violence in the Name of Honour: Theoretical and Political Challenges* (2004). She is currently conducting research on women, war, diaspora, and learning; women political prisoners in the Middle East; and war and transnational women's organizations (Women, War, Diaspora, and Learning: Research Resources: www.utoronto.ca/wwdl).

Sheila Riddell worked as an English teacher in a comprehensive school before doing a PhD at Bristol University in gender and education. Since 1988, she has lived and worked in Scotland, researching and writing on disability, additional support needs and equality in public policy. She is currently Director of the Centre for Research in Education Inclusion and Diversity at the Moray House School of Education, University of Edinburgh, and Professor of Inclusion and Diversity.

Lyn Tett is Professor of Community Education and Lifelong Learning at the University of Edinburgh. Her research interests are the factors such as class, gender, and 'race' that prevent people from participating in education and the action that can be taken to develop more inclusive institutions. Her latest book is *Adult Literacy, Numeracy and Language: Policy, Practice and Research* (Open University Press) edited with Mary Hamilton and Yvonne Hillier.

Acknowledgements

We would like to thank the Gender and Education Association (GEA), and particularly members of the GEA Lifelong Learning Group, for providing the initial inspiration and stimulus for this book.

We would also like to express our very special thanks to Lindsay Melling for her support and assistance in compiling the final manuscript.

Finally, thanks to Routledge for commissioning the book and, in particular, to our editors, Philip Mudd and Tom Young.

Introduction

Gendering lifelong learning

Carole Leathwood and Becky Francis

'Lifelong Learning' has dominated educational policy arenas in recent years in many countries around the world. It remains high on the agendas of the United Nations Scientific and Cultural Organization (UNESCO), the Organisation for Economic Co-operation and Development (OECD), the World Trade Organization and the European Union. The term has been used to describe all learning activities in both formal and informal settings 'from the cradle to the grave', although it is more often associated with post-secondary school education. In the UK and elsewhere, it has redefined this post-school educational landscape, encompassing adult and community education, as well as vocational education and training, work-based and distance learning, and higher education. It has contributed to the breaking down of institutional boundaries, and the reconfiguration of learners, learning and learning environments. These developments have been accompanied by the publication of a growing body of literature documenting the changes and analysing developments in policy and practice, but with one particularly notable omission: a consideration of issues of gender. Yet how can this be so when lifelong learning remains so obviously gendered?

Any examination of participation in lifelong learning across the world reveals a highly segmented system, with men predominating in vocational education, technical courses and work-based learning, and women more likely to participate in community education and the caring fields. While such patterns are globally evident, there are, of course, many differences between countries. In the UK, for example, women now outnumber men in further education colleges and university undergraduate study, while some other countries are still struggling to ensure children's, and especially girls', access to *primary* education, never mind to technical education and training. Yet as the chapters in this book ably demonstrate, gendered patterns of access, participation and outcomes, albeit differently configured in different contexts, remain stubbornly persistent across the field of lifelong learning.

The idea for the book came out of a series of meetings among participants of the Gender and Education Association[1] Lifelong Learning Group. Discussions ranged from a consideration of lifelong learning policies and developments to specific institutional contexts, cultures, and pedagogies. They encompassed reflections on identities, emotions and the construction of knowledge, on what lifelong learning is, who it is for, and what purposes it serves. Throughout all of this, gender was a key issue, yet there was recognition that little had been written which focused on gender, and, perhaps not unrelated, that most published work had been written by men. A feminist analysis was urgently needed.

This book offers a range of critical feminist engagements with lifelong learning. A feminist approach provides an analysis and problematisation of gender relations, and the book is concerned to make visible, to understand and to critique gender inequalities in lifelong learning. It highlights the ways in which the policies and practices of lifelong learning, in very different contexts and with different groups of learners, are gendered in their construction and effects. Gender, however, is not the only issue here; while lifelong learning is a highly gendered arena, it is also a classed and racialised one. As Brewer (1993: 17) argued, 'gender as a category of analysis cannot be understood decontextualised from race and class'. The ways in which gender, 'race', class and other socially constructed identities and inequalities interconnect with each other has been the subject of a considerable amount of feminist debate (see e.g. Bradley 1996; Anthias 2001; Archer *et al.* 2001a; Francis 2002a) and it is not our intention to rehearse the arguments here. Instead, the book takes as its starting point an understanding that gender relations are classed and racialised and intermesh with other socially constructed identities and inequalities. An analysis of the different and complex ways in which these relations are constituted and performed through lifelong learning policies and practices underpins much of the work presented here. The book focuses particularly on gender through a recognition that while the ideological underpinnings and structures of gender, racism, class relations, and other socially constructed divisions are interconnected, they also have different, albeit related, histories (see Brah 2000) and are (re)produced and sustained through different, though often similar, mechanisms of power. It is important, therefore, to acknowledge both the differences and the similarities, the interconnections and the dissonances, while doing justice to an analysis of the specifics of gender and gendered power relations within the field of lifelong learning.

The book addresses questions such as:

- To what extent can the policy discourses and institutional contexts of lifelong learning be seen as masculinised and/or feminised?
- What are the gender implications of lifelong learning policy?
- In what ways is access to lifelong learning inclusive and/or exclusive?
- How do students, differently positioned in relation to gender, 'race'/ethnicity, social class, age, disability and sexuality experience lifelong learning opportunities?
- In what ways are learners' (gendered, racialised, classed) identities (re)constructed through lifelong learning?

- How do the outcomes of lifelong learning differ for different groups of students?
- Does lifelong learning provide opportunities to challenge or transgress gender binaries?

Implicit in any feminist engagement is a commitment to social change and social justice, and this is reflected in this volume. The book not only problematises current policies and practices, but also offers reflections on alternative visions, different possibilities and new ways of conceptualising and practising lifelong learning that might better reflect social justice concerns.

While all the chapters in the book are united in their commitment to a feminist analysis, the theoretical approaches adopted by the authors differ significantly. They range from post-structuralist to historical materialist, from work that utilises a Foucauldian conceptualisation of discourse to that which incorporates concepts such as patriarchy, capitalism and imperialism. There are discussions which draw on frameworks from liberal, radical and socialist feminist traditions and authors who utilise post-structuralist understandings of identity while also insisting on the importance of holding onto a materialist analysis. The book is, therefore, theoretically rich, providing examples of both the value and the limitations of different theoretical traditions.

Methodologically, too, a range of approaches are represented. These include policy analysis, individual case studies, biography and life history approaches, interviews and focus groups, pedagogical initiatives, the secondary analysis of national quantitative datasets and questionnaire surveys. The analyses range from the macro to the micro, from discussions of global, regional and national trends to the experiences of an individual learner, and while most focus on the contemporary, there are historical insights too. Much of the work makes connections between these different levels and contexts, highlighting the relationships between global developments and local practices in specific historical, social, economic and political contexts.

Overview of the book

The book is divided into three parts. Part I is based on policy analysis, and Parts II and III on discussions of empirical data. Part I examines *The Policy Context* of lifelong learning. Jill Blackmore in Chapter 1 provides an analysis of global developments in lifelong learning policy. Drawing specifically on the Australian context, but with reference to policies and initiatives in other countries, Jill provides a detailed critique of neo-liberal educational reforms and the implications for women both as learners and workers. Jacky Brine in Chapter 2 then moves us on to the European arena, exploring the relationships between European, global and national policy developments. Her analysis of the lifelong learning policies of the European Union, and in particular of concepts such as the 'knowledge economy' and the 'knowledge society', highlight the ways in which they (re)construct power relations related to gender, class, ethnicity and age. Finally in this part, Carole Leathwood turns the focus on to UK lifelong learning policy. She highlights the ways in which the two key themes/rationales of government lifelong learning policy discourse – the economic and social inclusion/social justice – are gendered. She then examines the construction of the lifelong learner in this discursive context, and the forms of lifelong learning on offer, in terms of their relationship to social inequalities and social justice.

Part II focuses on *Accessing Lifelong Learning*. In Chapter 4, Becky Francis examines gendered subject 'choices' and their bearing on school to work trajectories. She discusses the range of explanations for the persistent gendered, classed and 'raced' patterns in course/subject participation, particularly in vocational/training provision. Becky contrasts liberal feminist and post-structuralist approaches to these issues, and highlights the dangers of explanations that rest on pupil 'choice'. In Chapter 5, Louise Archer focuses on non-participation in lifelong learning. She examines the ways in which people's investments in particular gender identities impact on their views of participation in post-compulsory, and particularly higher, education. She draws on a range of research evidence to illustrate how resistance to participation is tied up with constructions of classed masculinities and femininities, with implications not only for widening participation policy, but also for the cultures and practices of educational institutions. In Chapter 6, Penny Burke provides a critical analysis of the hegemonic discourses of 'raising aspirations' and 'fair access' within widening participation policy, and the ways in which they hide processes of selectivity and exclusion. She then turns her attention to what happens when 'widening participation' students enter HE, with a critique of the study skills movement, arguing that although this is an attempt to support students, it continues to position these students as the problem.

In Part III, the focus moves on to *Experiences of Lifelong Learning*. In Chapter 7, Lyn Tett begins this part with an exploration of the impact of gender and class on the participation of women in community education in Scotland, examining the role played by issues of risk and desire. Her focus is specifically on adult literacies provision, in which discourses of 'shame' and 'lack' are particularly evident. Drawing on research with working-class women, Lyn calls for a reconceptualisation of both knowledge and literacies education. Helen Colley in Chapter 8 then takes us into the world of further education (FE) in England. She examines learning from the perspective of participation in communities of practice, and explores issues of identity, class and gender within the vocational culture of childcare courses. Through a detailed account of an FE tutor's life history and learning, Helen argues that learning (and teaching) are not simply about the acquisition of skills and competences, but about processes of becoming within highly gendered and classed structures and learning cultures.

The focus then moves on to higher education (HE), with Sheila Riddell's examination of issues of disability, gender and social class. In Chapter 9, she draws on a secondary analysis of national datasets to illustrate how the social profile of disabled students in HE is different from that of the HE student population as a whole. She then analyses the ways in which three students with a dyslexia diagnosis negotiate their identities in relation to gender, social class and disability in the context of higher education participation in Scotland. We stay with the field of higher education for Heidi Safia Mirza's examination of the place of black women in HE in Chapter 10. Heidi explores the invisibility/ visibility of black women in the 'hideously white' historical and contemporary context of higher education in England. She provides an important analysis of the now ubiquitous discourse of 'diversity' in HE and what it does, or does not do, in terms of in/equalities.

Barbara Kamler in Chapter 11 takes us back to the field of community education. She explores the experiences of older women (aged 60–85) engaging in processes of writing, talking, performing and film-making in Australia. Women of this age group tend to be excluded from dominant constructions of lifelong learning, and Barbara's chapter provides an inspiring account of the potential and benefits of learning opportunities, but also a powerful case for a reconceptualisation of lifelong learning to actually mean 'life-long'. Finally, Shahzad Mojab in Chapter 12 examines the experiences of Kurdish women in Sweden to provide a feminist critical analysis of the ideological and social relations embedded in the concept of 'lifelong learning'. The women in her research recount their experiences of war and diaspora, and challenge the dominant constructions of learning, and of themselves as learners, in their new host country. In particular, Shahzad's research highlights the ways in which the needs of learners are neglected when the needs of the labour market predominate.

The concluding chapter highlights some of the key themes in the book and focuses on the implications for lifelong learning policy and practice.

Note

1   http://www2.warwick.ac.uk/fac/soc/sociology/gea/

Part I

The policy context

Chapter 1

Unprotected participation in lifelong learning and the politics of hope

A feminist reality check of discourses around flexibility, seamlessness and learner earners

Jill Blackmore

The politics of hope

Policy discourses over the past decade in most OECD nations have mobilised notions about lifelong learning as a new way of thinking about the relationship between work, education, training, family, and leisure (Delors 1996; Karmel 2004). The concept is not new, with its derivation in the 1960s referring to the interaction between work and formal education (e.g. apprenticeships), and then community-based non-formal education in the 1970s. Now the concept of lifelong learning (LLL), as utilised in policy, rhetorically captures formal and informal, non-formal, abstract and experiential learning in schools, universities, TAFE, communities, workplaces and homes. LLL is portrayed as the future way of living and learning for children, young people and adults, a 'wonder drug' (Coffield 1999). The implicit assumption is that we can learn something from any aspect of our daily lives that can inform how we do paid work more productively (Field 2000a).

Policy statements mobilising the discourse imply a broad conceptualisation of LLL as a key aspect of a learning society. LLL is about learning to be, learning to do, learning to work and learning to learn (Delors 1996). Knowledge economies can no longer rely upon an educated elite, but require constant retraining and upgrading of a renewable and higher skills base for all. LLL is the discourse mobilised in educational discourses as the panacea for youth 'at risk' (Dwyer and Wyn 2001; Knight 2004); in industry discourses to rectify skill deficiencies in training to maintain national productivity; in welfare discourses arguing about the need to update the skills of the adult unemployed to reduce welfare costs; in management discourses as a basic condition for individuals working in 'learning organisations'; in community service discourses as a key element in social capital building in disadvantaged communities and to counter social exclusion (Schuller and Field 1998; Tett 2003); in home–school discourses about the family as active participants in their children's learning (Lopez and

Scribner 1999); and in discourses of community education promoting LLL for leisure (Department of Victorian Communities 2005). LLL is, many argue, a basic premise of full citizenship in a democratic society, a means to impart agency and well-being. LLL, therefore, it would appear, is seen to benefit women, young people and a range of 'equity' groups.

While each discourse reinvents the meaning of LLL within its own parameters, there are common threads trans-nationally. One theme is that LLL facilitates a seamless flow between education/training/work/home, that it accrues for the individual personal benefits through ongoing education and training whether in terms of employment, personal well-being and empowerment, or career development. For the public, LLL accrues benefits in terms of maximising skills and public educational investment. LLL therefore requires structural and cultural reform of education systems and educational workers to facilitate multiple pathways. A second theme is that LLL requires greater flexibility on the part of the individual, and, that in turn, individuals, through LLL, gain greater flexibility and are committed to their ongoing self-improvement (and therefore, it is assumed, choice about lifestyle and career). The assumption here is that the new work order has supplanted the twentieth-century ideal of the full-time single career pathway with the 'portfolio' or 'boundaryless' career based on flexible, multi-skilled self-motivating workers (Gee *et al.* 1996). Flexibility, mobility and serial jobs require continual upskilling and retraining.

Third, it is assumed that LLL occurs in multiple contexts, with multiple providers; anywhere, anytime, in workplaces, communities, homes, as well as formal educational sites. The post-welfare state only seeks to regulate a range of self-managing public *and* private providers rather than provide LLL except to the marginalised. Fourth, the discourse of LLL is frequently connected to democratic notions of citizenship, agency and participation, implying LLL has democratising capabilities. LLL promises new opportunities for marginalised groups and increased access to education and training, building individual and community capacities to respond to a globalised new work order (Clegg and McNulty 2002; Edwards *et al.* 2002; Kilpatrick *et al.* 2003).

Finally, LLL recognises that adults are also learners, and, as 'learner earners' undertaking education/training/work simultaneously, they are self-managing their learning. This imparts the notion of innovative and resilient individuals who are independent and self-reliant citizens. LLL is therefore about identity formation, and schools, universities and further education are expected to produce learner identities:

> There are the personal and social contours of the risk society, which oblige schools to prepare children for creating and engaging in a learning society. Learning, in a risk society, becomes not merely enhancement of the self, or a means of social and economic advancement, but . . . an indispensable mode of being and acting in the world.
>
> (Strain 2000: 244)

Work and education/training (and therefore not being in work) increasingly define who we are and how we are valued.

Learning to earn and earning to learn: paradoxes, tensions, contradictions

The above optimistic account is contestable. The discourses of LLL and how they are mobilised with particular subjects in mind, whether 'at risk' youth, middle managers, or women not in paid work, cannot be de-contextualised from the cultural and structural re-formation of the education–work nexus of the past two decades in most Western nation-states. When scrutinised from a feminist perspective that works the binaries between public/private, family/work, unpaid/paid labour, and emotional/rational in relation to empirical studies of particular equity groups, a number of contradictions, paradoxes and tensions emerge. In particular, concepts of LLL such as seamlessness, boundary-lessness, flexibility and relevance when enacted through policy produce differential experiences for women and girls within what are for many more neo-Fordist than post-Fordist conditions of work and learning (Albeit 2000).

Individualisation of risk and responsibilisation

LLL took on discursive power in the early 1980s as rapidly changing labour markets were seen to be a condition of national productivity in more competitive times. In Western developed nation-states, and Australia and New Zealand in particular, de-industrialisation arose from the flow of manufacturing to cheaper labour fields in Asia and South-East Asia. Bipartisan policies informed by neo-liberal market ideologies of the OECD, the IMF and the World Bank during the 1990s imitated the structural adjustment reforms undertaken in South America, New Zealand and the UK in the 1980s (Henry *et al.* 2001). Structural adjustment meant that the democratising discourses of LLL, while mobilised most often in new 'regionalised state' formations such as the EU, were readily subverted, by the neo-colonial tendencies of global capitalism in developing nation-states, and multi lateral and unilateral trade agreements between developed nation-states (e.g. North American Free Trade Alliance (NAFTA), Asia Pacific Economic Community (APEC)), due to its neo-liberal assumptions of competitive individualism and deregulated markets (Brine 1999). Neo-liberal orthodoxy during the 1980s and 1990s of deregulation of financial and labour markets and structural devolution was prescribed in the case of Latin America and Africa by international funding bodies and voluntarily adopted in the case of Australia and New Zealand, on the periphery of emerging regionalised economies (Summerfield and Aslanbeigui 1998; Blackmore 2005).

The discourse of LLL was mobilised by Anglophone nation-states to restructure education and training to make it more relevant to the economy

(Brine 1999; Gaskell and Rubensen 2004). Education and training were a source of national income in expanding international education markets in Asia and South-East Asia, and the means to improve competitiveness globally by upskilling adult and new labour generally (Blackmore and Sachs 2006). New modes of educational governance characterised by devolved and marketised education systems now focused on self-managing organisations. Structural devolution of educational management, together with new technologies, facilitated the dispersion of management tasks and responsibilities down to individual organisations (schools, TAFE and universities), and within organisations to sub-units and individual teachers competing for limited funds within what were becoming more corporate, quasi-autonomous, and entrepreneurial public organisations. The infiltration of a market orientation into the structures and cultures of educational organisations affected what was taught, to whom and how. Under-funded public and private educational institutions reliant upon enrolments, particularly the non-elite unable to attract students (preferably full fee paying), struggled for survival. Markets do not deliver equity.

The effect of this restructuring has been the casualisation of educational labour markets, particularly in the training sector; increased market competition within and between sectors (e.g. use of competitive tendering to deliver government labour market and literacy programmes); and the shifting of costs to users. In this context, LLL has been defined as an individual responsibility requiring increased individual investment in schooling and higher education to compensate for reduced government funding in public education (schools and universities) (e.g. Australian government funding, excluding international and domestic student fees, has reduced from 85 per cent to less than 30 per cent recurrent university income since 1996) (Australian Vice Chancellor's Committee AVCC Statistics 2004). Australian disinvestment in education in real and relative terms (GDP expenditure on education reducing from 4.3 per cent to 3.8 per cent since 1992) stands in contrast to increased investment in education and training in Canada, the USA, the UK, the EU, and Asian Tiger states as a source of social cohesion and economic growth (AVCC 2002).

Welfare and labour market services have also been outsourced to private providers (e.g. churches), a trend most evident in NZ and the UK where national government policies are not mediated by state or provincial governments as they are in Canada, Australia and the USA. In the Australian federal system, provision for those at risk is maintained through increasingly marginalised public sector providers (schools, universities and TAFE) as federal education funding has shifted as a result of neo-liberal policies from public to private education, and from the state to users. Governments in all countries more closely target discrete groups 'at risk' to create new efficiencies. Again, the safety net for marginalised workers is being cut away with the deregulation and/or demise of industrial awards, the rise of individualised workplace contracts in Australia emulating the American labour market model of under-employment and low wages for the unskilled. Increasingly, in the UK, the USA and Australia, there is the expectation that the unemployed (in particular, single mothers) have a 'mutual obligation' to the state to work in return for receiving welfare, thus individualising the responsibility for children. Nearly all Australian workers, part- and full-time, now experience a sense of their precarious position in the workplace, as redundancy agreements and contracts undercut the notion of tenure even among middle-class professionals and managers (Pusey 2003).

Thus, since the 1980s, the nation-state has increasingly mediated global/local market relations by deregulating financial and labour markets to attract international capital. At the same time, an increasingly interventionist state has been failing to protect individuals, not only from the extremes of globalising markets, but also from the infringement of human rights with the rise of terrorism (Hesford and Kozol 2005). Similarly, neo-liberal education reforms have significantly altered relations between the individual and the state with the shift from government to governance (Rhodes 1997), signalling a move away from a citizen-based notion of rights associated with a sense of the public, to an individualistic client-based notion of rights based on contractual obligations (Pierre 2000). This shift from a welfare to a post-welfare state in most Anglophone states has transferred risk and responsibility from the state onto the individual and the family, and therefore women who traditionally assume the greater responsibility for the aged, the young and the sick. LLL has been portrayed as one measure to reduce risk, but it is increasingly an individual responsibility.

Narrowing not broadening of education

LLL in the 1970s and 1980s was discursively constructed as an ongoing educative process within a social democratic political frame. Education for all was the aim through greater participation in, access to, and equity from LLL, as in the case of the neighbourhood house movement. Policy texts during the 1990s have been informed by a limited version of human capital theory promoted from conservative think tanks and through international policy forums (e.g. OECD), drawing on neo-liberalism's assumptions about the self-maximising self-interested individual who is not gendered, raced or classed (Henry et al. 2001). This version of human capital theory neglects how social capital in communities, work and families maintains the invisible social infrastructure upon which fast capitalism relies. It assumes an unproblematic connection between levels of investment in education/training (as if only by choice) through LLL and the rewards obtained in paid work (as if only by merit). Education and work are treated as being neutral domains with regard to culture, race, gender and class. Within this policy frame, LLL focuses on skills-based training rather than personal development or citizenship formation, on 'employability skills' not generic skills, on compliance to standards and not critical and independent thought (Gee et al. 1996; Blackmore 1997; Mahony and Hextall 2001; Gaskell and Rubensen 2004). This has led to a narrowing rather than broadening of how LLL has been understood and enacted in education policies in the EU, North America and Australasia. Studies of choice indicate little evidence of the 'consumer rationalism' assumed in policy texts (Potts 2003; Reay *et al.* 2005).

Seamlessness and coordination

LLL is the premise upon which the post-compulsory sector is being restructured, co-ordinated and managed. In Australia, the UK and the EU, qualification frameworks have been developed to create 'flexible pathways' and provide 'seamlessness' between education sectors, and between states for cross-national credit transfer, e.g. the Bologna Agreement for universities. Australian federal and state-run programmes now manage and track individual young people's pathways into work and further education and training (e.g. Mapping Individual Pathways, On Track). The push for seamlessness, together with international pressures (e.g. PISA and TIMMS) for an ongoing improvement of outcomes as measured by student access, participation and retention, standardised achievement tests, and graduate outcomes, has led to new institutional formations. These have taken the form of neighbourhood clusters, increased curriculum specialisation of schools (e.g. specialist schools in the UK), 'network facilitation models' (e.g. Local Learning and Employment Networks or LLEN in Victoria to coordinate youth education and welfare services), and community capacity building such as Education Action Zones, Cities of Excellence in the UK and New Community Schools in Scotland (Gewirtz *et al.* 2005). In Australia, the focus on outcomes has led schools to be more responsive to the needs and interests of 'at risk' young people by widening the range of curriculum and pedagogies (e.g. Victorian Certificate of Applied Learning, Australian Vocational Education and Training in Schools or VET) in partnership with TAFEs to broaden student choice, whereas the tendency in the UK has been to 'exclude' students unable to engage with mainstream schooling (Ball *et al.* 2000; Campbell 2002).

Paradoxically, while there is a desire by government to divest responsibility in provision of education and training, there has been a push to introduce and re-regulate private and public providers. Seamlessness has required greater coordination and cooperation between schools, technical and higher education sectors, public and private institutions and produced new funding models (e.g. academies in the UK and proposed business-run, federally-funded Technical Colleges in Australia). LLL providers, informally connected during the 1970s and 1980s, are now governed through national frameworks of certification and accreditation (e.g. Australian Qualifications Framework) and converging modes of curriculum 'delivery' (e.g. competency-based approaches). Informal education has been replaced by multiple gradations of certification. Yet certification can mean fewer benefits in terms of accessing employment due to the rise of credentialism, while options for informal and non-formal education are reducing.

The rapid expansion in private sector provision (by churches and 'for profit' firms) of training and welfare programmes has introduced new players, leaving public providers catering for 'non-profitable' clients, many of them single-parent, female-headed families. There has been a blurring of education, training, welfare and employment programmes with increasingly complex welfare conditions for the unemployed. Thus private training bodies, churches and NGOs have become complicit in implementing and monitoring increasingly harsh welfare policies. The boundaries between sectors and their different responsibilities are blurring and being redrawn. For example, underfunded community and neighbourhood houses established in the 1970s for informal adult education in Australia are now moving into new fields in order to survive, picking up 'at risk' young students (aged 13–14), at a lower cost to government, early school leavers who find adult learning approaches more amenable.

Competencies and knowledge work: contractual or pedagogical relations?

The restructuring of education in line with 'the national interest', new efficiencies, and individualised choice (e.g. LLL) has been steered through strong policy frames by the state and by executive strategic planning in educational organisations. Outcomes-focused policies are part of the strong accountability frameworks based on performance-based funding that utilise the technologies of performance indicators, performance management and quality audits. These technologies of performativity facilitate governments and executive managers' capacities to steer individual self-managing workers and learners from a distance while the difficult decisions over distribution of people and resources and individualised needs are devolved to units and equity groups competing for reduced resources at the interface. In curriculum, for example, strong policy frames focusing on outcomes are evident with the imposition of competency-based approaches during the 1990s in the training sector, a mode now penetrating higher education and schools with the integration of TAFE and VET programmes into their provision and a focus on generic graduate attributes as defined by professional bodies and international standards movements.

Paradoxically, schools, like universities, are struggling with debates about the need for different modes of producing, transmitting and learning new forms of knowledge, together with pedagogies that produce learner identities more appropriate for the twenty-first century (Strain 2000; Young and Spours 1997). The focus of more critical pedagogies is holistic, on creativity, entrepreneurship, and personal agency as well as meta-cognitive skills of 'learning how to learn', rather than vocationally specific skills that will rapidly be out of date (e.g. New Basics in Queensland and Essential Learning in Tasmania) (Hayes *et al.* 2006). In the USA, many jurisdictions developed programmes that integrated academic and occupational curricula to improve the transition from school to work through a coherent sequence of courses (Kincheloe 1995); some sought to address underachievement marked by race and ethnicity by developing multi-cultural programmes; others sought to detrack with the hope to reduce inequality; and some looked to single sex schooling (e.g. black males) (Rubin and Silva 2003). Similar reforms in school curriculum are less evident in the UK with its prescriptive National Curriculum, curriculum specialisation, and return to ability grouping that encourages schools in the context of education markets and league tables to develop practices of 'triage', i.e. putting most resources with middle-level students where the most difference can be made on outcome measures, excluding/ignoring the most difficult low-achieving students, while encouraging the high achievers (Gillborn and Youdell 2000). Within the USA, as elsewhere, there is considerable debate as to whether standards-driven accountability frameworks can deliver, or may actually impede, more equitable outcomes (Sklra and Scheurich 2004).

Another articulation of the convergence between competencies and outcomes, leveraged by market demands for client, industry/profession responsiveness, is the development in universities of graduate attributes and workplace-based experiential learning where students integrate practical problem-based learning approaches with more theoretical positions, e.g. Coop programmes in Canada (Gaskell and Rubensen 2004). Such interdisciplinary, experiential and workplace-based learning could optimistically be considered to be more typical of what Gibbons *et al.* (1994) refer to as Mode 2 knowledge, focusing on problem solving and a theory–practice dialogue necessary for knowledge-based economies. A pessimistic reading is that the lock step approaches of competency/outcomes have normalising tendencies, intensify government control, are usually driven by strong externally defined standards that treat learning as a set of discrete outcomes and are not as situated and multi-dimensional (emotional, personal, cognitive, etc.), while viewing curriculum and pedagogy as vocational tools to produce learner earners and not citizens.

A third articulation is how literacy is increasingly treated as a vocational skill rather than a means of personal empowerment, a major shift in the Adult, Community and Further Education sector. Previously, literacy classes were as much about personal development and community as facilitating access to further training for work for women of non-English-speaking backgrounds (NESB). Such critical pedagogies, developed to build social capital within local communities, have been supplanted by packaged 'teacher-proof' curriculum based on generic competencies, reducing pedagogy to transmission (Smith and Keating 2003). Many teachers feel competency-based approaches reduce professional autonomy, thus de-professionalising more than re-professionalising (Sanguinetti 1998). User pays and vocationalism together have encouraged more instrumentalist attitudes to education, particularly to higher education, shaping academic/student interaction as a contractual rather than pedagogical relationship within a market-driven context.

Vocational education and training: an equity strategy?

Schools have also been expected to respond to the demands of the LLL agenda (Shacklock 2003, 2004). VET and vocational learning are now expected to act as an 'equity strategy' (Bowman 2004). But vocational education, whether within secondary school or the further and community education sector in most Anglophone education systems, has historically been treated as the lesser and marginalised relative to mainstream academic curricula. Thus institutional responses to break down barriers between vocational/academic sectors to improve the transition from education to work face systemic historical disposi-tions that nurture the minority of students pursuing the academic track into university (Teese and Polesel 2003). Competitive public and private education markets arising from parents' exercising choice, together with sys-temic accountability focusing on outcomes, mean academic performance for university entrance is *the* mark of a successful school and student. Schools there-fore take significant risks in terms of student markets, and therefore survival, by focusing on vocational or community programmes that are not 'marketable', such as providing a crèche for young mothers, welcoming a critical mass of students with disability, or offering alternative vocational programmes (Angwin *et al.* 2004). Finally, the cost is high to provide well-resourced vocational educa-tion in schools where demand is greatest, usually those which have the most disparate student needs in the more disadvantaged areas that have the fewest community resources or capacities to attract students. LLL, with its assumption of the integration of theory/practice and facilitating transition/pathways from school to work, is itself not valued in high stakes assessment and competitive education markets.

Despite this, in Australia as in Canada, VET and VCAL are popular with individual teachers, students and parents because these programmes impart personal achievement and local community relevance (Fenwick 2004). New school-based apprenticeships in hospitality and retail have provided increased access of girls in equal numbers predominantly in the public sector, but with a decline in numbers entering the traditionally male-dominated, blue-collar trades. There is also a flow-on effect from workplace VET in rural areas into local labour markets in the hospitality industry. But these jobs are highly casual-ised, part-time and traditionally feminised (Fenwick 2004). Butler *et al.* (2005: 10) argue that post-compulsory policies still operate within 'a masculinist VET frame'. VET policies and programmes reproduce rather than dismantle gender segmentation in education and work and are not preparing young women for the realities of the workplace as 'the current political agenda is to steer women and girls into the traditional institutionalised role' with little sense of what these jobs will offer in terms of employment opportunities, pay or career paths (ibid.: 11). While boys leaving school early are more likely to get into longer-term training, apprenticeships and full-time employment, girls who leave early disappear, falling into casual work without training possibilities and are less likely to have stable familial relationships or remunerative employment (Collins *et al.* 2001; Teese 2002: 188; Long and Dusseldorp Skills Forum 2004).

Those most at risk are the early school leavers who have to negotiate a complex mosaic of post-compulsory and youth support providers (thirty-eight in one regional Local Learning and Employment Network), geographically dispersed and often invisible, rather than follow the coherent linear pathway into higher education (Angwin *et al.* 2001). They are attracted by any form of work, perceiving work as a form of flight as they are disengaged and/or dissatisfied with school. Any work is an economic strategy for short-term survival. But this ultimately predetermines long-term intermittent employment in low-paid unskilled jobs (Teese 2002: 185). The most invisible of all are pregnant teenagers, pregnancy being the primary reason for young girls leaving school. They experience 'the difficulty of just juggling their education with managing a child. I think most of the girls do have ambitions and want to move forward in their lives, but they find the realities of a young baby too much for them' (Principal, quoted in Angwin *et al.* 2004: 7).

Therefore, for those most at risk, the emergence of new/old forms of vocational education and training provision promises new opportunities, but without challenging the gender order of work/family relations or the gender regime of organisations. Evaluations of VET indicate equity groups (indigenous students, NESB, young mothers, rural and remote people, people with disability), the primary VET targets, benefit least in terms of employment opportunities and economic benefits (Bowman 2004; Butler 2005; Lawrence 2005). Yet VET has improved these

> [students'] capacity for self direction and their capacity to relate well to others . . . [and]their perception of the relevance of livelong learning and their ability to exploit learning opportunities grows. Their horizons enlarge and new interests are formed. Their self-esteem in raised and their ability to communicate is enhanced.
>
> (Teese 2002: 188)

Such programmes create new flexible worker identities, inculcating the desire to work, and with both skills and capacities (Tennant *et al.* 2004). Relevance for work and even what girls enjoy means access to service work that is undervalued and underpaid. But the opportunity to gain secure and fulfilling work that meets their expectations, utilises their capacities and potential, and that provides a good and ongoing remuneration is not high. Despite relatively successful participation, progression and outcomes in the education of women, indigenous and rural/regional groups, obtaining positive and more equitable employment outcomes is now the issue (Quay Connection 2003; Dumbrell *et al.* 2004). Current policies on LLL do not engage with the social, economic and cultural contexts that shape young women's life chances.

Paying more, achieving more, but earning less

LLL is increasingly the learner's responsibility and a condition of their ongoing employment with the incremental creep towards user pays in all education sectors: schools, TAFE and universities. Self-funding of education and training is not new for women. Women in the education professions have historically invested in their own education and training more than men (e.g. paying for clerical training in the 1950s and 1960s, professional development and post-graduate degrees in teaching), whereas men in training have often been funded by government or employers (e.g. apprenticeships, MBAs in business) (Blackmore 1997; Pocock 1998). Transition from school to further education is now the point of greatest scarcity and where equity issues are highlighted. In universities, the Higher Education Contribution Scheme in 1992 offered a more equitable solution than upfront fees for non-traditional users of higher education. Yet women take significantly longer to repay their debt. Now they are confronted with increased fees (25 per cent increase in HECS in 2005) and full new fee paying places as government funding of higher education shrinks, with student support facilities such as child care threatened by the abolition of Compulsory Union Fees.

Despite women's ongoing educational achievement in school and higher education and their investment in professional development, they do not reap the same rewards for LLL in the workplace as their male counterparts, casting empirical doubt on the human capital thesis. The gender wage gap emerges and increases within three years between equivalent male and female university graduates (House of Representatives 2002). In Australia, government discourses justify this phenomenon by drawing on Hakim (2002), arguing that men have a career orientation and women have a family orientation to paid work, thus rationalising women's tenuous relationship to well-paid work. LLL is a discourse mobilised within increasingly risky and unprotected work conditions that require women to work and train harder and longer in part-time work, while still undertaking full-time home duties and self-funded training.

Spatially segmented work, spatially segmented learning

LLL is a discourse that can serve dominant economic interests in the changing capital/labour configurations of post-industrialism with the faster flows of people and ideas rather than individuals. Mobility and flexibility are the key to access and success in education and work. Yet family and social relations of intimacy and sense of efficacy are often about belonging, place, and a sense of security. Masculine as well as feminine identity is challenged as women become economically independent. Notions of family are challenged by female-headed households, extended families, and same sex parenting. Nor are women a homogenous 'equity' group. Differences among women arise due to class, indigeneity/'race'/ethnicity, linguistic background and location. Pockets of poverty and wealth coexist within close proximity in cities, and the gap between cities and rural regions is widening, with increased differentials in the provision of transport, communication, health and welfare infrastructure (Harding and Greenwall 2002).

LLL and informal learning is critical in rural communities where a higher proportion of women, for example, than men in rural and remote areas achieve higher level VET qualifications and participate in informal education but have limited occupational opportunities for skilled work locally (Golding 2004). Reverse gender segmentation exists in LLL here because:

> Women typically need to learn locally in order to adapt to changes in their lives, their family business and in the rapidly changing world of work. In the smaller and remoter towns, much of this women's learning takes place by necessity through adult and community education, work and informal training rather than through accredited vocational education and training (VET) . . . women are the new 'hunters and gatherers' for learning: for themselves for their families, and in some instance, for and behalf of their male partners . . . by contrast men are not as 'hungry' for the necessary learning or are unable to access a local, appropriate convivial space in all and remote towns to acquire that learning . . . they had traditionally learnt through work, on the job, on the farm and public organizations.
>
> (Golding 2004: 156)

Again, once in work, rural women, like their city sisters, do not receive commensurable income to men despite being greater consumers of LLL than their male counterparts. But as participants in LLL, they build social capacity in their families and as active citizens provide the social glue for communities, unrecognised by government.

Other studies in the UK and Canada that include women as co-participant researchers produce narratives that indicate how single parents on welfare (Butterwick 2004), Aboriginal women, and low-income female workers with children were 'not wanted' by employers. They also had the greatest difficulty in accessing education and training because they lacked affordable childcare that matched school hours against employment hours, i.e. the everyday routines of parenting, work, welfare rules and childcare did not synchronise (Tett 2003). As Tett's (2003) Scottish study indicated, policies failed to recognise the psycho-social effects of lack of control of material and social conditions of people's lives which impact on health and social relationship of communities as well as individual households. Thus marginalised women were expected to participate in community, in work, in LLL, and also maintain family without the necessary conditions that made this balancing act possible.

Flexibility, fluidity and boundarylessness

Gender identities are also increasingly under threat and in crisis (Connell 2000). Globalisation has seen fluidity between the transformed conditions of work, the changing social relations of gender, multiple modes of learning, and new patterns of career and family. LLL is itself a product of radically transformed relations between education/home/work/leisure with its assumption about the fluidity and flexibility between these domains. For example, the institutional flexibility required to meet the needs of volatile student markets and frequent government policy shifts has largely been achieved through radically changing the conditions of educational labour through its privatisation, feminisation and casualisation. Privatisation of labour has occurred with the blurring for academics and teachers between work and home, resulting from extended work hours under enterprise bargaining, the intensification of labour requiring more home-work, and the requirements for online teaching internationally, collectively eroding family time (Pocock 2003). Australian full-time employees now work the highest average number of hours per week in the OECD. Such patterns of work intensification are evident in UK, American and Canadian universities (Morley 2003) and schools (Mahony and Hextall 2001). Education systems and organisations as greedy organisations simultaneously rely on this privatisation of work and employee good will and passion, but ignore their employees' familial responsibilities in terms of organising workplaces flexibly *for* workers (Blackmore and Sachs 2006).

Flexibility of educational organisations also relies on increasing the already rapid rate of casualisation of the educational workforce in casual and part time work (rising from 8 to 24 per cent in Australian universities, 1992–2004), a marginal labour market already highly feminised (Australian Bureau of Statistics 2004; AVCC 2004). Casualisation arises from the strategies of downsizing, outsourcing and contractualism. TAFE in Australia, like the further education sector in the UK, was already highly reliant on contract and sessional labour (up to 50 per cent in some instances) (Gleeson and Shain 1999; Whitehead and Moodley 1999). Alice, a middle manager in a large suburban TAFE commented:

> Our teachers have been living with this for years now. The casualisation of the teaching profession in VET, which is predominantly women, means when the teachers' contracts come due, the teachers are pitted against each other in competition for their own and others' jobs. They're all on six-month contracts, the coordinators on three years. Seven of our coordinators positions are all up in December, competing against each other for our jobs. I don't know whether to go for my coordination position again or go back into teaching. Doing something else, being 46, the realities are bleak. But here we've got no pathways, no career prospects except marking time and grabbing whatever we can get. The name of the game is surviving.

People will work for below award conditions, with less job security and fewer ongoing positions. Each year we're told there's cut-backs again.

In these peripheral education labour markets, women lack the benefits of institutional collegial relationships and support as well as professional development and institutional commitment to their well-being (Blackmore and Angwin 1997). Flexibility in most organisations has become less about individual flexibility to be family friendly and caring for worker well-being or careers and more about institutional flexibility to meet the demands of volatile markets. In Australia, such trends will worsen with the introduction of Australian Workplace Agreements removing union protection and reducing award conditions to a minimal, and work contracts negotiated by individuals. AWA will impact most on marginalised casual workers who tend not to be in unions, but also women, even in senior management, who can have less negotiating power in male-dominated institutions because of familial responsibilities. Women more often negotiate away salary increments and bonuses for family time (a pattern already evident in collective Enterprise Agreements of the 1990s).

Any discussion of women's work as educators and indeed leader/managers in all sectors not only referred to the boundarylessness between work, community and family, but also how work decisions (promotion, mobility, part-/full-time) were contingent upon familial responsibilities and relationships (Blackmore and Sachs 2006). Biographical narratives of women, even in leadership positions, indicate complex life courses characterised by 'flexible' 'portfolio' careers, and frequent movement between paid work, unpaid family duties, community work and education/training (Pocock 2003; Probert 2001). It signals the disappearance of the twentieth-century male model of full-time career in one job, now putting both working-class and middle-class men and women at risk, as experienced by the older male workers in rural areas (Pusey 2003).

Women's increasing participation in paid work is emulating the US core–periphery model of work that is gendered, raced and classed. Reich (1997) refers to the core of professional managerial class of symbolic analysts, largely white and male, supported by a middle circle of skills-based technicians including the quasi-professions of teaching and nursing, and serviced by a periphery of semi-skilled workers in casualised employment, predominantly women, recent immigrants and people of colour. Most Western post-industrial societies are rapidly moving towards this model of flexible specialisation. But portfolio careers are the privilege of the core where the attributes of LLL (credentials, experiential learning, mobility, flexibility) accrue primarily to the transnational, usually male, symbolic analysts who are mobile and skilled within an elite global labour market (Connell 2000). The same attributes of multiskilling, continuous upskilling, certification and flexibility have become the condition for marginalised educational workers to merely *retain* their low-paid 'serial jobs' (Blackmore and Angwin 1997). Furthermore, transnational masculinities rely upon the social capital building and domestic labour role of women and peripheral service workers. Flexibility, therefore, usually means increased risk and increased demand for the constant upgrading of skills through certification for those on the periphery, but is advantageous to those in the professional managerial class at the hard core of the new work order where training is largely in-house, experiential and seen to be readily transferable.

LLL for learning organisations

Finally, our study of women leaders in schools, universities and TAFE during the 1990s (Blackmore and Sachs 2006), focused on a cohort who had been educated in the public sector during the 1960s, trained in the universities in the 1970s when feminism troubled dominant epistemologies and politics, and taught in public schools in the 1980s when top-down policies converged with bottom-up activism to focus on participation and equity. It was these women's flexibility, adaptability and experiential learning in multiple sites of paid and unpaid work that now made them highly employable as change agents and managers of educational restructuring during the 1990s. Merilyn's story characterises the 'accidental' nature of their careers that produced a professional and leadership habitus infused with a passion for education and social change (Blackmore and Sachs 2006).

> I fell into jobs . . . I was manager of the Australian Competency Research Centre, a commercial, autonomous unit . . . a huge experience of change and reform in that sector. I had a teaching background, secondary. This combination . . . was the ticket to this job. The critical thing is to do with change. My TAFE institute made the decision to restructure, and spill positions: they wanted people in there that knew what change was about. Change is how I have operated most of my working life . . . I've always been in relatively tenuous employment situations . . . The cultural pattern is very strong: my father was a teacher and a Principal. The educational influence was always pretty strong at home.

This pattern of recruitment of women into middle management (deans, heads of school, directors, principals) was also evident in all UK education sectors, where women took on the responsibility for the 'domestic' labour, i.e. emotional management work, risk management and quality assurance in systems undergoing radical workplace re-ordering (Deem and Ozga 1997; Whitehead and Moodley 1999; Gleeson and Shain 1999; Blackmore and Sachs 2006). As middle managers, they were trapped ambiguously between implementing policies in antithesis to their leadership habitus focusing on students, learning and social justice, and 'managing' a new social order based on the corporate values of markets and managerialism (Gleeson and Shain 1999). Their former colleagues, women teachers and academics, were increasingly positioned as technicians within this managerialist frame of technical professionalism emerging in the 1990s. Discourses of learning organisations and innovation were downplayed to a focus on competencies, attributes, and the privileging of student and employer notions of relevance over teacher professional knowledge and judgement. As middle managers in corporatised schools, universities and further education they mediated relations between increased top-down, executive managerial power and reduced local autonomy and professional judgement arising from the multiple accountabilities of the audit and outcomes-based education. These were not the post-Fordist, horizontally structured learning organisations based on relationships of trust that encouraged collegiality, innovation and creativity that they preferred (Blackmore and Sachs 2006). While these wo-managers displayed the attributes of LLL desirable for learning organisations experiencing continuous change, readjustment and realignment, the burden of managing risk in organisations in crisis was dangerous in terms of their personal health, well-being, and relations with colleagues, families and friends. Many women contested the purpose of reform and how the resources/power/knowledge are unequally distributed, often to their detriment. Yet they, as individual teachers and academics, were held responsible for outcomes over which they had little control. Indeed, the corporatised educational organisation was less about learning and more about how 'employees are compelled to share their job related informal learning to enhance productivity' (Livingstone 1999a: 165).

Thus, the LLL discourse is mobilised at a time when education is now delivered through a complex set of contractual, consensual, competitive and cooperative arrangements, bewildering for both providers and users alike in their multiplicity, contradictions and array of choices, to 'service changes going on elsewhere in the economy and social formation' (Edwards 1997: 67). These arrangements are recasting and realigning work/home/education relations, fixing them into new patterns that could arguably be seen to be more controlling and exploitative in terms of daily work relations and practices than previous rigid boundaries between the domains of work, home and education.

So despite the discourse of LLL as a means by which to reduce risk for particular equity groups, the policies that inform the material conditions under which these groups live and work do not support an inclusive, reflexive or empowering lifelong learning for women now, nor for the future generation. There is little systemic and systematic recognition of the changed conditions in which choices are made by women and equity groups. While schools, TAFE and universities are producing flexible and self-reliant worker identities, the workplace does not meet their expectations, often being more alienating than satisfying. The discourse of LLL has been mobilised in the context of neoliberal educational and economic policies, post-welfarism associated with a rhetoric of self-help and mutual obligation, and a re-privatisation of work and care. These have added to women's paid and unpaid labour and marginalise young women without the minimum educational credentials.

Despite this, the discourse of LLL is appealing to women educators and managers, themselves high achievers in LLL, seeking to improve women's opportunities through LLL and to promote social change. The logic of the discourse is seductive and difficult to refute. LLL is powerful discourse because it penetrates to the soul of educational work about self-improvement, while making individuals more self-managing of their own LLL. The danger lies in the assumptions embedded in LLL as conceptualised in policy and practice. The material conditions of both work and family life are arguably worsening for some, through work intensification, employment insecurity, and more expensive education and training. It is also a period of high risk even for the middle class (Pusey 2003). Dual family incomes are essential to maintain living standards. Women and children in single parent families now constitute the majority of those living in poverty, with a widening gap between rich and poor (Harding and Greenwall 2002) reflected in rising educational inequality based on location, class and indigeneity/'race'/ethnicity with significant implications for schools in these locations in New Zealand, Australia, the UK, the USA and Canada (Waslander 1995; Teese and Polesel 2003; Canadian Statistics 2004; Vinson 2004; Street 2005). The paradox of LLL is that if women and girls are not learner earners, they will be further marginalised, yet the benefits they accrue from their participation in LLL do not bring comparable rewards to many men. Increasingly, both men and women outside the 'hard core' of tenured and/or high paying contract transnational professional/managers are now 'unprotected' in the new work order.

New possibilities, old problems

Girls and women, as other equity groups, are doing more LLL successfully, but without the rewards (Fenwick 2004). The instrumentalist conceptualisation of LLL arising from human capital theories leaves untroubled shifts in the public/private upon which worker flexibility is premised, ignores the complex networks 'at risk' young people and other equity groups negotiate, and negates the professional knowledge production of learner earners in organisations. VET continues to be a masculinised area that enourages girls to enter traditional pathways, while failing to meet the needs of women in small business (Kempinch et al. 1999). Policies that take seriously the differential benefits of LLL need to protect the family–work balance rather than undermine it; create conditions of work and learning that facilitate LLL; develop more sophisticated indicators of what counts as educational success; and realise LLL is about building social as well as economic capital.

Alternative perspectives to official discourses about LLL focus on reflexivity (Edwards et al. 2002), social capital (Kilpatrick et al. 2003) and inclusion (Clegg and McNulty 2002). These perspectives, as have feminists' perspectives on pedagogy for some time, take the position that why and how people engage with learning is not merely dependent on the provision of opportunity through institutional networks, but also the conditions of learning and the negotiation of social networks or 'networks of intimacy' (friends, family and community). School/parent partnerships, for example, are more likely to work if they actually 'engage with the social realities of women's lives to foster learner identities' (Clegg and McNulty 2002: 572), as opposed to one premised upon middle-class femininity where parents are compliant with teachers' notions of 'good' parenting (Tett 2003). Learning is not just about gaining employment, it is about identity. Students learn about education and work through their families and friends, their networks of intimacy. The availability of the learning opportunities is an insufficient condition, as it does not 'create the structurally located dispositions involved in participation' (Clegg and McNulty 2002: 582). This is particularly applicable to more marginalised women and young women, where identity and education are not closely interlinked in their networks of intimacy, as they were, for example, among the professional managers. Yet even for this relatively privileged group of women, who had invested significantly in LLL in the production of leadership/managerial habitus, the current conditions of work shaped by markets and managerialism are producing alienation and disengagement. Work may be the primary source of status and identity, but educational work no longer sustains the motivating disposition among many educators for social justice (Bourdieu 1997). Learning is a social and collective practice. It contributes to social capital in that individuals and groups will cooperate to achieve things they may not otherwise desire, do or attain (Kilpatrick et al. 2003: 417).

Governments seek through policy to dictate behaviours, but fail to draw upon the habitus and dispositions of all the actors in the partnership as a 'resource on which to build' (Clegg and McNulty 2002: 582). Schools and more informal modes of learning can, in some instances, mediate between an individual's networks of intimacy and institutional networks of learning, providing a space in which social capital is exploited productively for both individuals and the collective. Thus social capital is considered to be a 'resource' based on relationships among people, and not merely an individual attribute, a positional good, mobilised to exclude or gain comparative advantage over others (Kilpatrick et al. 2003: 419) At the same time, as Bourdieu (1997) points out, social capital is also about power, place, as it is inflected by gender, class and race distinctions. Social capital is not a social panacea for economic ills that are structurally produced, as I have argued, with the slip of responsibility from the state to voluntarism, largely borne by women (Gewirtz et al. 2005). But in the existing political economy of LLL with its unequal distribution of possibilities, inclusions and rewards, individuals are increasingly responsible for both their ability to access education, and for their failure in education and work, and at the same time they are increasingly dependent on education and their successes are claimed as exemplifying the learning society (Coffield 1999). We are living in a knowledge society, therefore, 'in which the collective learning achievements of adults [and young people] far outpace the requirements of the economy as paid work is currently organised' (Livingstone 1999a: 164).

Chapter 2

Locating the learner within EU policy

Trajectories, complexities, identities

Jacky Brine

This chapter focuses on the lifelong learning policies of the European Union and develops a feminist analysis that asks, from within a theoretical framework of class and gender, which learners, what learning, when and why. This is pursued through a close analysis of the policy texts that are considered from within a framework of three trajectories: (1) the trajectory of governance; (2) the trajectory of time; and (3) the trajectory of contemporary textual influence.

The analysis begins with the trajectory of governance. The policies of the European Union play a significant mid-way role in an increasingly complex model of governance that, framed by geo-political, social and economic contexts, includes the national and the global. This is not a straightforward trajectory from the Organisation for Economic Cooperation and Development (OECD) or the General Agreement on Trade in Services (GATS) through the EU and the Council of Europe to the nation-state; key national politicians and civil servants are actively involved in the construction of policy at both the European and the global levels also. And the European Commission is not only involved at other European levels and the global, but is often in a position of 'checking and auditing' the implementation of EU policy at the national level. Thus, the policy is less a straight line but a constantly looping back and forth. This chapter begins by contextualising the EU within this complex (backtracking) trajectory of inter-looping governance in order to highlight the significance of the focus upon it as a major policy-making level.

Second, is the trajectory of time. The concept of lifelong learning can be traced back to the Council of Europe's (CoE) Janne Report (CoE 1973) that introduced several new concepts that subsequently re-emerged within the policies of the European Union; the CoE's permanent education became the EU's lifelong learning. This chronology will focus on the texts that are exclusively and explicitly concerned with lifelong learning. The chronological trajectory will end with the most recent key EU explicit policy text on lifelong learning – the Resolution of 27 June 2002 (CEC 2002). This provides a definition that includes *all* learning (formal, non-formal and informal) across a person's life, from pre-school to post-retirement, the aim of which is to improve knowledge, skills and competences within a personal, civic social and/or employment-related perspective, previously more fully described as active citizenship, personal fulfilment, social inclusion and employability. This construction of an all-enquiring, curious, inquisitive, knowledge-hungry learner, taking all opportunities to learn, is repeatedly referred to as 'everyone', the 'individual who is the subject of learning' who must be presented with 'an authentic equality of opportunities'. However, although the EU Resolution begins by constructing a homogeneous learner, one defined neither by gender, class, age or ethnicity, the 'devil' as they say 'is in the detail'. In this section of the chapter I begin the close textual analysis to identify which learners the text does construct, what learning is identified with them, when, where and why.

The third trajectory is that of contemporary textual influence. This is based on the recognition that EU policy does not consist of single separate strands of influence but that actions and priorities introduced in one context, and legally approved or granted legal competency, then influence and are integrated into other policies, frequently those most concerned with directing member state action. Thus, the trajectory of contemporary influence occupies a crucial space between the prime policy intention, as expressed in the Resolution, and the implementation at national level. Significantly, the 'devilish detail' is less immediately obvious when included as part of, for instance, the Lisbon Council *Presidency Conclusions* (CEC 2000a), the European Employment Strategy (CEC 1999a), the European Social Fund (CEC 1999b) or the Youth Programme (CEC 2000b). In this section, continuing the close textual analysis of the previous section, I search for the identities of the learners within contemporary policy texts.

Drawing together the insights from the three trajectories, I conclude with a further consideration of the primarily gendered (but clearly also classed and raced) learners constructed through the EU policies.

Trajectory of governance

It is no longer possible to consider the policies of the European nation-state without contextualising and considering them in relation to the policies of the European Union. Similarly, it is necessary to locate the policies of the EU within the global – economic, cultural and geo-political. This is not a simple deterministic policy trajectory from the global to the national, but a complex system of multi-level governance where particular nation-states are major players at both multi-national (EU) and global levels, with the nation-state as 'constituent units of a new transnational political system' (Jachtenfuchs 2001: 256). Much of the nation-state involvement, however, is obscured behind a bureaucratic mask of apparent anonymity. Bourdieu in his exploration of these new forms of governance speaks of decoys, of 'a screen which prevents citizens . . . from perceiving their disempowerment and from discovering the loci and stakes of a genuine politics' (2003: 14). Thus, the global world is constructed not only by the unfettered transfer of capital and goods, as seen by those who focus solely on economic influences and, ignoring nation-states, treat the multinational corporation as the dominant actor, but by 'the state', the political actors acting primarily through the processes of policy-making. The United Kingdom, for instance, is a member state of the European Union, the Council of Europe, the WTO (World Trade Organization), the GATS and the G8. The European Union is, as a distinct 'body', also a participant in G8 meetings, and, since 1995, a member of the WTO. The aim of this chapter is not to focus specifically on *why* this is so, but to note that it is so, and that this is the policy context within which the concept and the policies of lifelong learning are generated.

However, the focus of this chapter is explicitly on the lifelong learning policies of the European Union, and thus I turn now to briefly sketch the EU policy-making process, described by Richardson (1996) as a 'garbage can' – a view of complexity agreed with by many other EU theorists: intergovernmentalists, neofunctionalists/supranationalists and multilevel governmentalists. My own leaning is towards the latter for they present less deterministic interpretations that are based on a perceived intermingling of European and national affairs (Majone 1993; Pollack 1997, 2001). This is a far more complex reading of the European 'project', of the role of member states and the Commission, of a process in which the traditional nation-state is transformed into 'a new transnational political system' (Jachtenfuchs 2001: 256). Hooghe and Marks (2001) define multilevel governance by three characteristics. First, decision-making competences are shared by actors at different levels, and, as illustrated above, the supranational institutions, such as the Commission, become actors in their own right. Second, new modes of collective decision-making emerge (such as the EU's open method of co-ordination (OMC)). Third, the traditional separations of domestic and international politics are blurred. Theorists of multilevel governance see the nation-state as a key actor in European politics while at the same time the Commission is seen as independently impacting on member state policy-making. The EU–member state relationship is 'far more complex, flexible, ... far more post-modern' (Aalbert 2004: 29, 41).

The significance of multi-level governance for this chapter is first, that the UK nation-state is an active player, an active maker of policy, at all levels: European and global, as well as national. Without access to these elite policy-makers, it is extremely difficult to determine the origins and the trajectory of the policy idea, thus allowing the nation-state to appear either as 'maker' of policy or as a 'receiver' of it – dependent on the policy itself and on the particular political need. In this way, as I have argued elsewhere (Brine 2002a), it is possible for the UK government (Conservative or Labour) to blame or ignore the EU as it sees fit. Moreover, the complexity of the multi-level role of the nation-state is further obscured by the similar multi-level roles of influence: of non-government organisations, interest groups, senior civil servants/administrators and epistemic communities of academics (Brine 2000; Nóvoa and Lawn 2002).

The second significance is that the concept (lifelong learning) emerges within a short timespan from many places, (for instance, the OECD, UNESCO, the Council of Europe, the GATS, the EU and the member state, the UK), thus both consolidating through repeated use, and confusing through differing or absent definitions.

The third significance is that, from its multi-authorship and multi-text location, the discourse is similarly multi-layered for, as will be discussed below, despite the apparent homogeneity of the lifelong learner, three main categories of learner are constructed and each of these is further fragmented by gender, class, age, race and ethnicity. Despite the assumption by many theorists that the study of global geo-political relations of governance and policy-making, and the related concerns of economics, are an ungendered field of study, it is, as I have argued elsewhere, not so. For the policies that are made, the discourses they construct, the practices by which they are implemented, and even the methods by which they are audited, (re)construct, and are constructed by, relations of gender, race and class.

Different EU texts are presented at particular stages of the policy-making process, and carry different levels of legislative power. The textual process is one that moves from consultation to legislation or recommendation. It begins with a discussion or consultation document from the Commission. This is most likely to be a Memorandum that welcomes comments. This then leads to a Commission Communication that provides the detailed information that might eventually lead to a more concise legislative document. Thus, with regard to the explicit development of the policy on lifelong learning, there is a Memorandum, a Communication and a Resolution (CEC 2000c, 2001a, 2002). The strength of an explicit policy lies in its interrelationship with other policies and action programmes so that it moves outward on a multiple and mutually reinforcing policy trajectory into the member states. This policy merging often involves more than one directorate general (DG); the DGs of this chapter are the DG for employment and social affairs and the DG for education and culture – although generally the sole authors of a text, they are the joint authors of the detailed Communication on Lifelong Learning (CEC 2001a).

Trajectory of time

I begin the time trajectory with the EU *White Paper: Growth, Competitiveness, Employment* (CEC 1993), the aim of which was to increase and create jobs, to raise levels of education and to address the perceived threat to social cohesion. Stating that 'the Community now faces the danger of *not only a dual labour market but also a dual society*' (CEC 1993: 134, original emphasis), this key White Paper placed 'lifelong education and training' at the top of its list of priorities (ibid.: 16). Although *Growth* made only two explicit references to lifelong learning, they are both significant. First, it defined the concept:

All measures must therefore necessarily be based on the *concept of developing, generalizing and systematizing lifelong learning and continuing training.* This means that education and training systems must be reworked in order to take account of the need – which is already growing and is set to grow even more in the future – for the *permanent recomposition and redevelopment of knowledge and know-how.*

(CEC 1993: 120, original emphasis)

In the second reference to lifelong learning, *Growth* made the connection between this and what subsequently becomes known as the 'knowledge economy', and in particular, the role to be played by higher education.

As well as defining lifelong learning and relating it to the knowledge economy, *Growth* also, for the first time, identified three types of learner. The first is the higher education learner, the learner for the 'information society'. The second is the unemployed, low-skilled, 'disadvantaged' person in need of 'training', and the third is the unemployed school leaver and young person (under 25). Subsequent texts continue to construct these three distinct learners. There are many reasons why this White Paper represents a pivotal point in EU policy-making (Brine 2002b) but here its significance lies in the three-way fragmentation of the homogeneous learner.

The subsequent *White Paper: Education and Training* (CEC 1995) pushed the three learners into two main routes of learning: the traditional and the modern. The traditional route was described as that based on formal, high-level, academic qualifications whereas the modern route was based on the accreditation of experiences and competencies. The 'information society' learner following the traditional route would gain high-value cultural capital through formal, transferable, qualifications. The unemployed learner (school-leaver, young person or adult) following the modern route would be encouraged to record their learning on a 'personal skills card'. In either case, the individual learners would themselves be responsible for their own learning – and their related 'employability'. The significance of this White Paper is that it defined differing curricula leading to outcomes of differing value – in itself and in its exchange. Moreover, as the responsibility is individualised, so is the risk; as opportunity is individualised, so is failure. The concept of individualism is thus closely linked to blame and pathologization – a model of social integration defined by Levitas (1998) as that based on the morals and behaviour of a perceived underclass. Whereas the concept of individualism is an inherent feature of all lifelong learners, that of an immoral underclass applies predominantly to the low-knowledge skilled unemployed. Significantly, as Beck argues, although the individual is set adrift from 'class commitments', 'the *relations* of inequality remain stable' (1992: 89), and I argue that these relations remain classed, gendered and raced.

Two key EU events took place in 1997. First, the Treaty of Amsterdam (CEC 1997a), which stressed the emergence of a 'knowledge economy', one based on information and communication technology, on knowledge construction and transfer. It also stated that education and training were critical to this 'new' economy, addressing needs related to occupational change and to unemployment. The second event was the Luxembourg Council (CEC 1997b) where, despite an emergent discourse of the knowledge economy, nevertheless was greatly concerned with youth and long-term adult unemployment. Individualisation was strengthened, and the EU's concern with employment morphed into *employability* – the ability to *become* employed rather than the state of employment itself. As the concept of individualisation was linked with that of employability, the lifelong learner was placed in a state of constant becoming, of readiness for employment.

Three years after Amsterdam and Luxembourg, the policy chronology moves to Lisbon. Lifelong learning at this time remained an ill-defined concept – as did the newly arrived concept of the knowledge economy. The Lisbon Strategy marked a key point in the EU development of the employment strategy, the knowledge economy/society and lifelong learning. Although the Lisbon Strategy made many references to a knowledge economy, it made little attempt to define it, relying instead on an assumption of shared definition and understanding. The terms of knowledge-based *economy* and knowledge *society* were used apparently interchangeably – but not as randomly as it would at first appear: the knowledge-based *economy* was used only when referring to the need for higher-level graduate and postgraduate information and knowledge skills. Conversely, the knowledge *society* was used when referring to the unemployed, to those with low-level knowledge skills, and those socially excluded. Significantly, despite the surface sparkle of the new bright knowledge economy, the main focus of the Lisbon Strategy is on the knowledge society and the perceived underlying threat of the dual society.

In the same year as the Lisbon Strategy the Commission produced the first of the lifelong learning trilogy of documents: the Memorandum (CEC 2000c), the Communication (CEC 2001a) and the Resolution (CEC 2002). The *Memorandum*, a consultation document, defined lifelong learning as 'all purposeful learning activity, undertaken on an ongoing basis with the aim of improving knowledge, skills and competence' (CEC 2000c: 3). The Memorandum emphasises the opportunities that the new knowledge economy will bring, but also risks and uncertainties: it is the individual's responsibility to take the opportunity and to limit the risk. Lifelong learning, education and training throughout life, the 'capacity to create and use knowledge effectively and intelligently . . . and . . . on a continually changing basis' (ibid.: 7) are the responsibility of the individual. This infers that the person who does not do this, the person who does not take the opportunity, and the responsibility, for doing so, will 'fall by the wayside' (ibid.: 7). Moreover, the theme of individualism is also the driver of provision: 'education and training systems should adapt to individual needs and demands rather than the other way round' (ibid.: 8). The Memorandum construct two groups of learners: those *with* knowledge skills and those *without*. These are the main vertical categories which are cut horizontally by age, gender, class, race and ethnicity.

Following the consultation of the Memorandum, the Commission produced the Communication which detailed their proposals to establish a 'European area of lifelong learning'. The definition of lifelong learning was amended: 'All learning activity undertaken throughout life, with the aim of improving knowledge, skills and competencies within a person, civic, social and/or employment-related perspective.' This wider definition was further supplemented by a new concept of life*wide* learning: formal, non-formal or informal. Thus, life*long* and life*wide* learning covered absolutely *all* learning at all times, in all sites. Nevertheless, the *Communication* continued to prioritise the relationship between lifelong learning and employability – that is the emphasis continued to be on the 'unemployed' learner.

There are four observations to make regarding the Communication. First, it confirmed and extended the concept of individualism; second, it introduced the notion of quality assurance and the need for guidance and counselling; third, it emphasised the need for recognition and transfer of qualifications (not only in relation to Bologna, to those of higher education, but also to those of lower-level and vocational attainment); and fourth, the knowledge economy was eclipsed by the knowledge society. So much so that even the reference to the key statement from the Lisbon Strategy quoted above read: 'To become the most competitive and dynamic knowledge-based *society* in the world' (CEC 2001a: 3, emphasis added).

The shifting discourse of economy–society signals the complex construction of European lifelong learners. The knowledge *economy* is consistently related only to higher-level graduate and postgraduate learners, whereas the knowledge *society* is equally consistently associated with low-knowledge-skilled unemployed learners.

In referring to the graduate and postgraduate learner, those with high-level knowledge skills, the emphasis is on provision, not on further identifying the learner. The text echoes the Bologna Declaration (CEC 1999c), highlighting the need for higher education to implement the systems for the recognition and transferability of qualifications, and for widening participation. Conversely, when referring to the low-knowledge skilled and unemployed learner, the emphasis is less on provision and more on identifying the learner. It reiterated the 1993 threat of a dual society and identified specific groups who were especially 'at risk of exclusion' – and hence in need of lifelong learning as follows:

people on low incomes
disabled people
ethnic minorities and immigrants
early school leavers
lone parents
unemployed people
parents returning to the labour market

workers with low levels of education and training
people outside the labour market
senior citizens (including older workers)
ex-offenders

(CEC 2001a: 13)

The Communication spoke of the 'considerable risks and uncertainties associated with the knowledge-based society', and added that it threatened to 'bring about greater inequalities and social exclusion' (CEC 2001a: 6), especially as there are almost 150 million people within the EU of fifteen member states without a basic level of education, and who therefore, they argued, faced a higher risk of marginalisation (ibid.: 6). Thus the themes of, on the one hand, change, opportunity and individual choice, and on the other, risk, uncertainty and individual responsibility, described by Field (1998) as a discourse of crisis, continue, and lifelong learning is consistently constructed as a major solution to the problem of social exclusion and unemployment.

The subsequent Resolution on lifelong learning (CEC 2002) recorded the European Council's confirmation of the Commission's proposed policy direction for lifelong learning. Most significantly it confirmed the definitions of life*long* and life*wide* learning, reinforced the concept of individualism and referred throughout to the knowledge society rather than economy.

From the *White Paper: Growth* (CEC 1993) to the Resolution (CEC 2002), the concepts of knowledge economy and society interweave but are consistently related to different constructs of learner: the former to the high-knowledge skilled graduate and postgraduate; the latter to the low-knowledge skilled, and the unemployed school-leaver, young person or adult. In both cases this is accompanied by the concept of individualism, of opportunity and risk, blame and failure. Whereas the focus on the high-knowledge skilled learner is on transferability and mobility, that of the low-knowledge skilled is on the identification of the learners themselves. Three dominant concerns continue to underpin these specific policies: (1) the construction of the EU itself – the European project (the discourse of integration); (2) global economic competitiveness (the knowledge economy and the discourse of economic growth); and (3) the threat of the dual society (the knowledge society and the discourse of political stability).

Trajectory of contemporary textual influence

As illustrated in the previous section, EU documents related to lifelong learning are interspersed with others, either broader or with a different specific focus – with only the most important papers chosen for this particular analysis. This illustrates the multi-sited, consistently cross-referencing approach that is fundamental to EU policy-making that ultimately refers back to the prime legal competency – that is a reference to an article within a treaty, and to the subsequent genealogy of that policy. But whereas this provides the trace for legal competency, it does not so easily locate the construction of the discourse itself: this, as illustrated in Brine (2002b), requires a detailed exploration of many texts that is not possible in one chapter.

However, to illustrate the complexity of the connections I search now for the way in which lifelong learning, the knowledge economy–society and the identities of learners are represented in a selection of contemporary Commission documents.

I begin with the *White Paper: A New Impetus for European Youth* (CEC 2001b) which is based on a large consultation exercise with young people across the EU. Its section on education mirrors the traditional/modern division of the *White Paper: Education and Training*, (1995) as it points to two groups of learners: those who need to be encouraged towards 'a career in science or technology' and for whom subjects such as research and technology must be made more attractive, and those who 'leave school and training before acquiring formal qualifications'. The emphasis here is on a ' "blended" (correctly mixed) education' that uses 'the internet and multimedia, theoretical classroom methods and studying at home, as well as youth activities, practical experience and work' (ibid.:32). The paper takes pains to add training to each reference to learning, thus linking the more vocational to the academic. Here we see again the construction of two main groups of learner. The first is the young high-knowledge skilled person destined for formal learning in higher education, accumulating a wealth of cultural capital that is contained in her/his, increasingly recognisable, transferable academic qualifications. The second is the early school leaver who, without academic qualifications is, in this paper, encouraged towards a 'blended' learning mix of primarily non-formal and informal learning, which despite the push towards recognition and accreditation, the currency does not hold a similar value. The paper makes no explicit distinction of gender, ethnicity or class.

The high-knowledge skilled learner is, not surprisingly, the focus of the report from the Conference of European Higher Education Ministers (CEC 2005a) tracking the implementation of the Bologna Declaration (CEC 1999c). This report returns to and strengthens the discourse of the knowledge economy and the need for higher level knowledge-skills. Whereas we would not expect the low-knowledge learners to be included here, it is noteworthy that there is no explicit reference to lifelong learning. Despite the obvious progression from undergraduate to postgraduate, doctoral or professional development within higher education, these learners are far less frequently located within the discourse of lifelong learning; whereas lifelong learning is increasingly synonymous with the low-knowledge learner. I return to this point below. Despite the allure of the knowledge economy discourse, across the EU 25 member states, only 21 per cent of the working-age population have achieved tertiary education (USA 38 per cent, Canada 43 per cent). Moreover, the report points out that this is a significant increase brought about by those new entry states which have higher levels of tertiary participation. The knowledge-economy is for the few.

In sharp contrast to the HE paper, the Commission's review of the key 1999 employment strategy (CEC 2004a) focuses entirely on the low-knowledge learner. Given its prime focus on (un)employment, there was no reference whatsoever to the knowledge-economy or society: 'knowledge' Europe has vanished: this is not the Europe of the low-knowledge learner. As with the *Communication from the Commission: Making a European Area of Lifelong Learning a Reality* (CEC 2001a), this paper offers a rare elaboration of the low-skilled learner. They are 'people at a disadvantage', women, young people (particularly early school leavers), ethnic minorities, immigrants, the low-skilled and older workers. There is no elaboration, in any text, of the high-knowledge learner. We can only discern this learner as the 'other': that is, they are not disadvantaged, men, not an early school leaver, white, British born, and not old.

As stated above, the Lisbon Strategy (CEC 2000a) was a pivotal point in the development of the employment strategy and the concepts of the knowledge economy and lifelong learning. However, in response to a growing suggestion that it be abandoned, the Commission published the *Communication to the Spring European Council: Working Together for Growth and Jobs: New Start for the Lisbon Strategy* (CEC 2005b). The paper returned to the concept of global competition and reintroduced the concept of a knowledge *economy* dependent on high-level knowledge skills. Yet, the contradiction between economy and society evident throughout this analysis is replayed again as the linked paper reviewing the specific objectives of education and training (CEC 2005c) instead stressed the knowledge *society* and focused on youth, primarily the high numbers of early school leavers, with only secondary attention given to the high-knowledge learners and the desired areas of maths, science and technology. While it stressed the all-encompassing nature of lifelong learning, there is a significant discursive shift in its definition: 'The new social and economic formation also demands increased recognition of knowledge and skills acquired outside the formal education system, and increased support for non-formal and informal training for all age and social groups' (CEC 2005c: 12).

The paper constructs a dichotomy between formal learning, that of the education system that leads to transferable recognisable academic qualifications, and non-formal and informal *training*: a re-strengthening of the academic–vocational divide that is a pervasive classed and gendered feature of much education – particularly in Britain.

From the late 1970s, with the establishment within the Commission of the Equal Opportunities Unit, there has been a consistent focus on gender equality. Since the early 1980s there have been a series of equal opportunities programmes that both provided funded programmes to external networks and lobbied within the Commission. A key shift occurred with the mainstreaming of equal opportunities into the Structural Funds (CEC 1999b); a further shift occurred with its expansion into the area of access and supply of goods and services (CEC 2004b). The latest report on equality between women and men (CEC 2005d) implicitly defined 'life-long learning' (now hyphenised) as adult education and training; a much truncated version of the Communication definition (CEC 2001a), but which nevertheless is more reflective of one strand of common sense usage – synonymous with post-compulsory education and training. The report states that in twenty-one member states, more women than men participate in (this particular type of) lifelong learning – that is, adult education and training.

The discourse of lifelong learning is less obvious in these contemporary texts: rarely referred to explicitly, and when it is, it is either in relation to the low-knowledge skilled learners and early school leavers, or in an adult education way to women. With the exception of the Communication (CEC 2001a) and the review of the employment strategy (CEC 2004a) with its detailed definition of specific social groups, for the most part, the explicit construction of learners is simply through their skill level or age.

The learners and their learning

As stated in the Memorandum, the Communication and the Resolution, lifelong learning is directly related to the labour market, to employability, and in order to further identify the learners and to understand the learning that they do, we must look to their place in the knowledge economy/society.

Walby (2005), in her continuing work on the gendered labour market, identified two main industries related to the 'knowledge economy': the 'high tech' manufacturing industry and the knowledge-intensive industries. Very few people work in the 'high tech' manufacturing industries; for instance, only 1.26 per cent within the UK, and even this figure is decreasing. It is also a strongly gendered industry in employing twice as many men as women. Quoting EU statistics, Walby adds that, despite its apparent high-level knowledge position, (and despite its centrality to the discourse of the knowledge economy and lifelong learning), only 30 per cent are considered 'high skilled', that is with at least graduate qualifications. Similarly the EU gender equality report (CEC 2005d: 14) stated that although in 2001 almost 25 per cent of all graduates were in the fields of maths, science and technology, only 31 per cent of these were women.

There are far more people working in *knowledge-intensive* industries (for instance, within the UK, 41 per cent and increasing), but this wide-ranging labour market classification includes areas of both knowledge *reproduction* and knowledge *creation*. Moreover, many differing sectors are included within it. Many of these are more commonly recognised as services: banks and insurances, real estate, research and development, advertising, water services, air transport, post and telecommunications, sporting activities and legal services; or public sector provision: education, health and social work. All these areas are covered by the WTO's General Agreement on Trade in Services. Although there are slightly more women than men in this sector, many differing occupations are included within it: within the EU only 42 per cent of people working in know-ledge-intensive industries are high-knowledge skilled: graduate or postgraduate, for example, the higher education sector includes people who work as porters, cleaners, secretaries, gardeners as well as academics.

The gender equality report (CEC 2005d) shows that the pay gap between women and men continues with EU national women earning 16 per cent less than men. More women continue to work part-time (30.4 compared with 6.6 per cent), and slightly more are unemployed (10 per cent compared with 8.3). At management levels the figures are reversed with women at 31 per cent compared with men at 69, at executive level 10 per cent are women, and 90 per cent are men.

These statistics, while generally indicative of a gendered/classed EU labour market, are only useful up to a point. As is common with EU statistics, their primary classification is the nation-state, and thus differences of class and eth-nicity are difficult to ascertain, and a reading of this sort must be based on other research findings that show, for instance, that low-knowledge skill is classed and linked to poverty, social exclusion and under-education (Brine 1999; CoE 1992). Nevertheless, the report does provide a certain degree of complexity within gender as it distinguishes, where it can, between EU 'national' women, and EU immigrant women, showing unemployment rates are significantly higher for immigrant women, both in comparison with EU national women and with immigrant men, and correspondingly lower in terms of educational attainment. The only other variable shown is age: older women have higher rates of unemployment and low educational qualifications.

It may be that this gendering of the knowledge economy is due to women being less successful learners, and most especially less successful than men in formal education and hence without the cultural capital that will take them into the knowledge economy. The discourse leads to the assumption that those learners with high academic qualifications, the high-knowledge skilled workers, would be those most visible within the knowledge industries – and this is not so. Yet the EU gender equality report (CEC 2005d) shows the opposite, that women and girls are increasingly successful within the formal learning sector: women aged 20–24 are achieving a higher educational attainment level than men: 58 per cent of graduates and 41 per cent of PhD graduates were women (CEC 2005d). The majority of the 19.8 per cent of early school leavers (in the EU of 25 member states) are boys (CEC 2005d). Thus, based on formal learning qualifications, the high-knowledge learner can as easily be a woman as a man.

The above analysis has highlighted the discursive relationship between the constructs of lifelong learning and the knowledge economy–society. The argument is that the knowledge-economy requires high-level knowledge skills and therefore the individual must strive to achieve this – or at least to achieve the best they can – to 'achieve their full potential'. The technological change of the knowledge-economy demands a constant updating of that learning: hence *lifelong* learning. This concept of the bright 'brain-based' future is a 'hook' to which lifelong learning is attached; it is a bright surface discourse that glimmers in the sun of the European horizon – a world of clean and non-physical knowledge work that hides the bulk – around 80 per cent (CEC 2005a) – of lesser- or non-knowledge work that includes servicing both the knowledge economy and the knowledge workers. Nevertheless, the 80 per cent must still be lifelong learners, indeed as shown above, these are those who are most often targeted as such; they are the learners most specifically demographically identified; they are the learners with the most prescriptive curricula in terms of (new) basic skills and vocational training; they are the learners who, without easily recognisable qualifications, must gather, record and attempt to gain accreditation for non-formal and informal learning.

The primary classification of learner is through the level of knowledge-skill, and as shown above, women and men are found in each category. However, as also shown above, women, although equally represented as high-knowledge learners, are not as likely to be a high-level worker in the knowledge economy. It may be that high-knowledge skill women are as caught in the accreditation cycle, albeit within the formal learning sector, as the low-knowledge skilled are in the non-/informal.

Like that of 'equal opportunities', the discourse of lifelong learning is cloaked in 'inherent goodness', by which I mean it is extremely difficult to disagree with 'learning', with 'personal fulfilment', with reaching one's 'full potential', with the (neo-)liberal focus on individual rights and responsibilities. However, beneath this cloak, lifelong learning is a discourse of competition, of personal striving, of constant becoming, of inclusion and exclusion that continues to (re)construct educational and labour market power relations of gender, class, ethnicity and age. As shown above, lifelong learning is repeatedly linked with the discourse of the bright beckoning future of the knowledge economy, yet, as predicted in numerous EU reports of the 1980s (Brine 1999), the same technological changes that underpin the knowledge economy are those that have led to the technological replacement of numerous workers in both the manufacturing and the service industries: the ones leading to large numbers of unemployed people, Bauman's (2004) 'outcasts', constructed in EU policies as the 'threat of the dual society'.

Chapter 3

Gendered constructions of lifelong learning and the learner in the UK policy context

Carole Leathwood

This chapter turns the focus on to contemporary policy discourses of lifelong learning in the UK, and examines constructions of the lifelong learner in this context. Lifelong learning has been a key theme for the new Labour government since its election in 1997, but a commitment to adult, and lifelong, education has a much longer history. In 1919, the Adult Education Committee of the Ministry of Reconstruction insisted that:

> Adult education must not be regarded as a luxury for a few exceptional persons here and there, nor as a thing which concerns only a short span of early adulthood, but it is a permanent national necessity, an inseparable aspect of citizenship, and therefore should be both universal and lifelong.
>
> (Cited in Field and Leicester 2000: 4)

Adult education in the UK has a long history of education for progressive social change. Demand from working-class and feminist movements was instrumental in building a commitment within adult education to developing provision for marginalised groups, and as Jackson (2004a) notes, support for working-class education has been a persistent and powerful theme within this tradition. This was not only provision 'from above', with middle-class educationalists catering for the working classes, but autonomous educational provision organised within and by working-class and feminist organisations. One example was that of the Co-operative Women's Guilds established in the late nineteenth century, which were 'primarily about working-class women's struggle for their own educational, social and political agenda and self-determination' (Swindells 1995: 39). The Guilds played a key role in campaigns for suffrage, free education and a range of social issues such as pensions, and the education they provided was explicitly political and geared to social change. Within feminism and other progressive movements, there has long been an awareness that education can be both liberatory and oppressive, hence a demand not only for *access* to education, but for access to the *kinds* of education that can support and facilitate emancipatory goals. This does not mean, however, that working-class education necessarily embraced feminist concerns, or that feminist education was free of classed, racialised and indeed gendered assumptions, processes and outcomes. The education for women initially offered in the working men's colleges, for example, included daytime classes in 'ladylike' activities for middle-class women, while evening classes in basic skills and sewing were provided for working-class women (ibid.).

Unfortunately, such classed and gendered patterns of participation are not that far removed from today's stratified configurations of lifelong learning, as discussed, for example, in Becky Francis's chapter (this volume). Yet there is a powerful presumption within dominant discourses of lifelong learning that education is neutral, and/or inevitably a force for good. Contemporary government policy on lifelong learning is particularly focused on increasing access and participation for those with little previous access to education and with the fewest qualifications, and hence in many ways is to be welcomed. Yet, as will be seen, it is far removed from some of the earlier and rather more radical formulations of lifelong education.

In this chapter, I will begin with a discussion of key themes within UK lifelong learning policy and an examination of the ways in which these are gendered. I will then move on to an analysis of the constructions of the lifelong learner in this policy context, and finally consider the forms of lifelong learning that are available. Lifelong learning offers tremendous potential to reduce inequalities and enhance social justice. It will be argued, however, that despite the emphasis on social inclusion and social justice in contemporary UK lifelong learning policy, the dominance of an economic rationality within these policy formulations suggests that persistent inequalities in the labour market and society as a whole will be reinforced and reconstituted.

Lifelong learning policy

The election of the new Labour government in 1997, with its oft repeated mantra of 'education, education, education', brought a renewed commitment to lifelong learning. Key national reports, consultation documents and Acts of Parliament have been accompanied by new targets, funding commitments, organisational arrangements and partnerships which have impacted upon all sectors of education and training. The impetus for this flurry of policies and activities rests, however, not simply with a belief in the importance of education for all citizens, but with the perceived need to respond to global economic developments. The Learning Age Green Paper states:

> We are in a new age – the age of information and of global competition.
> Familiar certainties and old ways of doing things are disappearing. The
> types of jobs we do have changed as have the industries in which we work
> and the skills they need. At the same time, new opportunities are opening
> up as we see the potential of new technologies to change our lives for the
> better. We have no choice but to prepare for this new age in which the key

to success will be the continuous education and development of the human mind and imagination.

(DfEE 1998, section 1, para. 1)

It is, of course, tempting to immediately point out that while some things clearly are changing, some 'old ways of doing things' – like the continued under-valuing of women's work and the ongoing assumption that it is pre-dominantly women who will provide the caring and domestic labour in our society – are proving to be all too resistant to change.

But to return to the economic rationale for lifelong learning. There is an assumed inevitability about all this – *'we have no choice'* – and lifelong learning is seen as the answer. The human capital assumptions are evident in the Foreword to the above Green Paper by David Blunkett, then Secretary of State for Education and Employment, who wrote:

> Learning is the key to prosperity – for each of us as individuals, as well as for the nation as a whole. Investment in human capital will be the foundation of success in the knowledge-based global economy of the twenty-first century.

And the key to this investment is skills development: 'Skills are now top of our agenda. We need highly qualified people in the workforce if we are to remain competitive in an increasingly global market' (Hope 2005).

Yet as the Learning Age Green Paper makes clear, lifelong learning is about more than jobs and skills:

> The development of a culture of learning will help to build a united soci-ety, assist in the creation of personal independence, and encourage our creativity and innovation. Learning builds self-confidence and independ-ence . . . Learning offers excitement and the opportunity for discovery. It stimulates enquiring minds and nourishes our souls. It takes us in directions we never expected, sometimes changing our lives.

(DfEE 1998: 10)

In this discourse, lifelong learning is constructed as an unconditional 'good thing' – for every individual and for society as a whole. The twin themes of global economic competitiveness and social inclusion/social justice run throughout the government's lifelong learning policy documents, although as many have commented, it is the economic rationale rather than the social justice concerns that have remained dominant (Leathwood and Hayton 2002; Taylor 2005), with, as will be seen, implications for the kinds of lifelong learning opportunities that are available. What is less commented upon in the main-stream literature is the way that both of these themes/rationales are gendered (and classed and racialised) – something to which I will now turn.

Gender and the economic rationale for lifelong learning

The construction of the economic within lifelong learning policy, and indeed the discipline of economics itself, is highly gendered, resting on masculinist and ethno-centric assumptions and values (see Ferber and Nelson 1993; Williams 1993). The economic arena is conceptualised entirely in terms of paid work, with women's unpaid labour in the home/family/community (and indeed in the workplace) rendered invisible. As Waring (1989) notes, women simply 'don't count' in mainstream economic theory and practices.

Blackmore (1997) has shown how human capital theory rests not only on simplistic assumptions of a straightforward and linear relationship between education and work, and between educational achievements/credentials and economic productivity, but also on fixed technical notions of skill which privilege the needs of both capital and of male workers. Instead she illustrates how skills are socially constructed – with the value attributed to particular 'skills' depending on how those skills are gained (e.g. through formal training, experience or learning in the home), who has them (e.g. men or women), and the context in which they are used (e.g. in paid work or the home). Skill, she argues, like gender, is relational, and reflects relations of power, with women's skills being valued less than those of men.

The decline of the manufacturing base in the UK, and hence of the traditional employment patterns for working-class men, has contributed to a concern about men's educational participation and levels of achievement. The demands of the service sector for employees with personal and social skills has been seen by some as a feminisation of the workforce (see e.g. Walkerdine *et al.* 1999), with worrying consequences for men to whom such skills are not assumed to come 'naturally'. A gender essentialism underpins this discourse – women are assumed to 'naturally' have/be able to acquire such skills, although they have not traditionally been recognised or valued as skills. A key aspect of the lifelong learning agenda has been to construct a particular kind of employable subject, something that is discussed further below. The focus for the new subject is less on the technical skills previously demanded by the manufacturing industry and more on generic and transferable skills. Yet as Blackmore (1997) has articulated, this move from an emphasis on technical skills to generic skills is no less gendered. Although the multiskilled manager is required to incorporate the generic skills of interpersonal team working and communication skills, these are framed instrumentally and do not have the same connotations of ethical commitment as those associated with the on-going caring that is central to dominant constructions of femininity.

Lifelong learning policy focuses not only on the economic benefits of a globally competitive workforce for society as a whole, but also emphasises the economic benefits of ongoing learning for individuals. This ignores, however, the ways in which the labour market is gendered, classed and racialised. Vertical

and horizontal segregation persist, and women at all qualifications levels continue to be paid significantly less than men (DfES 2004). Many working-class
women are trapped in 'lifelong earning' in low-paid and low-status jobs
(Jackson 2003), with lifelong learning unlikely to challenge the structural
relationships through which working-class and particularly minority ethnic
working-class women are positioned in low-paid work. The economic benefits
of higher education participation are extolled by the government in its widening participation policy, but although students with a degree do on average earn
more than those without, earnings levels still reflect the gendered, classed and
racialised labour market (Conlon and Chevalier 2002). Students in HE now
accrue significant levels of debt in order to fund their studies – and poorer
students have the highest debt levels (Callender and Wilkinson 2003) – but
lower levels of pay for women, minority ethnic and working-class graduates
mean that these graduates are likely to take longer to pay off this debt.

Yet the economic rationale for lifelong learning assumes that such learning is
inevitably good and beneficial for both society as a whole and individuals who
become lifelong learners. There is little recognition of differential costs and
benefits, nor of the differential opportunities to engage in lifelong learning in
the first place. Engaging in lifelong learning is presented as the logical/rational
choice for individuals, with no acknowledgement of the ways in which the
choice-making individual of neo-liberal economic policy – 'economic man'
(Ferber and Nelson 1993) is a gendered, classed and racialised one.

Gender and the social justice/social inclusion
rationale for lifelong learning

Lifelong learning to enhance social inclusion is a key aspect of the policy
discourse, yet here too, the economic underpinnings are evident. Social inclusion is largely framed in terms of inclusion in the paid workforce (Levitas 1998),
once more ignoring women's unpaid work in the home and community. And
although there is a concern to address the needs of the socially excluded, this is
largely about getting people into paid work:

> We will also need to renew our efforts to achieve equality of opportunity,
> recognising that some groups are harder to reach and last to benefit from
> policies to tackle social exclusion. As policies help people back into
> work, training or other opportunities, the pool of people who remain will
> inevitably be those who are harder to help.
>
> (Office of the Deputy Prime Minister 2004)

Yet paid work is not the only focus of government policy on social exclusion.
David Miliband, Communities Minister, recently said:

> Social exclusion is not just about basic conditions. It is about not having

access to the things most people take for granted – basic skills, a job, a decent home, a sufficient income and contact with friends and family. It is about not having power over your life and your future.

(Miliband 2005)

Yet for many (and it is almost always women) with children or other caring responsibilities, getting a job, as well as access to education and training, depends on being able to obtain affordable and good quality childcare, while achieving a 'sufficient income' often remains a pipedream for low-paid workers. Some assistance with childcare costs is available through some government return to work/study programmes, e.g. those aimed at lone parents, but as Toynbee (2003) discovered in her account of life in low-pay Britain, poorly-paid work rarely offers a route out of social exclusion, and of course it is women who are most likely to be in the lowest paid jobs.

The social inclusion rationale for lifelong learning also begs the question – inclusion in what? There is no critique of existing structures or power relations in government lifelong learning policy, but instead an emphasis on building social capital, social cohesion and a unified society. The unified society is unproblematised, and the emphasis on social capital and social cohesion fails to recognise the unpaid work women do in families and communities (Jackson 2003). Yet the concept of the 'learning society' is widely used in lifelong learning literature. It conjures up a cosy image of everyone happily engaged in a wide variety of learning opportunities, and accruing a broad range of benefits for themselves, their families, their communities and society as a whole. Yet this also tends to be seen in instrumental ways as necessary to ensure economic competitiveness: 'In the next century, the economically successful nations will be those which become learning societies: where all are committed, through effective education and training, to lifelong learning' (NCIHE 1997, 1.1).

Morley (2002: 90) describes the learning society as 'a seductive discourse' which is nevertheless strongly influenced by human capital theory and hence focuses on wealth creation rather than distribution. She argues that the discourse of the learning society disguises inequalities by ignoring barriers to participation, social positioning and 'psychic narratives/internalised oppression' such as confidence.

Increased confidence is frequently discussed as one of the wider personal/social benefits of lifelong learning, while lack of confidence is seen as a barrier. It is usually assumed to be the working classes, women and some minority ethnic groups, however, who are thought to be lacking in confidence, and the confidence they lack is the 'confidence' to fit into white, masculinist, middle-class educational arenas and values. Of course, students often do talk about their lack of confidence, or of an increased confidence that results from educational participation and achievement, but like Bartky (1990), I would argue that this 'lack of confidence' is more usefully theorised sociologically, and in terms of access to particular forms of cultural, social and material capital than as a matter of individual psychology and personality characteristics or failings. The emphasis on confidence within current policy discourse is an example of the way in which responsibility (and, therefore, blame) become individualised in this discursive context.

The emphasis on social inclusion in 'the learning society' ensures that some other barriers to lifelong learning are recognised in the policy literature. Childcare responsibilities, for example, are assumed to be a barrier for many women, hence the provision of some financial assistance with childcare costs in some government programmes. The difficulties of being caught between two 'greedy institutions' of education and family have long been recognised (Edwards 1993: 62), but the time involved in domestic and caring work is still not acknowledged, nor are the consequences for women who are unable to attend classes when children are ill and regularly miss out on the informal learning opportunities that take place in the café/bar after class. Such commitments tend to be seen as private individual/family matters (Gouthro 2005) and as a 'normal' aspect of women's participation – hence are naturalised as part of being a woman (Stalker 2001). Hence gender issues are recognised to some extent – but perhaps only when these are conceptualised as an aspect of women's traditional role, and so not a threat to traditional gender relations. For example, while childcare might be acknowledged, the time women are expected to devote to looking after male partners is not (Delphy and Leonard 1992), nor is the resistance and/or hostility that some women receive from such partners when they engage in educational activities (Stalker 2001). Some report feelings of guilt for 'neglecting' their families, and attempt to minimise the impact of their studies in the home, for example, by studying late at night and trying not to appear too clever (Blaxter and Tight 1994; Gouthro 2004, 2005).

While barriers constructed as 'individual' or 'personal' might be acknowledged, middle-class, masculinist and ethnocentric academic cultures, curricula and institutions are not identified as barriers, yet they ensure that many feel that lifelong learning is not for them and has no relevance to their lives (see Louise Archer's chapter in this volume and Archer *et al.* 2003; Quinn 2003; Read *et al.* 2003).

Within the social justice/social inclusion rationale for lifelong learning, therefore, despite an explicit focus on social justice concerns, inequalities are disguised, minimised or individualised, and the status quo remains largely unproblematised.

Constructioning the lifelong learner

A new subject – the lifelong learner who takes full responsibility for their own learning – is constructed through these policy discourses. This theme of individual responsibility is evident throughout current government policy, reflecting the neo-liberal shift away from state responsibility to that of the individual in a market economy. All individuals are expected to adapt to these 'new times', with the implications that those not doing so will need to change. For example, the Fryer Report which emphasised the importance of establishing a culture of lifelong learning, insisted that this would require changes from the government, funders and providers of lifelong learning, but it also states:

> The biggest change of all will be required in the attitudes of individuals and groups, particularly among those who are not currently engaged in lifelong learning activities, who demonstrate no inclination to become involved, or enjoy few opportunities to develop their abilities, interests or capacities through learning.
>
> (Fryer 1997: 4)

> Individuals should increasingly accept more control over the development of their own learning throughout life and, within their available resources, be ready to invest more in it themselves.
>
> (ibid.: 5)

A deficit discourse, so familiar in policy discourses about the working classes, is again very evident here. It is clear that some, for example, those with 'no inclination to become involved' are lacking in the right attitudes, and will need to change. The compulsory element within lifelong learning policy noted by Coffield (1999) can also be seen here.

This new lifelong learning subject is also an 'employable' one, with Ivan Lewis, the Skills Minister, stating, 'I think we have, through education, training and the concept of lifelong learning, the opportunity to replace a "job for life", if you like, with a new imperative of "employability for life" (Lewis 2004). Again this shifts the responsibility onto the individual and away from the government responsibility to provide full employment. As Charles Clarke, Secretary of State for Education at the time, explained:

> We want every adult to address their own skills that they need for employ-ability, but also to be responsible for taking action to address their own skill needs. So, acquiring skills is not something that somebody does for you, it is something that you acquire for yourself with help and support in the way that you need it.
>
> (Clarke 2004)

The theme of independence which is implicit in the above runs throughout lifelong learning policy. The Learning Age Green Paper states: 'For individuals, learning will encourage independence. For the nation, learning will offer a way out of dependency and low-expectation towards self-reliance and self-confidence' (DfEE 1998: 6). Yet as can be seen from Charles Clarke's speech above, independence is not simply a product of education, but a required characteristic of the lifelong learner – it is an aspect of the self-responsible and self-managing subject. In this discourse, independence is valorised and dependency denigrated. Yet the dependence/independence dichotomy is highly gendered as well as classed and racialised (Leathwood 2006). It disguises the interdependencies of social relations, denigrates those who need support, and assumes a self unencumbered by domestic and caring responsibilities, with sufficient material and other resources and capitals to maintain the myth of independence. The lifelong learner is the new subject of neo-liberalism – independent, confident, and taking responsibility for themselves and their futures. They are to be an 'entrepreneur of the self' (du Gay 1996), creating themselves through continual lifelong learning and re-skilling, as the ideal employable subject. This is also, I suggest, a masculine subject, embodying characteristics traditionally associated with masculinity rather than femininity.

Coffield (1999: 488) argues that this construction of the lifelong learner is also about social control:

> Lifelong learning is being used to socialise workers to the escalating demands of employers, who use '*empowerment*' to disguise an intensification of workloads via increased delegation; '*employability*' to make the historic retreat from the policy of full employment and periodic unemployment between jobs more acceptable; and '*flexibility*' to cover a variety of strategies to reduce costs which increase job insecurity.

Similarly, Crowther (2004: 125) argues that the dominant discourse of lifelong learning 'acts as a new disciplinary technology to make people more compliant and adaptable for work in the era of flexible capitalism'. Although class relations might be implied here, there is little recognition in the mainstream literature of the ways in which gendered and racialised power relations are reconstructed within this discursive framing. As Morley (2001) argues, the discourse of employability ignores gender, ethnicity, social class and other markers of identity that impact on students' experience and entry to the labour market. Where lifelong learning activities are directed at producing 'employable' subjects, they are also reproducing the gendered (as well as classed and racialised) worker identities of the labour market. Yates, for example, discusses how a vocational teacher of hospitality courses focused on developing in students the appropriate worker identities which included not only the technical skills for the job (using tools, etc.) but also being punctual, obedient and tolerant of being shouted at, i.e. the 'appropriate' worker identity for the bottom of the hierarchy in the catering industry. Yet these are not neutral attributes but classed, gendered and racialised. For example, being an attractive young women 'is one "employability" characteristic' for the hospitality industry (Yates 2004: 8). Similarly, Blackmore (1997) notes that vocational education is often more about social and attitudinal skills than high level technical ones, for example, secretarial courses for young women which emphasise particular constructions of femininity. These courses are directly serving the needs of the labour market, and in this way helping to sustain the inequalities integral to capitalism. Morley's (2001: 137) suggestion that we need a discourse of 'employer-ability' to ensure that employers become attuned to issues of inequality is very welcome, but it is hard to see this being taken up in the current economic and political context.

The lifelong learner is therefore constructed as a compliant employable subject, able to fit into the existing gendered, classed and racialised social order, rather than a critical thinker and citizen. Yet surely this contradicts a notion of the lifelong learner/worker for the twenty-first century as flexible, creative, highly skilled and able to adapt to meet the demands of the new economy? Broadfoot and Pollard (2000) also point to this contradiction in their suggestion that current school (over-)assessment policies are unlikely to instil a commitment to lifelong learning in pupils. Instead, I suggest, such policies privilege conformity rather than a creative and critical disposition. Jacky Brine's analysis (Chapter 2 in this volume) of the classed distinctions between the knowledge society and the knowledge economy is pertinent here, with the compliant subject who does not question the status quo particularly necessary for the lower echelons of the labour market in a capitalist economy. The economic and social justice elements of lifelong learning policy are not, therefore, as contradictory as they might appear at face value; rather, both are concerned with inclusion into, conformity to, and the legitimation of, a starkly unequal and highly stratified society.

What lifelong learning, or lifelong learning for what?

A key question in relation to lifelong learning policy must be lifelong learning *of* what and *for* what? In particular, what knowledges, skills and understandings are on offer within lifelong learning provision, what is valued and prioritised, and whose values are these (Jackson 2004a)?

From the above discussion it will come as no surprise that the emphasis in UK policy is on skills for work – both basic skills (literacy, numeracy, IT) and vocational education/training. This is evident in two of the three key targets that have been set for adult learning:

- to improve the basic skills of 1.5 m adults between 2001 and 2007;
- to reduce by 40 per cent the number of adults in work who lack NVQ[1] level 2 or equivalent by 2010.

The third, that 50 per cent of 18–30-year-olds should enter higher education by 2010, appears to be about a broader academic education, but there is a not very well hidden agenda to target the new 'widening participation' (predominantly working-class) students into two-year vocational 'foundation degrees', rather than into the full three-year degree programmes (Leathwood and O'Connell 2003). This is indicative of the differentiated routes, qualifications and educational institutions available to different groups (see e.g. Leathwood and Hutchings 2003; Leathwood 2004) which serve to perpetuate inequalities.

The targets reflect the general trend of LL policy in being predominantly about skills for work to meet the needs of the labour market, and directed primarily at 'the disadvantaged' and socially excluded. This emphasis on skills for work provision is also justified in terms of social justice. For example, the 2003 Skills White Paper stresses that:

> Our Skills Strategy aims to ensure equality of access to opportunities by ensuring that public funds are focused on those most in need. Achieving basic skills reduces inequalities. Level 2 qualifications are associated with enhanced prospects and promotion of equality for some groups.
>
> (DfES 2003a, para. 4.43)

While the Foster Report states that: 'an emphasis on skills development will in itself turn out to be a huge driver for social inclusion and improved personal self esteem, achieving a valuable synergy between societal and personal need' (Foster 2005: 16). The extent to which this succeeds, however, will depend on what skills for work are being developed, by/for whom and how. Workplace learning is a key part of the lifelong learning agenda, and this is reflected in the government targets discussed above. However, lower qualified employees – and more women are in this category – receive less training, with the trade union 'Amicus' stating that employers were sometimes reluctant to offer training to women as they feared they might then have to pay them more (House of Commons Trade and Industry Committee 2005). 'The material of male power' (Cockburn 1981) still has resonance. Part-time employees and those working for employment agencies, both of whom are also more likely to be women, also receive less training (DfES 2003a).

As has already been noted, skills training that leads only to low-paid, low-skilled work is unlikely to promote social inclusion in any meaningful sense of the term. It is clear that there is little in the policy on vocational education which is concerned to seriously challenge the gendered patterns of participation, and hence of identity construction, discussed by Becky Francis in her chapter (Chapter 4 in this volume). The general move towards outcomes-based education focussing on skills and competencies that Jill Blackmore discusses (Chapter 1 in this volume) has also been evident in the UK, and such developments are not 'innocent'. Kilminster (1994) examined the reformulation of vocational education following the introduction of new competency-based General National Vocational Qualifications in the UK. She argues that these new qualifications privilege a conservative ideology that valorises the market and individualism, and that this impacts particularly on working-class students who make up the majority in further education colleges. She compares the new curriculum to the previous curriculum for two specific modules and notes how references to social factors are excluded in the later versions. Furthermore, the opportunities for teachers to subvert the new ideological stance are severely curtailed by external tests which demand the 'right' answers (e.g. supportive of market philosophy). Kilminster argues that to expect students to both understand the broader issues and perform correctly in the tests would be asking for a far more sophisticated understanding of the social construction of knowledge than can be expected at this level within the time constraints of the courses.

When vocational education is geared solely to serving the needs of the labour market, it is likely to reinforce social inclusion as compliance, and reconstruct the gendered, classed and racialised worker identities demanded by employers. There is little in government policy on lifelong learning which indicates that vocational education and 'skills for work' should incorporate a broader and critical education in which work is placed within its social, economic, political and historical context.

There are, however, commitments to learning that extend beyond a narrow 'skills for work' focus. The 2003 Skills White Paper (DfES 2003a) recognises that people may be reluctant to embark on courses linked to qualifications, and/or may want to learn 'for its own sake'. It therefore concludes with a commitment to providing a minimum budget for adult and community learning. However, funding allocations for further education colleges for 2005–6 prioritise basic skills and work-related learning, resulting in reduced funding for other provision. The Association of Colleges insists that this will mean cuts in course provision, a rise in course fees for students, fewer fee concessions, e.g. for pensioners, and less support with childcare costs (AoC 2005). There will, therefore, be fewer opportunities to 'learn for its own sake'.

Yet 'learning for its own sake' or 'learning for pleasure' has also been problematised as part of the liberal tradition of adult education which, insists Thompson, 'was always concerned with "individual" outcomes and "personal" growth in the context of predominantly middle-class assumptions and value systems' (1995: 125). Instead Thompson argues for drawing on the alternative tradition of adult education for social change. This is not simply about self-fulfilment and personal development, but for useful knowledge in relation to helping people to understand what is happening in their lives to enable them to change it: 'The radical tradition in adult education based on "really useful knowledge" implies the development of critical thinking, the recognition of human agency, political growth and the confidence to challenge what is generally taken for granted as inevitable' (Thompson 1997: 145). Such formulations of lifelong learning would enhance active citizenship and benefit social democracy, while also helping to construct critically aware learners and workers whose breadth of knowledge and skills, for example, in critical analysis and creative thinking, would, I suggest, be far better suited to (collective and individual) social and economic 'success' than any unquestioning compliance is likely to be. As Thompson (2000: 44) notes:

Freire's insight that education either functions to conform people to the logic of the present system, or else it enables them to deal critically and creatively with their world in order to change it, remains a useful reminder about the tension between 'really useful knowledge' and 'merely useful knowledge' in the history – and the future – of educational struggle.

Conclusion

Lifelong learning policy, as currently formulated in the UK, is more likely to disguise, reinforce and reconstruct inequalities than act as a force for social justice. A feminist analysis makes visible the gendered, classed and racialised aspects of lifelong learning policy and practice, in a context in which white middle-class men and masculinist values continue to dominate education policy-making and the management of educational institutions. The key life-long learning policy documents, while offering some recognition of 'diversity' and the need to bring in previously excluded groups, frame participation and non-participation as individual success and failure, with few, if any, reference to structural inequalities. Recent policy on the curriculum for the 14–19 age range, for example, almost completely ignores gender – despite considerable gender stratification in this area. Where gendered patterns are recognised, these are constructed as a matter of individual choice, hence again shifting the responsibility onto the individual (Leathwood 2007). Social inclusion is framed in terms of an unquestioning inclusion within a highly stratified and unequal labour market, with little in the policy texts suggesting a commitment to lifelong learning for an active, creative and critical citizenship.

Yet as Fullick (2004) notes, the current lifelong learning strategy is likely to fail if the narrow skills-driven approach which alienates potential learners continues to be pursued. There is already a healthy resistance to participation from many who regard the education on offer as middle-class and alien (Archer *et al.* 2003; Leathwood 2005a), and without any attempt to address the reasons for such resistance, and to ensure that educational opportunities offer positive and relevant experiences and benefits, many of those who are the intended recipients of lifelong learning policy are likely to continue to resist it. Furthermore, without a commitment to developing critical understandings of existing knowledges and practices, lifelong learning offers little more than the learning of compliance.

Of course, feminist and other critical educators have always found and created spaces for more positive educational approaches, even within the confines of narrow and potentially restrictive curricula (see e.g. Jackson 2004b), and students bring their own experiences and critical faculties to the education on offer. There is a long tradition of education for social change in the UK, and of a feminist critical pedagogy which challenges competitive individualism, aims to change the culture of educational and other public institutions, and emphasises the importance of a liberatory education (hooks 1994; Thompson 1997). And many opportunities for life-changing (and, potentially, society-changing) lifelong learning occur on a daily basis outside formal educational provision, not only in the ordinary activities of everyday life but also in social and political activities. The miners strike in the UK in the 1980s, for example, provided a very powerful learning opportunity for working-class women in the mining communities (Elliott 2000). Of course we need to provide opportunities for people to develop their basic skills – literacy, for example, is a powerful tool for social justice, but until lifelong learning policy reflects people's interests, needs, commitments and desires not only for personal opportunities but also for social change, its relevance to many will remain limited.

Note

1   NVQs (National Vocational Qualifications) are work-related qualifications offered at five levels, from level 1 (foundation skills) to level 5 (professional and/or senior management skills).

Part II

Accessing lifelong learning

Chapter 4

Troubling trajectories

Gendered 'choices' and pathways from school to work

Becky Francis

Introduction

The general assumption underpinning mainstream education commentary in Britain is that as young women are outperforming boys at GCSE and A-level exams,[1] and increasingly at undergraduate level too, they are clearly no longer a concern and we should redirect our attention and resources to meeting boys/young men's needs.[2] Indeed, this has been the actual case in the British compulsory sector for some time, with targets and resources allocated by the Department for Education and Skills aimed at improving male achievement. The jettisoning of attention to issues concerning girls and women in education has been particularly justified by the 'poor boys' discourse that is hegemonic in contemporary debates on gender and achievement (Epstein *et al.* 1998). This discourse positions boys as victims of the 'feminisation' of schooling, blaming female teachers and a 'feminised schooling environment' for the 'gender gap', in spite of a complete lack of evidence – and indeed the existence of a raft of contradictory evidence – to support this case (see Francis and Skelton 2005, for discussion). Given that in Britain women are now outnumbering men in Further and Higher education (David and Woodward 1998; TES 2005), it is unsurprising that such arguments are increasingly being applied to the post-16 sector too (Quinn 2003). The task of highlighting continuing inequalities that disadvantage girls and women is therefore particularly imperative.

Curriculum subject preference and uptake forms one of the areas reflecting persistent gender inequality in spite of somewhat changing trends in gender and educational attainment. In this chapter I will endeavour to elucidate some of the key trends regarding gender, curriculum subject preferences and uptake, and their bearing on school-to-work trajectories. I hope to illustrate the ways in which gendered (and 'raced' and classed) discourses of selfhood and appropriate behaviour carry women (and men) down particular routes, reproducing gendered inequalities (such as pay gap, and so on) in their future lives.

Gendered academic subject choice

Since the introduction of the National Curriculum in Britain, girls and boys
have been forced to take the same core subjects up to age 16, largely ironing out
the previously endemic gender difference in curriculum subjects pursued by
secondary school pupils (see Arnot *et al.* 1999). However, discrepancies remain:
for example, in the numbers of pupils entered for GCSE exams in traditionally
gendered subjects (Francis and Skelton 2005). And although research has shown
that subject preference is less gender-bound than was the case in the 1970s and
1980s (Miller and Budd 1999; Francis 2000), stereotypical patterns persist, particularly regarding pupils' *least* favourite subjects (Francis 2000; Francis *et al.*
2003). Further, gender difference remains strikingly apparent in the non-
mandatory subject areas at Key Stage 4, particularly in 'training routes' such as
GNVQs and vocational GCSEs, where uptake remains highly patterned by
gender and class. And as Table 4.1 illustrates, as soon as choice is reintroduced at
post-16, gender re-emerges as a key factor in subject uptake. These patterns are

Table 4.1 Qualifications obtained by students on HE courses in the UK by gender and
subject area

| | First degree | |
| | 2003 | |
	Female	Male
Medicine and dentistry	3.3	2.8
Subjects allied to medicine	18.1	4.2
Biological sciences	15.2	8.0
Veterinary science	0.4	0.1
Agriculture and related subjects	1.3	0.8
Physical sciences	5.2	6.9
Mathematical sciences	2.1	2.9
Computer science	4.2	13.4
Engineering and technology	3.1	15.7
Architecture, building and planning	1.8	4.5
Social, economic and political studies	14.7	9.9
Law	7.2	4.2
Business and administrative studies	21.2	17.5
Librarianship and information science	4.6	2.6
Languages	14.6	5.2
Humanities	7.4	5.7
Creative arts and design	16.0	10.1
Education	7.5	1.8
Combined	5.4	3.9
All subjects	**153.1**	**120.3**

Source: From HESA/JACS data, 2004, Francis and Skelton (2005).

by no means exclusive to the UK (see Leathwood 2007, for a discussion of the international context).

This entrenched tendency towards gender-stereotypical subject uptake is a particular concern given that recent British educational policy is set to locate choice making of routes for study earlier in compulsory schooling than has been the case to date (Crace 2005), suggesting that these gendered trends will be exacerbated by this move.

A-level uptake continues to reflect the trends identified in the feminist literature of the 1970s and 1980s (e.g. Sharpe 1976; Stanworth 1981; Spender 1982; Kelly 1985) with young women more likely to take up arts subjects, and young men more likely to take up maths and the 'hard' sciences. For example, DfES data show vastly more men than women taking A levels in maths and physics (though interestingly, no longer in chemistry), and girls more often taking language and social science subjects (with the exception of economics) (see DFES Statistics Gateway at <http://www.dfes.gov.uk/rsgateway/DB/SFR/s000630/SFR01-2006v1.pdf> for details). Although the figures show that young women are tending to perform better than their male counterparts (and are taking A levels in greater numbers) (see Francis and Skelton 2005, for detailed analysis), these gendered choices have strong consequences for the types of career that students are able to pursue (Thomas 1990; Francis 2002b; DTI 2004; Madden 2004).

These trends carry through to degree level. Table 4.1 shows how nearly three times as many women as men are studying languages, four times as many study education, and women also predominate in the humanities, creative arts, and social sciences. They maintain their traditional numerical dominance of biology at undergraduate level, and constitute the vast majority of those pursuing subjects allied to medicine (which include subjects such as physiotherapy, nursing, etc.). A well-documented digression from traditional patterns has been that women have established numerical dominance in the traditionally male-dominated areas of law, medicine and veterinary science; prestigious subjects, the latter of which are related to the 'hard' sciences (although career routes within law and medicine are shown to remain gendered with more women becoming GPs and more men specialising, and more men becoming barristers). Men overwhelmingly outnumber women in engineering and computer science, and less heavily in the physical sciences and maths. Hence the subjects that undergraduates pursue still tend to reflect the gendered construction of subject areas as masculine or feminine, and hence as more appropriate for one gender or the other (Paechter 2000).

Paechter (2004) reminds us that these gendered 'choices' occur within the parameters of an educational curriculum which remains itself inherently gendered and classed (as well as 'raced'). She argues that the current curriculum is 'very firmly rooted' in the elite male curriculum developed in the nineteenth century to enable upper-class and middle-class boys to manage their estates, or to enter the professions or civil service. The values reflected in this curriculum,

Paechter maintains, reflect those of the Enlightenment in which rationality is elevated over empathy, and this valuing of abstraction and 'reason' is reflected in the hierarchy of subject status still evident today, in which traditionally masculine subjects such as maths and science are seen as of greater importance, and 'harder', than traditionally feminine subjects such as languages and arts (Thomas 1990; Harding 1991; Francis 2000; Paechter 2000). Hence these constructions are imbued with power and lack: it is not simply that the subjects which men and women pursue tend to differ; rather, power and status are disproportionately invested in those subjects which tend to be pursued by men, and those more frequently pursued by women tend to be positioned as 'softer', easier and more esoteric (Francis 2000).

We know also that these 'choices' are heavily 'raced' and classed: research has shown how women from certain minority ethnic groups tend to have less gender-stereotypical subject preferences and choices than their white working-class counterparts (e.g. Mirza 1992; Biggart 2002; Francis and Archer 2005). This may be due to various factors: the impact of ethnicity and/or diasporic experiences on the construction of gendered subjectivity; the impact of 'race' stereotyping on career guidance, teacher expectations, etc., and a recognition by minoritised young people of the constraints of racism in a Western employment market (see Mirza 1992, or Archer and Francis 2006, for discussion). In terms of social class, there remains a tendency for working-class young men and women to follow vocational rather than academic routes. But as work by Archer *et al.* (2003) and Reay *et al.* (2001) has shown, where minority ethnic and working-class men and women do enter higher education, they tend to be concentrated in the lower-status post-1992 universities.[3] It is therefore suggested that for those who complete their course of study, their resulting degrees bear less 'cultural capital' in the eyes of employers than do degrees from students frequenting the elite sector.

Gendered training choices

These trends for gender divergence are, if anything, exacerbated in the vocational training sector. In Britain, this area of post-compulsory education remains predominantly populated by working-class students. Further Education (FE) colleges, where the majority of vocational courses are concentrated, are particularly likely to attract working-class and minority ethnic students; and while in the past male students have been a majority, recently more women than men entered FE for the first time. Yet work-based training routes remain disproportionately subscribed to by men. And in terms of the pursuit of particular areas, Modern Apprenticeships (MAs) are strikingly gendered: Miller *et al.* (2005) note how engineering and construction MAs are overwhelmingly dominated by men; and childcare MAs by women. And Payne (2003) notes that seven in ten men who were in Government Supported Training at age 16/17 were training in handcraft occupations, whereas over half female trainees were in personal service occupations, with another fifth in clerical or secretarial work.[4] The entrenchment of these patterns is bound up with issues of social class and status: vocational options remain denigrated in comparison with academic routes within schools and society at large (Leathwood and Hutchings 2003). Hence MAs are often overlooked by careers guidance within schools and within families: young people have been found to have limited knowledge of them (Fuller *et al.* 2005). The same issues apply to other vocational routes, which are equally gendered: Madden (2004) notes the high proportions of girls taking vocational GCSEs in childcare and hair and beauty in contrast to tiny numbers of boys, and the converse pattern in uptake of construction and engineering vocational GCSEs.

The extent of gender delineation in uptake of these vocational courses inevitably impacts directly on gendered employment patterns. Fuller *et al.* (2005) have shown how employers in traditionally masculine or feminine sectors receive very few Modern Apprenticeship (MA) applications from the non-traditional gender: '95 per cent of plumbing, construction and engineering employers received none or very few applications for MAs from women; 90 per cent of childcare employers received none or very few applications from men' (ibid.: v).

Gendered aspirations and trajectories to work

The UK workplace remains highly gendered, with horizontal and vertical segregation clearly evident across occupational sectors (EOC 2004). For example, women comprise just 1 per cent of employment in construction occupations; and only 8 per cent in engineering occupations (ibid.). Rolfe (2005) shows that men still comprise only 2–3 per cent of a burgeoning childcare workforce, in spite of local and national campaigns to recruit more men into this shortage area. The EOC maintains that such occupational segregation is damaging the UK economy by contributing to skill shortages (as there are skill shortages in many particularly 'gendered' work areas, such as construction, plumbing and childcare). This occupational segregation is a central factor in the persistence of the gender pay gap in Britain (EOC 2004). Clearly, the gendered subject choices discussed above constitute a key explanation for these continuing trends. The curriculum subjects that pupils pursue facilitate routes to particular occupations and curtail others. Gendered aspirations contribute a further explanation.

Schoolgirls' occupational aspirations have broadened considerably and become more ambitious over the last two decades (Riddell 1992; Francis 1996, 2002b; Sharpe 1994; Arnot *et al.* 1999; Wikeley and Stables 1999). Researching in the 1980s, Spender (1982), Gaskell (1992) and others found that girls planned to work until they were married, and then to stop work or assume the role of secondary breadwinner. Recent studies in primary and secondary schools show that girls have since become far more career-oriented (Sharpe 1994; Lightbody and Durndell 1996; Francis 1998, 2002b). Many girls now choose jobs that normally require a degree, demonstrating a high level of ambition (Lightbody and Durndell 1996; Francis 2002b), and they appear to see their chosen career as reflecting their identity, rather than as simply a stopgap before marriage.

These findings might, then, seem to suggest that equality has been realised: girls are now as ambitious as boys, and see an equal range of jobs as open to them. However, as we have seen, this is far from being the case. Girls' post-compulsory pathways have been shown to differ significantly according to socio-economic group and ethnicity, with white girls from lower socio-economic groups more likely to pursue gender-stereotypical future occupations (Biggart 2002; Francis et al. 2003; Archer et al. 2005a). A closer examination of the data regarding choice of future occupation reveals that the types of jobs chosen by boys and girls generally remain very different. Boys tend to avoid jobs that have been seen as stereotypically feminine (Riddell 1992; Whitehead 1996; Francis 1998, 2002b; Miller and Budd 1999). Furthermore, It has been shown that the reason that there is little overlap between the jobs chosen by girls and boys despite increased diversity of choice is that the *attributes* of the jobs chosen by girls and boys are stereotypically gendered (Francis 2002b; Francis et al. 2003). So that, for example, girls tend to choose jobs with attributes that can be classed as 'caring or creative', supporting a construction of appropriate feminin-ity; while boys choose jobs that are scientific, technical, or business oriented, aiding their production of themselves as appropriately masculine.

These constructions are, of course, inflected by other aspects of social identity such as social class and ethnicity. The work of Archer and Yamashita (2003b) and Archer et al. (2005a) among others shows how young people's trajectories are informed (and constrained) by local information networks, and what is seen as appropriate for 'people like me' (in terms of social class, ethnicity and gen-der). Working-class and minority ethnic pupils tend to follow known 'safe routes' (Archer and Yamashita 2003b), often for minority ethnic youths in recognition that the labour market continues to discriminate against them (Mirza 1992; Pang 1999). Hence gendered, classed and 'raced' subjectivities inscribe the patterns of aspiration among young people.

Research has shown that young people have little information on the issues surrounding gender and career, or the implications of their choices at Key Stage 4 for future job sector access, remuneration, status, etc. (Francis 2000; Archer et al. 2005a). Young women's common ignorance of the implications of their choices is illustrated by Fuller et al.'s (2005) finding that two-thirds of girls said they would be tempted to try a non-traditional sector if it had better pay rates and opportunities for progression than gender traditional sectors – that mascu-line sectors so commonly *do* involve superior remuneration had obviously passed them by.[5] Fuller et al. (2005) found no evidence that schools or the Connexions service were deliberately trying to challenge young people's gen-der stereotypes or flag up non-traditional possibilities. Even employers believe that if schools promoted MAs and non-traditional options more effectively, young people would be more likely to apply to such sectors (Fuller *et al.* 2005).

Work experience

Research has documented how the vast majority of schoolgirls, and a (smaller) majority of schoolboys, say that they would consider taking up and/or learning to do a non-traditional job (Francis *et al.* 2005; Fuller *et al.* 2005; Whitehead 1996). Fuller *et al.* (2005) found further that over half of boys and three-quarters of girls in their sample said that they would be more likely to take up non-gender traditional occupations if they were allowed to try working in a non-traditional sector before making a final choice. This finding illuminates the potential contribution of work experience placements in providing such 'trial' opportunities – however, this opportunity is currently being squandered (Rolfe 1999; Francis *et al.* 2005). Indeed, a study[6] for the Equal Opportunities Commission (Francis *et al.* 2005) shows that not only does work experience placement practice currently not broaden horizons, but that it often actively constrains and further narrows them. It is worth spending a moment reporting the explanations for this phenomenon, as arguably they are indicative of the discourses and resulting discursive productions permeating educational policy and practice regarding 'choice' and 'opportunities'.

Approximately 90–95 per cent of school pupils in England engage in block work experience placements as an aspect of mandatory work-related learning. These placements are usually of one- or two-week duration, normally during the final term of Year 10, or early in Year 11. We found that the types of work placement taken up by young people were overwhelmingly gender-stereotypical – indeed the pattern was even more stereotypical than in the actual labour market itself (Table 4.2).

Education Business Partnership (EBP) managers and work experience coordinators responsible for facilitating and/or organising work experience placements were well aware that uptake of placements is highly gender stereotypical, although there was less awareness of 'race' and social class issues. However, although a few were concerned about the persistence of stereotypical uptake, for many other coordinators gender stereotyping was seen as inevitable and less of a concern. Very few were prioritising it as an issue to address in spite of their acknowledgement of the extent of the problem. Like EBP managers, many teachers clearly thought that attempts to tackle gender stereotypes were frustrating and as one work-experience coordinator said, 'I just do not see this as a major issue'. Many saw stereotypical uptake as 'inevitable', and resulting from sexism and low expectations (deficit) within the family, rather than from structural and institutional discrimination. The extent of gender segregation has caused some teachers to ignore the problem, rather than find even more creative ways to respond to it. This lethargy seemed partly the result of a lack of prioritisation and target-setting at a national and local level (as other issues were being

Table 4.2 Employment sectors in which work experience placements had been undertaken

Sector	No. of females	No. of males	Total
Agriculture and horticulture	0	8	8
Animal work – semi/unskilled	13	5	18
Animal work – professional	3	0	3
Armed forces	0	5	5
Arts, fine	2	1	3
Arts, performing	1	1	2
Arts and crafts	1	2	3
Automotive/transport	1	4	5
Business	2	1	3
Catering	8	13	21
Charitable/public sector	1	2	3
Children (working with)	43	2	45
Design	1	17	18
Education	34	15	49
Emergency services	1	4	5
Engineering	0	31	31
Finance	4	7	11
General care industry	9	0	9
Hair and beauty	23	2	25
IT	1	18	19
Legal	7	6	13
Leisure/travel/tourism	9	10	19
Marketing/sales	5	6	11
Media production	3	6	9
Medical – professional level	2	2	4
Nursing	3	0	3
Office work	23	33	56
Para medical professions	1	6	7
Printed media/literary arts	3	3	6
Retail	26	44	70
Science	1	4	5
Semi/unskilled manual labour	1	26	27
Skilled/semi-skilled manual trades	0	6	6
Sports	1	6	7
Odd/joke answers	0	4	4
Uncodable	4	9	13
TOTAL	237	309	546

Source: Francis et al. (2005).

Note: Numbers based on respondent choices. There are more boys than girls in our sample, which needs to be taken into account when considering the data in Table 4.2. However, it is evident that placement uptake among our sample is strongly gender-stereotypical. Further, the different roles/ jobs within these categories tended to reflect strong differences in terms of gendered uptake (for example, within media production more boys were in areas connected to technical production, where girls tended to be in artistic production). Francis et al.'s (2005) report for the Equal Opportunities Commission also contains far larger figures from the Learning and Skills Council, which illustrate similar patterns.

prioritised). However, this lack of prioritisation also reflected the main explan-ation, which relates to notions of 'choice'.

Some EBP managers appeared to feel that strong measures to address gender stereotyping would be beyond their remit, as their duty is simply to provide pupils with experiences of the workplace and to facilitate individual student choices. For example, some talked about how pupils were welcome to approach employers under their own initiative, and that such individualised practices are actively encouraged and celebrated as entrepreneurial. The emphasis on individual freedom of choice belies the fact that there is segregation in the labour market and in work experience placements. This emphasis on individual freedom of choice was reflected in the systems for placement allocation across the schools in our sample, in which over half of work experience coordinator respondents reported that the majority of placements are identified by individual pupils.

The onus on pupils to identify their own placements has limitations, and raises equity issues in relation to gender and socio-economic group. First, the approach has implications for the diversity of work placement available, as some pupils have knowledge of, and access to, a limited number. Following on from this, there are implications regarding socio-economic group and ethnicity with respect to the sorts of jobs that pupils are aware of, and have access to (for example, in relation to the sorts of jobs which family members and friends are working in, from which they can facilitate placements). The well-connected pupils from higher socio-economic groups in the case study schools in our study appeared able to secure both more prestigious and often more meaningful work placements than their counterparts in lower socio-economic groups. Many pupils went on placements with relatives: this satisfied the common con-cern of parents and some teachers and EBP managers that pupils are 'at risk' when travelling to placements and/or on the placements, but also meant that pupils were more likely to be channelled into occupations linked to socio-economic group and gender. Gender issues compound those of socio-economic group, as boys are found consistently to have greater levels of confidence than girls (Jones and Jones 1989; AAUW 1992; Walkerdine *et al*. 2001), and may therefore be more likely to feel able to approach employers independently.

Some coordinators perceived encouragement to undertake non-traditional placements as over-intervention. As one responded with irritation, 'I have boys doing childcare and girls doing carpentry because it is what they want to do, not to meet equal ops agenda.' This reaction again reflects the opinions of many work experience coordinators that equality of opportunity pertaining to work experience placements lies in the offer of freedom of choice to all pupils, rather than in encouraging pupils to undertake non-traditional placements. As another coordinator explained, 'Quite frankly, it really does not worry me. Jobs are jobs and it does not matter which sex does them. I do not think people should be forcing the issue.' Contrastingly, however, we found that many young people are interested in trying non-traditional placements (see Francis *et al.* 2005, Chapter 4) and are lacking the opportunity to do so.

Embedded within these views is a discourse of equal opportunity, but here equality is projected as concerning equal freedom of choice, rather than equal outcomes. Hence the lack of uptake of non-gender traditional placements becomes discursively produced not as the result of barriers or discrimination, but simply a reflection of the individual choices of pupils (which happen to be gender-stereotypical). Freedom of choice was seen as paramount by our adult respondents. One coordinator summed up this position when she explained that equal opportunities are 'at the forefront of everything we do' and:

> it just comes naturally to us now. It may not come naturally to some students who are still making choices which are generally stereotypical, but I think they're making informed choices within their realms of being informed. There's not much else we can do about that. I don't actually have a problem with it if that's what they want to do. I don't think we should be forcing students.

Within this view of equal opportunities such gender stereotyping is not perceived to be a concern (this coordinator went on to admit that non-traditional placement take up in her school is 'very low, unfortunately').

This discourse of individual freedom of choice, supported by that of equal opportunity (to 'choose'), positions pupils' 'failure' to take up non-traditional placements as due to their own individual failings rather than institutional issues. Deficit and responsibility are projected onto the individual students (incorrigibly pursuing their perversely stereotypical choices in spite of the opportunities apparently open to them), and institutions/policy are hence positioned as benign and innocent. This discursive construction that a commitment to equal opportunities at policy level contextualises all activities and hence no further action is required percolated through all levels, from LSCs, to EBP managers to teachers.

The limitations of social learning theory and liberal feminist approaches

A raft of factors have been shown to contribute to the patterning of curriculum choice and school-to-work routes by gender. We have discussed those of career choice, aspiration, and work-related learning. There are other explanations: for example, the (interconnected) low status and low pay of many traditionally feminine occupations have been shown to deter men from entering those occupations (Hutchings 2002; EOC 2004; Rolfe 2005). However, within all this it is widely recognised that societal constructions of what is 'appropriate' for one gender or the other continue to have a profound bearing on trajectories. These gendered constructions have been variously theorised as gender roles expressing gender stereotyping (in sex role theory); as social norms reflecting socio-economic imperatives (in functionalist and Marxist-feminist theories); and as produced by gender discourses (in post-structuralist perspectives). Yet although social learning and 'role' theories have been widely critiqued in the sociological literature, theories of gender stereotyping that see stereotypes 'taught' to individuals through social institutions remains hegemonic in the literature on school-to-work 'choices'.

Hence individuals are seen as learning gender stereotypical roles by drawing on information from family, education, the media, peer-group, and so on (Miller and Budd 1999). I do not mean to contest the power of stereotyping, but I do see this social learning approach as limited in a number of ways. Not only does it suffer from the problems associated with a view of the self as fixed and coherent identified by many researchers, and challenged by post-modern theories (see e.g. Davies 1989; Connell 1989, for discussion); but also it seems to echo the liberal feminist approach that it so often supports in locating the issues at stake *with individuals*. There is an assumption that if individuals have been taught to think stereotypically by social institutions, it may be possible to simply un/re-teach them, to ensure they take up less stereotypical ways of thinking and behaving. This logic has galvanised numerous liberal-feminist intervention projects, from the famous Girls Into Science and Technology (GIST) project of the 1980s, to organisations such as WISE and JIVE which continue to operate today. Such approaches reflect the liberal feminist tendency to see equality about access to male-dominated systems, rather than dedication to changing those systems and the epistemological assumptions upon which they rest (Weiner 1993). As a number of feminists writing on gendered curriculum subjects have pointed out, this liberal feminist approach actually perpetuates a deficit view of girls. It positions gender inequalities as perpetuated by girls/women who may be educated to change their misguidedly stereotypical behaviours, rather than analysing institutional or discursive factors which might be perpetuating these behaviours (e.g. Walkerdine *et al.* 1989; Henwood 1996; Henwood and Miller 2001).

Structuralist critiques reveal how this liberal feminist position does not adequately recognise the invested power differentials inherent in the perpetuation of gender difference, and the way in which structural/institutional factors limit and constrain opportunities to reject stereotypes (Archer *et al.* 2003; Lucey and Reay 2002; Reay *et al.* 2001). Further, how 'stereotypical choices' in some cases constitute a perfectly rational response to institutional gender discrimination. For example, Henwood (1996) shows how girls in her study recognised the sexism endemic in science and technology workplaces and quite reasonably chose to preclude experiencing this by avoiding such occupations. Likewise, Archer *et al.* (2005a) and Archer and Yamashita (2003b) illustrate the ways in which young people's 'choices' are constrained by financial considerations, by habitus-driven perceptions of what is appropriate 'for people like me', and by the racisms and other discriminations practised in local jobs markets.

From a post-structuralist feminist perspective, social learning and liberal feminist approaches fail to account for fluidity and power of gender discourses, which produce people in different ways in different discursive environments, and powerfully inscribe themselves in productions of selfhood. For example, the extent to which many men, drawing on gender discourses prevalent in society at large, are precluded from even considering fields such as childcare due to its construction as 'a job for women' – to do so would be to risk compromising their (relational) construction of masculinity.[7] Equal Opportunities Commission research such as that by Rolfe (2005) does recognise that the status (and pay) of childcare work are low due to its association with mothering, but argues for raising its status via 'emphasis on training and qualifications' (ibid.: v), rather than challenging the devaluing of 'mothering' (and indeed the construction of childcare as a female domain – 'mothering' rather than 'parenting') upon which this lack of status is founded.

Discourse analytical (and radical feminist) approaches deconstruct the dichotomy which invests power and status in (masculine) scientific/technical and business-oriented jobs, along with the rationale (often adopted by liberal feminists) that these are preferable to caring/creative occupations, simply because they may be better paid and attributed greater kudos in a masculinist society. Many European Union gender mainstreaming directives appear to be based on these notions that equality means women working the same hours, and practising as little childcare as men (as these practices will narrow the gender pay gap), rather than questioning the assumption that work (and remuneration) are the most important aspects of life, or why it is that men undertake less childcare than women.

The key point must be that girls/women/boys/men should not be restricted and their talents wasted due to the persistence of the discursive construction of gender as relational. Issues of gender, social class and ethnicity must be addressed both by schools, and by employers. In doing so, there needs to be full recognition of two aspects: (1) the way in which gendered 'choices' reflect investments in gender constructions fundamental to young people's sense of social identity and what is 'normal' and/or 'acceptable'; and (2) the continued gender dominance and discrimination which young people are subject to in opting for non-gender traditional routes. In Chapter 10 in this book Heidi Mirza (2006) quotes Simmons as saying that, as a black woman operating in a white academic world, she is 'a freshwater fish that swims in sea-water', and describes feeling 'the weight of the water on my body'. This powerful analogy of the psychic costs involved in being continually positioned as 'the Other', as operating in the wrong habitus and even the wrong body – these are the realities that confront young people in making their 'choices'. Choices which are never, then, equal. The challenge remains for us as feminist educationalists to retain our outrage at the perpetuation of these inequalities, and to challenge the neo-liberal discursive practices that propagate and exacerbate them while projecting blame for unequal outcomes onto the individuals concerned.

Notes

1   GCSEs are the exams taken at the end of compulsory schooling at 16 in Britain. A levels are post-compulsory exams traditionally taken two years later at 18.

2   The extent of 'boys' underachievement' remains highly contested. Although girls from the vast majority of social groups outperform their direct male contemporaries in terms of general attainment at the various Key Stages in compulsory education, researchers have pointed out that for the majority of British pupils, 'race' and social class have a greater bearing on 'achievement gaps' than does gender (e.g. Gillborn and Mirza 2000; Francis and Skelton 2005; Archer and Francis 2006). For example, middle-class White British boys continue to substantially outperform White British working-class girls, and Black Caribbean and Black African pupils of both genders achieve below the average. This complexity in achievement patterns according to multiple factors of identity has led to the avocation of the approach termed 'Which Girls? Which Boys?', by social justice researchers. For a developed analysis of the gender and achievement debate as it relates to schooling, see Francis and Skelton (2005).

3   That is, ex-polytechnics or colleges of Higher Education which were incorporated as universities in 1992 UK legislation.

4   These authors also note that male-dominated apprenticeships tend to be better paid, higher level and higher in status than those dominated by women (see Payne 2003; Madden 2004).

5   Research for the EOC in one region showed that the hourly pay rates in hairdressing and childcare were less than half those paid to engineers and plumbers (Madden 2004).

6   Jayne Osgood, Jacinta Dalgety and Louise Archer.

7   Indeed, research has documented the extent to which some male primary school teachers will go to in order to construct themselves as 'properly' masculine within their stereotypically feminine occupational spaces (e.g. Skelton 2001) (although this is not, of course, the case for all men teachers).

Chapter 5

Masculinities, femininities and resistance to participation in post-compulsory education

Louise Archer

Gender and HE participation

Within the UK government's ongoing commitment to widen participation in higher education, particular emphasis has been placed on tackling the under-representation of (white) working-class men (McGivney 1999; NCIHE 1997). This moral panic continues to garner popular, policy and media attention (e.g. 'Where have all the young men gone?' Berliner 2004) as women's participation rates increase at a faster rate than their male counterparts – despite the fact that working-class women are still (also) severely under-represented within HE (Robertson and Hillman 1997). Indeed, there is little popular recognition that, in general, working-class and minority ethnic students continue to be concentrated within less prestigious institutions and subject areas and (along with women) seem to earn less on graduation than their middle-class, white (and male) counterparts (Audas and Dolton 1999). Furthermore, the specific concern with *white* working-class men's participation also hides patterns of under-representation among other groups of men, such as African Caribbean and Bangladeshi young men.

My intention here is not to set up an *either/or* model of concern or to argue that one group is more, or less, deserving of attention and resources than another. Rather, I want to begin to contextualise the current media and policy preoccupation with (white) male non-participation and broaden it out into a more critical discussion of (non-)participation. Indeed, I would argue that the current focus on white, working-class male university participation has not simply arisen from the publication of particular data sets and statistical evidence on participation. Rather, I suggest that this focus needs to be understood as produced within a wider cluster of public discourses around 'race', class, gender and educational achievement and participation. In particular, I see the current panic around white, male, working-class (non-)participation as emanating from wider discourses concerning the (supposed) 'crisis in masculinity', the boys' educational underachievement debate (see Epstein *et al.* 1998; Francis and Skelton 2005, for critical discussions) and racist/ethnocentric assumptions around whiteness and academic achievement. Hence, I feel that understanding non-participation among *all* working-class groups (minority and majority ethnic; male and female) is an important social justice task.

Within educational policy, working-class non-participation in HE has predominantly been framed in terms of 'lack' – as resulting, for instance, from a lack of aspirations or a lack of knowledge about HE (e.g. the government's *Aim Higher* initiative). This approach has been criticised for adopting a deficit model towards working-class groups (Thomas 2001) that does not fully engage with the complexity of structural inequalities (Archer *et al.* 2003). Critique has also been directed at the tendency for policy to conceptualise educational choices and participation within a rationalistic, individualist framework, which assumes that people make calculated educational choices (e.g. by weighing up the evidence for and against participation). This approach, I would argue, ignores the important and complex role played by feelings, emotions and identities.

Drawing on this critical perspective, in this chapter I discuss how people's investments in, and performance of, gender identities (masculinities and femininities) are an important consideration when seeking to understand patterns of non-participation among ethnically diverse working-class men and women.

Conceptual approach

My conceptual approach can be described as feminist poststructuralist. From this position, gender is understood as non-essential, fluid, contested, processual and produced through discourse. In other words, gender is not treated as the product of genetic or biological differences. Instead, masculinities and femininities are understood as 'real fictions' that are constructed through relations of power. These relations of power are not simply external to people (they do not act 'one-way'), rather they are taken up, internalised and performed through the minds, bodies and behaviours of social actors (Foucault 1978; Butler 1990). This approach understands gender as inherently relationally constructed. That is, notions of 'maleness'/'masculinity' are only intelligible and produced in relation to notions of 'femaleness'/'femininity', and vice versa (e.g. see Davies 1989, 1993; Francis and Skelton 2005).

This conceptual framework draws considerably on research that has been conducted within the sphere of compulsory education (on the ways in which children 'do boy' and 'do girl'), and extends this into the field of relationships in post-compulsory education. It thus enables an understanding of how some (working-class) men and women come to see higher education as incompatible with their own notions of masculinity/femininity and as incommensurable with their feelings about the most desirable and/or acceptable ways of 'being' a man or woman.

Contextualising the focus on gender/identities within reasons for non-participation

In my discussion, I shall be drawing on several studies that I have been involved with over the past few years, all conducted with working-class young men's and women's views of education and post-compulsory education. These include the *Social Class and Higher Education* study (e.g. Archer *et al.* 2001a; Archer *et al.* 2001b; Archer *et al.* 2003; Archer and Hutchings 2000); the *Identities and Inequalities* study (Archer and Yamashita 2003a, b) and the *Dropping Out and Drifting Away* study (Archer *et al.* 2005a; Archer *et al.* forthcoming). Details on the methodologies of these studies can be found in other publications, as listed. However, a thumbnail sketch of the specific data sets[1] that I am drawing on from each study is provided below, for ease:

* The *Higher Education and Social Class* study: group discussions with 118 'non-participants' aged 16–30 years old, who were not in higher education and unlikely to enter it.
* The *Identities and Inequalities* study: interviews and group discussions with 20 Year 11 pupils (aged 15/16 years old) in an inner-London 'failing' school.
* The *Dropping Out and Drifting Away* study: individual, longitudinal tracking interviews and discussion groups with 89 Year 10 and 11 pupils (aged 14–16 years) who had been identified by schools as 'at risk of dropping out and/or not progressing into post-16 education'.

All the studies were conducted in London and all comprised an ethnically diverse sample of respondents. The primary focus in this chapter will be on access to HE, but reference will also be made to post-compulsory educational participation.

Before moving on to a closer consideration of the role of gender and non-participation in HE, it is first important to flag up that all these studies identified a complex mix of factors that combine to produce under-representation and non-participation. All, for instance, discuss the role of finance/money, knowledge/information and risk alongside identity. All the studies found that university simply did not feature on working-class young people's 'horizons of choice'. Most did not have family histories of HE participation and therefore university was seen as an alien and unknown world. All the projects also flagged up how universities were seen as places that are 'not for me', being regarded as the preserve of 'posh' and 'brainy' people. For instance, university students were imagined to be 'all smart and just all clever', compared to respondents' views of themselves as 'non-smart' (and 'common'). Consequently, university was typically described as 'it seems good, but it's not for me', 'I just can't see myself there' and 'I don't reckon I'd fit in there'. In sum, working-class young people viewed HE as a place in which 'you can't be your true self'.

In addition, the process of studying at university was widely viewed as being too expensive, too long and too risky. Structural inequalities played an important role in excluding the young people from HE. For instance, all the studies found examples of young people being subject to low staff expectations of their abilities and/or being channelled into lower status academic routes that render HE participation more difficult and unlikely. They were also disadvantaged by the hierarchy of universities (see Leathwood 2004) and recognised that only less prestigious, 'crap' universities were open to them. Furthermore, young people tended to defer making post-16 'choices' (the 'wait and see' approach) as a means of managing uncertainty in their lives, but this also disadvantaged them because they tended to miss out on preferred courses and institutions. Finally, as various respondents emphasised, the content and format of education itself were often regarded as 'boring' and irrelevant to their own lives.

Into this mix of factors and inequalities, gender and identity also emerged as important concerns, as I shall now discuss.

Masculinities and HE non-participation

Across the studies, boys and men constructed going to university as undesirable and incompatible with their working-class masculine identities. As the following sections discuss, this was because: (1) (higher) education was constructed as feminised and as antithetical to undertaking paid work/employment (which was constructed as a corner stone of working-class masculinity), and (2) university was allied with an unattractive and undesirable form of middle-class masculinity, which (3) was seen as oppositional to performances of popular, 'cool' masculinities.

Education as feminised – 'work' as masculine

As has been noted in relation to compulsory education (see Francis and Skelton 2005, for discussion), boys and men across the three studies framed their resistance to educational participation through an education–work dichotomy, in which the former element is read as feminine and the latter as masculine. Post-compulsory education (particularly higher education) was widely seen as 'feminised' and thus 'not manly'. It was regarded as prolonging childhood through continued financial dependency, with studying preventing, delaying and/or constraining men from undertaking paid work. Employment was valued as more than just a source of income – it constituted a defining feature of adult masculinity (Morgan 1992) and social status (Archer *et al.* 2001b). Indeed, many schoolboys aspired to leave education as soon as possible, in order to achieve adult male status through entry into the labour market and, across the studies, boys and men all agreed that they would 'rather be earning than learning'. 'If you've got to be there swotting over a book, you can't be out grafting, can you? And you can't have a social life, if you're like me and you've got to do so many other things' (Derek, 29, white Irish labourer). Consequently, post-compulsory educational participation was viewed as incommensurable with the performance of hegemonic (valued, dominant) forms of masculinity.

Distinctions were also made between different types of work – with some being valued over others as epitomising a 'real' man's job. In particular, boys and men expressed a keen interest and pride in 'practical' jobs and skilled manual trades like mechanic, electrican, plumber and joiner (see Archer *et al.* 2001b). Various boys also aspired to the 'ultimate' hegemonic working-class masculine job of becoming a professional sportsman – with professional footballer topping the dream list. These jobs were associated with strength, prowess, competition, 'coolness' and 'big money' – all of which were seen to be achievable without extensive educational credentials or qualifications.

As Willis (1977) noted, within this framework, 'tough' and 'physical' work comes to symbolise 'hard' working-class masculine identities, whereas education is equated with 'soft', feminised and/or middle-class identities. Young men thus regarded education as being the preserve of 'other' (effeminate, weak) men who cannot cope with 'real' work (Mac an Ghaill 1996). This conflation of social class and gender was also amplified across 'race', as some 'professional' jobs (i.e. those that require a degree) were associated with whiteness alongside middle classness. For instance, a black Caribbean teacher in the *Identities and Inequalities* study described his struggle to get black Caribbean boys in his school to recognise that his own position as a teacher who 'wears a suit' could be a 'real' or valued version of black Caribbean masculinity.[2]

Higher education as the preserve of (undesirable) middle-class masculinity

Against the lure of 'working-class', 'masculine' jobs – and their promise to confer status and a socially valued form of working-class masculinity – higher education was seen as a rather unattractive option. Its undesirability was reinforced and amplified through its construction as an arena of middle-class masculinity. This form of middle-class student masculinity was depicted as effeminate, geekish and decidedly 'uncool'. For instance, when asked to describe university students, boys and men evoked socially inadequate, bookish types, whom they called 'boffins' and 'bods': 'There's a general stereotype isn't there? The Tefal man with a big head. Someone who needs glasses' (Steve, 24, white male builder).

Indeed, this notion of uptight, uncool masculinity was associated with all spaces of post-compulsory education, through from A levels to university. For example, Abdul described with a mixture of horror and amusement, how he had entered an A-level class in which the other students read *The Times* and discussed politics (and 'John's Major's haircut'). This caused Abdul to flee the class, as he realised that it was 'not me'.

Boys and men also constructed students as immature men (i.e. feminised, child-like), for instance, suggesting that students are unable to 'hold their drink' like 'real' men:

> They sort of go to uni and they just sort of don't know how to handle sort of the spare time and freedom . . . they all go out and they get absolutely tanked up down the student bar and they . . . they sort of like to swear and shout a lot and, er, kick dustbins. I couldn't believe it.
>
> (Seb, white male, 18, FE)

These constructions of HE as commensurate with undesirable middle-class masculinities were also inflected by 'race'/ethnicity. For instance, whereas white working-class men tended to portray themselves in individualistic terms, Muslim Bangladeshi boys flagged up how their responsibilities as 'breadwinners' to their extended families (in Britain and abroad) rendered studying/'not working' an impossibility. Furthermore, some Muslim young men associated the student drinker image with undesirable (un-religious) forms of masculinity, which they felt excluded their own participation.

The notion of middle-class student masculinity was thus derided on multiple fronts. Indeed, the vast majority of men (including those in the wider *Social Class and HE* study who actually wanted to go to and/or were already at university[3]), resisted any notion of wanting to 'change'. For instance, no men admitted to wanting to embody a more middle-class form of masculinity as a result of university participation. Instead, it was agreed that university participation was only acceptable if, as Fela put it, 'you go through university, university doesn't go through you'.

These associations of HE as a middle-class male space can be understood as exemplifying how the construction of masculinity is a contested ideological project. Power is central to performances of masculinity, and the above examples might be read as discursive struggles over the meanings and symbols of hegemonic masculinity. Hegemonic masculinities are 'those dominant and dominating modes of masculinity which claim the highest status and exercise the greatest influence and authority' within particular contexts (Skelton 2001: 50). These tend to be organised around the discursive subordination of Others, notably women and gay men (Connell 1989; Edley and Wetherell 1995; Paechter 1998). However, the dominance and power of 'hegemonic' identities can be highly localised, as identities are produced and contested within particular contexts of time, space and social relations (Archer 2003a). Consequently, for the non-participant men and boys in these studies, participation in higher education was felt to entail a potential loss – of identity and of power – as it would necessitate moving into a space that is associated with (and dominated by) middle-class masculinity. Thus participation was viewed as something that might potentially interrupt men's local hegemony and their ability to perform valued working-class gender identities.

'Cool' masculinities

In addition to being seen as undesirable and disrupting participation in the labour market, going to university was widely felt to interfere with young men's performances of popular, 'cool' masculinities. 'Cool' masculinities were positioned as highly desirable and pleasurable to perform – they could convey status and a sense of value and self-worth. The most popular forms of 'cool' masculinity were formulated in terms of 'bling' and 'bad boy' masculinity. These were culturally entangled (Hesse 2000) embodied performances which took various racially-inflected forms.

University participation was regarded as potentially denying or preventing these performances, not least due to its association with poverty and student debt. Hence many young men argued that they would rather work and be able to buy 'my trainers and my jewellery' than go to university. Student identity was closely equated with being unfashionable and 'uncool':

> When I see it in the media, I can see pure books. People is walking with their books on their arm all the time, looking all sad and cold and that. They should just like, just relax, be like cool! Put some shades on, maybe a little cap, cut the hair here and there.
>
> (Patrick, 18, black Caribbean male FE student)

The performance of 'cool' and 'bling' masculinities was closely bound up with notions of space and territoriality. In particular, they were described as entailing a 'duty' to maintaining the symbols of popular masculinity (e.g. 'style', car, home, girlfriend) and defence of this image within a young man's local area: 'Now I'm living on my jays, yes? I've got a car to look after, I've got my yard to look after. I can't be going to uni' (Drew, 21, black Caribbean shop assistant).

As Westwood (1990) notes, working-class urban masculinities are closely associated with place/locality and territoriality (see also Connolly and Neill 2001; Archer and Yamashita 2003b). In this way, non-participation is justified as part of a practice of 'staying local' that is intimately linked to 'staying safe' (i.e. staying within the known local area) and performing highly localised, territorial versions of 'cool'. In particular, because being 'cool' is linked to the performance of reputation and 'being known', it depends upon young men occupying a space in which their particular (classed, racialised) performances of cool are recognisable/recognised.

Femininities and HE non-participation

While education is popularly associated with the feminine, it was notable that not all girls and women identified with education nor wanted to participate in post-compulsory education. Some non-participant women did suggest that while they would like to go to university, they were constrained by situational factors (e.g. lack of time, money, childcare and other family responsibilities). However, a number of women also directly resisted the potential value or desirability of HE participation. As I shall now discuss, this relationship seemed to be underpinned by: (1) the othering of working-class femininity within educational discourse; (2) the dominance of a middle-class, masculine culture within HE; and (3) the association of HE with de-(hetero)sexualised, unglamorous, middle-class femininities.

The othering of working-class femininity within educational discourse ('feeling stupid')

A number of girls and women across the studies indicated that they were completely put off the idea of continuing in education due to their own traumatic experiences of compulsory schooling – which was typically described as 'dreadful'. In particular, various girls and women worried that they might be made to feel 'stupid' at university and would not understand what was going on in lectures and classes. These anxieties seemed to flow from their own experiences of 'feeling stupid' at school – and it was notable that a number of girls and young women across the studies felt that they were not receiving/had not received sufficient help and support at school. Certainly, the feminist literature indicates that, in comparison to boys, girls do tend to receive less attention and support from teachers and are targeted for fewer resources (Skelton and Francis 2005). They are also more likely to be channelled into gender-stereotypical subject areas and post-16 routes, and are more likely to have their abilities underestimated by teachers (Walkerdine 1990; Francis and Skelton 2005; Archer et al. 2003).

Furthermore, whereas working-class boys appear to be more likely to blame their underchievement on factors external to themselves, working-class girls have been found to internalise underachievement and blame themselves (Archer et al. 2004). Indeed, just as girls in a study by Archer et al. (2004) described themselves as 'not knowing anything' and 'no good', girls and young women in these studies labelled themselves as 'not the brightest', 'not a star student', 'stupid', and so on. It was therefore unsurprising that so many, like Elizabeth, complained that they were 'fed up' of education.

This psychic burden of blame echoes what Greed (1991) describes as the intellectual carnage inflicted on working-class girls within the education system. Girls and women tended to rule out higher education because they lacked confidence in themselves and their abilities and because they imagined that (as experienced at school) they would not receive sufficient support to enable them to succeed. This was imagined to be a particular problem at university, where they imagined there would be even larger classes and an emphasis placed upon independent study.

As I argue elsewhere (Archer 2005), for working-class and minority ethnic girls, the 'successful female student/learner' is a desired yet refused subject position. This is because working-class femininities are always already positioned as the 'wrong' sort of learner due to being positioned as 'other' to discourses of the 'ideal pupil' (who is assumed to be male, white, middle class, and so on – see also Archer and Francis 2006). For instance, many working-class, urban young women within the school-based studies performed assertive, highly visible and audible, agentic femininities, which were overwhelmingly interpreted by staff as antithetical to educational success (see also Archer et al. forthcoming). Indeed, 'never feeling good enough' in relation to education has been identified as a prevalent experience among working-class women and even among those who become educationally 'successful', success is experienced as inauthentic and fragile (e.g. see Mahony and Zmroczek 1997; Reay 1997; Lawler 1999; Hey 2004).

The classed and masculine culture of HE

While many men positioned higher education as a feminised (middle-class) space, working-class girls and women were more likely to construct universities in masculine (middle-class) terms. HE was imagined as a big, intimidating place in which young women might get 'lost' and 'swallowed up':

> I was just, oh my God, it was just the hugest thing you've ever seen in your life, and I thought why would little old me want to go somewhere like that? You know, it just swallowed me up, it was huge.
>
> (Lucy, 20, white hairdresser)

The perceived lack of fit between their own femininities and the sphere of higher education was also conveyed in the feelings of embarrassment and shame that Jodie associated with the idea of asking for a university prospectus – which she likened to asking in a newsagent's for a 'mucky book'.

Indeed, it has been noted that working-class women university students experience the culture of higher education as masculine, (white) and middle class irrespective of the gender, class and ethnic make-up of the student body at the university and on their particular courses (Quinn 2003). For instance, Read et al. (2003) discuss how non-traditional students (but particularly working-class women) can still feel othered by the dominant academic culture of post-1992 universities, where they are more likely to be studying with other students who are 'like me'. As Carole Leathwood (2006) also discusses, the dominant academic culture within universities continues to privilege an ideal of the young, white, male, middle-class 'independent learner', against which 'other' students can feel inferior and excluded.

HE as the preserve of undesirable (de-heterosexualised, unglamorous) middle-class feminininities

Just as boys/men resisted higher education through its association with undesirable, middle-class masculinities, girls and women identified universities with undesirable, middle-class femininities. For instance, Tina described university students as 'snobs, trendies' and Kim thought students were young women 'with money – hippified people who smoke pot in the toilets and just get stoned every night and drink' (Kim, 18, white secretary).

As Carole Leathwood and I have written elsewhere (Archer *et al.* 2003), young women positioned higher education and middle-class femininity as counter to their own investments in 'respectable' working-class hetero-femininities. For instance, Elizabeth was a white young woman who was adamant that she would not go to university, despite holding a qualification that could allow entry. She located herself in terms of a 'safe' and 'respectable' heterosexual femininity (as a 'family person') and asserted: 'I'm not being funny, but, like, the people that go to university are gay'. She justified her views using the example of a girl who had 'changed' as a result of going to university, and who now (in Elizabeth's eyes) performed an unacceptable version of femininity: 'like, I knew this girl, a couple of girls I know, and they come back and they look like grungers. Well, they are now- it's not the way they went'.

Higher education was thus positioned by these young women as incompatible with 'normal', 'respectable' working-class femininity. 'Normal', desirable femininity was epitomised by the dream of 'settling down' with a husband, car, house and children. This narrative evoked a poweful influence across the studies. For instance, over the course of the *Dropping Out* study, Jane and Nadira both came to relinquish their plans to go to university in favour of a more 'acceptable' form of femininity that involved 'staying close' to their families and 'settling down' with/marrying their boyfriends (Archer *et al.* forthcoming).

The strength of this discourse of 'normal', 'respectable' (Skeggs 1997) working-class hetero-femininity was also evident in the experiences of those working-class young women who had gone to university (Archer *et al.* 2003). These women described experiencing considerable hostility from their families over their decision – being criticised for 'getting above your station' and 'failing' to perform a 'normal' femininity:

> where I'm from . . . the area is just very sort of working class – I had these dreams above my station, you know? . . . It was all very sort of [acts indignation] 'well, like, what, is this not sort of good enough for you?' . . . I've been really shunned for coming here actually.
>
> (Sally, 22, white student)

Similarly Stephanie (26, white student) complained of her family: 'They compare me to my cousins who haven't been to university or anything like that but they have got children and a mortgage and they are married or have a steady boyfriend . . .'

As all these examples illustrate, the young women's constructions of popular, desirable working-class femininities coalesced around heterosexuality. This form of femininity was performed (and read) via the production of a 'glamorous' appearance (Skeggs 1997) and through being a wife/girlfriend and/or mother. These forms of femininity were perceived as being diametrically opposed to student femininities, which were seen to be 'unglamorous' (e.g. grunger) and privileging individualism, social mobility and 'career' over responsibilities to family, home and partner.

Women students were not only described as 'unglamorous' and 'gay' (and hence unfeminine), but the student lifestyle was also judged to prevent working-class young women from performing their own 'glamorous' and 'cool' femininities. For instance, Jordan did not see university as an attractive or viable option – it simply did not fit with her sense of femininity, identity and lifestyle:

> I don't see that [university] as a path for me. [Interviewer: Why?] Living on them grants. I like to have new Nike trainers and Nike tops and a new chain every month so I don't think the grant would suit me.
>
> (Jordan, 15, white Year 10 girl)

Many girls and young women aspired instead to work in traditionally working-class, feminine occupations, such as the beauty industry and care work. These were seen as 'normal' and acceptable areas of employment that were congruent with the performance of hetero-femininities (involving care of the self/body/appearance and care of others). These also constituted 'known', strategic, 'safe' routes into employment, that would not require girls to undertake further 'formal' education but would use their existing practical competencies (thus providing an escape from 'feeling stupid'). Furthermore, young women recognised that they could draw on their existing social capital and 'hot knowledge' (Ball and Vincent 1998) to increase their liklihood of successfully entering this line of work:

> My step-mum does her own nails and it looks good and my aunt and that have moved to Spain and they have a salon, so I thought if I become a beautician I can go and work for them.
>
> (Lacie, white)

> I want to be a hairdresser. I always do my own hair by myself.
>
> (Jermina, black)

> I like doing hair and stuff like that: I'm interested.
>
> (Kemisha, black)

In many ways, there is a clear parallel between the young men's and women's gendered resistances of higher education, for instance, both involve the resistance of middle-class forms of masculinity and femininity as undesirable and uncool. There is also, however, a subtle yet important difference: the men and boys in the studies did indeed resist participation as undesirable, but they also constructed participation in purely instrumental terms, e.g. as accruing 'a bit of paper' or 'connections' that could be attached to their (unchanged) self as a means for progressing them in the labour market (see Archer and Hutchings 2000; Archer *et al.* 2003). Girls and women, however, negotiated the prospect of HE participation in terms of an internalised re-working of their own identities, such that the decision to participate (or not) was essentially a question of whether to 'escape' (or not) from working-class femininity. For instance, working-class women students described their engagement in HE as a means of 'bettering myself' ('to be a rounded, complete woman', Violet) and to 'escape' from being 'that person'. Bearing in mind working-class women's deficit positioning in relation to education and the 'ideal student/learner' discourse, I would argue that for working-class women, HE participation is predicated upon the recognition of a position of inferiority and a subsequent investment in 'change'. Hence some women's resistance to participation might also be read as part of their resistance to wider discourses of derision surrounding working-class femininity.

Conclusion

In this chapter I have attempted to discuss how HE participation and non-participation are bound up with the expression and resistance of classed masculinities and femininities. While it is not my intention to reduce this to a set of coherent, unified implications for policy and practice, I would suggest that the issues raised do point to the need for current widening participation policy to better engage with the entangled, 'messy' reality of people's lives and identities. Indeed, as I have attempted to argue, gender identities can have a strong influence on the extent to which HE is seen as a desirable or relevant post-16 possibility. Yet these identities are also difficult to 'pin down' – they do not operate in the rational, calculating manner that many policy texts assume (Ball 1990). Rather, they exist at the level of the 'felt', as powerful, emotional, intuitive relationships to education that can be resistant to 'rational' intervention.

My discussion has also raised various social justice concerns – not least the way in which working-class masculinities and femininities continue to be positioned in deficit terms within dominant educational discourse. Resistance to university participation needs to be understood as grounded within wider relations of inequality. Furthermore, there needs to be a greater recognition of how working-class masculinities and femininities can provide sites of pleasure, fun and agency for young people – and that HE participation may appear to demand that these identities are suppressed or given up. This impels us to consider the continued middle-class dominance of academic culture and suggests that if we are to meaningfully widen participation for working-class men and women, then we will have to find new ways to disrupt the gendered, racialised and classed hegemony within (higher) education.

Notes

1   All the studies comprised of larger data sets – here I concentrate only on data that are referred to in this chapter.
2   Across both of the studies conducted in schools, 'streetwear' (particularly brands like Nike) were coded as 'cool' – conveyed through its association with black masculinity, see Archer *et al.* (2005b).
3   The Social Class and HE study also interviewed first year students in a post-1992 university, see Archer *et al.* (2003) for details.

Chapter 6

Fair access?

Exploring gender, access and participation beyond entry to higher education

Penny Jane Burke

The aim of this chapter is to critique the hegemonic discourses currently at play in policy on widening participation and the ways these might serve to perpetuate gendered relations and practices. In the first sections I deconstruct the discourses of 'raising aspirations' and 'fair access' to examine the underlying assumptions and to reveal the ways these discourses are classed, gendered and racialised. I interrogate these discourses to examine the mechanisms by which educational exclusions and inequalities are reconstituted and to uncover the complex processes of selectivity, which are interconnected with institutional categorisations and conventional academic practices. A key argument is that 'access' is an issue that requires attention, not only in terms of admissions and selectivity, but also in terms of epistemologies and pedagogical practices within higher education institutions and in relation to complex gender relations.

Drawing on a feminist poststructural framework, I use the conceptual tool of 'discourse' to capture the ways that knowledge and power are intertwined, profoundly shaping national, local and institutional practices and policies, structures and disciplinary technologies. Discourses are produced within shifting cultural contexts and continually refashioned through changing power relations. Discourses constrain and create the kinds of spaces we live in, the ways we give meaning to our experiences, the positions we take and the kinds of questions we raise (Foucault 1972, 1973). Discourses regarding widening participation institutionalise, normalise and regulate gendered understandings about what higher education is and who should, and who should not, have access to university study.

I also draw on New Literacy Studies (NLS), which conceptualise academic literacies as social practices that are located in complex gender relations. This framework enables a critique of the 'study skills' approach that many higher education institutions adopt in an attempt to support 'widening participation students'. I will use the insights of NLS to examine the study skills approach and its limitations, arguing that the approach might contribute to the re-privileging of exclusionary epistemological frameworks within the academy.

In order to illuminate some of the key points made in this chapter, I draw on qualitative data from two different studies of widening educational participation. The first was an ESRC-funded, ethnographic study, conducted from 1997 to 2001 (Burke 2002). This ethnography took a case study approach within a suburban further education college in the UK, focusing on the accounts of access students returning to study through Access to Higher Education and Return to Study courses. The twenty-three students were all white and most were working-class women. The second study is an ESRC-funded research project on masculinities and educational participation. This study focuses on men accessing education through Access to Higher Education courses or Foundation programmes in London. The forty men in this qualitative study come from a range of class and ethnic backgrounds and are aged 18–54 and participated in interviews that focused on their educational histories, as well as their experiences of their current courses.

Hegemonic discourses of widening educational participation

Raising aspirations

In current policy texts on widening educational participation, the discourse of 'raising aspirations' has a hegemonic position and shapes educational practices and understandings. 'Raising aspirations' is central to key UK policy initiatives for widening educational participation such as 'Aim Higher'. The emphasis of Aim Higher is on working with young people in order to motivate them to aspire to higher education. As the hegemonic discourse of 'raising aspirations' has a major impact on the framework of Aim Higher, it is important to unpack the assumptions that are taken for granted and that underpin it.

The 'raising aspirations' discourse constructs the main problem for widening educational participation as those individuals and communities who fail to recognise the value of participating in higher education. This leads to the assumption that the main work of Aim Higher staff lies with 'raising the aspirations' of those individuals. The logic is that certain individuals, who might have inherent potential, lack the motivation, confidence and the 'right' values and skills to aspire to higher education, due to their 'disadvantaged' backgrounds. The discourse locates such problems of deficit in individuals, families and communities that are pathologised within hegemonic discourses of 'social exclusion'. It is assumed that educational professionals, such as Aim Higher staff, are able to identify those individuals who demonstrate 'untapped potential' and ability, and raise their aspirations by pointing out the value of higher education. Currently, this has a particular gendered undercurrent in relation to the perceived 'crisis' of masculinity, which is supported by recent research claiming that being female increases the chances of higher education participation by 18 per cent (HEFCE 2005). As a result of the ongoing construction of boys as victims of the educational system, and the dominant reasoning that if women are doing well, then men are losing out, the concern to raise aspirations has shifted firmly from girls to boys (Epstein *et al.* 1998).

The deconstruction of 'raising aspirations' exposes the underlying and problematic assumptions of this hegemonic discourse. First, those targeted by the discourse are seen as an identifiable group of 'potentially excluded', constructed as not knowing what is good for them, while professionals, such as teachers and Aim Higher representatives, do know. These professionals are seen as able to identify who has the potential to aspire to higher education (and who does not), and to 'empower' those selected individuals to recognise and act upon that potential. Such assumptions ignore the structural, cultural, discursive and material constraints that particular social groups face. Raising aspirations is constructed as a straightforward process that occurs outside of social relations and the micro-politics of educational organisations and institutions (Morley 1999).

The discourse of 'raising aspirations' ignores the ways that identifications are re/fashioned through the discursive sites and practices of schools, colleges and universities. It emphasises individual aspirations without understanding the interconnections between a subject's aspirations and their social positioning, ignoring the cultural contexts in which certain subjects are constructed, and construct themselves, as not/having potential or ability or indeed not choosing to participate in higher education for a range of valid reasons (Archer and Leathwood 2003). When gender is recognised, it is often because boys are seen to be losing out in comparison to girls. This perspective takes an anti-feminist stance that perceives girls' and women's success as always at a cost to boys and men. Men are seen as victims of the feminist movement, which has undermined their masculinity and natural position in the order of things (Epstein *et al.* 1998; Archer and Yamashita 2003b).

Gendered identifications interconnect with classed and racialised positionings and this profoundly shapes the educational choices and experiences of different individuals and social groups (Reay *et al.* 2005). Skeggs has argued, for example, that class divisions operate as 'structures of feeling' in which working-class subjects construct themselves as inferior and undeserving:

> Categories of class operate not only as an organising principle which enable access to and limitations on social movement and interaction but are also reproduced at the intimate level as a 'structure of feeling' in which doubt, anxiety and fear inform the production of subjectivity. To be working-classed . . . generates a constant fear of never having 'got it right'.
>
> (Skeggs 1997: 6)

A quote from Kerry's learning journal below highlights how 'structures of feeling' play out. Kerry is a white, working-class Access to Higher Education student and her words illuminate the complex ways that class and gender interlink to create feelings of not belonging within academic discursive sites:

First day back after the summer holidays. What a shock!! I didn't expect Sociology to get so heavy so quickly. The teacher seems like an approachable guy thank god, because I will probably be going to him for lots of help. Question: Why do I always feel that I am not good enough to do the work? Answer: I don't know. I must look into it.

(Kerry, learning journal entry, 1999)

Identifications of 'being good enough' to access higher education are tied in with notions of ability and the construction of the 'able student' with potential. The raising aspirations discourse ignores the ways that 'ability' is classed, gendered and racialised in the interests of particular social groups, treating 'ability' as something that is measurable, fixed and related to general academic potential (Gillborn 2002). Gillborn and Youdell (2000) argue that such discourses of ability are deeply flawed. Students take up these discourses, in struggling to be recognised as deserving of access to higher education. For example, Paul, an Access to Higher Education student, explains that he will prove himself to have, or not to have, the potential to participate in a degree course through the end of year exam: 'I know I can do it, and I'm on the course, obviously, but the proof is in the pudding when it comes to the end of next July when I've gotta take the exams' (Paul, interviewed in 2004).

Paul understands his life and educational trajectories in relation to classed and racialised structures and equates having middle-class parents with a 'normal background'. He constructs himself as middle class, which he justifies in relation to the value of his house and explains that 'he couldn't be bothered' in the past with educational participation because his working-class parents did not push him. In this way, Paul takes up the hegemonic discourses that place the blame of educational exclusion on the deficit cultures of working-class parents (Gewirtz 2001). This allows him to reconstruct his class identity in relation to his perceived natural ability, explaining that if he had middle-class parents, then he would have been a professor:

If I had a normal background, I'd probably be a professor by now. Truth, if I was pushed, if I had the model middle-class parents, yes, I would have got me As and me BAs, but because I wasn't pushed, I couldn't be bothered. If you notice I put on my thing middle class, because I am middle class, I look at myself middle class but I was brought up in a lower class. I live in a half a million pound house around the corner.

Paul's narrative reveals the importance of classed auto/biographies in authoring the self and in imagining what is im/possible to access:

Once I get over this bridge it will be a lot easier, because I'll know what I'm doing, for college, for university. We are not walking in as naïve students, we are walking in as proper students. Because I don't feel that any of us, at the moment, feel like we are proper students. I think we just feel like we are just, you know, school children. But once we are halfway through the course we will be like proper students. That's it. And once we leave here and go to university, if it all goes to plan, it will be easier, because we will have done the majority of what we had to do in the first place. We won't be walking in there blinkered, we will be walking in there, because we know what we have got to do, focused, basically. And not walking around in the dark.

Significantly, until he learns how to become a 'proper student', he likens himself and his adult peers to school children, representative of wider class politics and the construction of working-class groups as infantile and not knowing what is best for them. The Access course is seen as a bridge and once the student crosses to the other side, proving her or his ability by passing exams, the Access student becomes a 'proper student', worthy of university entry, which supports notions of 'fair access'.

Fair access

A second hegemonic discourse at play in current policy of widening edu-cational participation in the UK is 'fair access'. This discourse is premised on the assumption that through 'transparent' sets of criteria, procedures, rules and regulations, admissions tutors and personnel are able to make fair decisions about accepting some candidates onto a course over others. Such decisions are seen as outside of wider social relations and contexts assuming that candidates apply to higher education on a level playing field. Candidates can be selected on 'merit alone' and assumptions are made about processes of identifying those with talent, ability and potential. Talent, ability and potential are constructed in this discourse as inherent natural characteristics of individuals rather than socially constructed discourses that are tied to classed, gendered and racialised values and perspectives. Inequalities are hidden within this discourse, except where reference is made to discrimination, but sets of admissions criteria are seen as the tools to overcome discrimination (Schwartz 2004). The ways that certain (middle-class) tastes, values and cultural capital are reprivileged through admissions criteria and through complex power relations are hidden.

The discourse of 'fair access' ignores the operations of selectivity, embedded in specific cultural values and assumptions, which serve to reinforce social inequalities. Wider social discourses that legitimate certain sets of cultural cap-ital ensure that candidates are identified and identify themselves as deserving or undeserving and this significantly affects decisions and choices (Williams 1997; Reay et al. 2005). Although Access to Higher Education courses have been significantly expanded over the past decade and brought into the mainstream through the efforts of the QAA to standardise Access courses, A levels continue to be constructed as the preferred route into HE (Bekhradnia 2003). Such preferences are institutionalised through policy texts such as *The Future of Higher*

Education (DfES 2003b), which gives Access courses one brief mention, and this has particular implications for the ways that Access students are viewed by higher education institutions. The perceptions of Access students are particularly characterised by assumptions that such students require special help and more resources (Bowl 2003; Burke and Hermerschmidt 2005).

Yet, students themselves contest this normalised construction of A levels as the ideal route into higher education. John, who has taken A levels and is now on a Foundation programme, explains:

> But the Science and Engineering Foundation Programme, you know, it gives you an introduction to university because it's like the same. You have all these subjects that relate to university. So it's like a much better course than just sitting a test as, for example, A levels.
>
> (John, interviewed in 2004)

Sadie, a Return to Study student taking A levels as part of her programme, argues that examinations make students feel that they 'must be awful' and yet, she explains, it is the assessment method, rather than the student's ability, that is responsible for letting students down:

> I do think exams are unfair. Some people just get on with them and don't pain over them, but they do let you down. Which is why I try to do my best in my coursework, try to make up my grade . . . I know, even if I revised every day from now to my exams, I wouldn't do any better than if I left it to a couple of months before, because I blank anyway when I get in there. It does gradually come back, but then you've run out of time. And your writing's all messy and you've got spelling mistakes and . . . things like that. It's awful. I hate them. I know you've got to have them, but I don't think they show who you really are. You can end up getting a grade you don't deserve. There'd be a lot more people out there doing well in education and moving on, but they just don't get recognised in exams. And then they feel 'gawd, I must be awful' but they're not really. You just panic too much. And that's what I'm dreading, that I'll know in myself if I don't do that well, I'll know it's not me.
>
> (Sadie, interviewed in 2000)

Sadie's account exposes the ways that conventional assessment practices regulate exclusions, mis/recognitions and complex identifications: 'There'd be a lot more people out there doing well in education and moving on, but they just don't get recognised in exams.' Both Sadie and John contest the logic that A levels are the best preparation for higher education. They expose that the traditional pedagogical and assessment approaches do not necessarily support access and participation, which leads to questions about widening participation strategies beyond entry.

Access and participation beyond entry

The discourse of 'raising aspirations' and 'fair access' is particularly problematic because it assumes that access and widening participation are largely a concern *prior* to entry to higher education. Yet access and widening participation continue to produce challenges *within* higher education and this must be addressed by higher education institutions, in terms of the gendered nature of current pedagogy, curriculum, support and resources and the ongoing re/privileging of classed, gendered and racialised knowledge through HE. Much WP research has revealed that contradictory and complex gendered exclusions take place within HE. For example, Jocey Quinn (2003) has argued that although women's participation in higher education has dramatically increased, the curriculum has largely stayed the same. Her research makes an important contribution to examining changing gendered participation patterns, reconsidering women's positioning in higher education institutions in the twenty-first century. Interrogating the increasing moral panics that women are 'taking over' the university, she provides a convincing argument that far from taking over, universities continue to be male-centred institutions (Quinn 2003: 21–32). While acknowledging that women's participation in higher education has certainly increased, Quinn claims that 'it is clearly premature to shift equality debates entirely onto men' (ibid.: 22), drawing on compelling evidence to support her case. For example, there is evidence that many women enter less prestigious universities and that many are mature and/or part-time students. Further evidence reveals that working-class and minority ethnic women students 'face acute problems of access and integration' (ibid.). Also, subject choices remain heavily gendered with women students being over-represented in Arts, Humanities, Education and medicine-related subjects such as Nursing.

Ways of addressing issues of access and widening participation within higher education institutions have been limited. However, there has been one key intervention – the provision of study skills support for 'non-traditional' students. I will argue that although it is valuable that study skills support has acknowledged the need to develop strategies within HEIs for widening participation, the assumptions underpinning such support might further reinforce the deficit construction of the 'widening participation student' against the normalised undergraduate student.

Critiquing study skills

Much of the attention given to WP support is in the form of 'study skills' support. This too rests on assumptions of deficit and lack rather than exploring the valuable sets of cultural capital and knowledge that students from different groups bring to HE (Burke and Hermerschmidt 2005). Drawing on the theoretical framework of 'new literacy studies' (NLS) (Street 1984; Lillis and Ramsey 1997; Ivanic 1998; Rose 1998; Lea and Street 2000; Lillis 2001;

Street 2001), helps to deconstruct the taken-for-granted assumptions around study skills. Although study skills has been developed to help students from under-represented groups participate in higher education, I argue that study skills might exacerbate existing inequalities, reinforcing certain students as having problems and measuring them against a normalised, idealised, 'traditional' student.

NLS draws on the work of Street (Street 1984; Street 2001) and others, which conceptualises literacies as multiple, contested, discursive and socially situated sets of practices. Lillis (2001) argues that the dominant literacy practice within Western higher education is 'essayist literacy', which has several key characteristics. She argues that the features of the essay contribute to 'a fictionalisation of both writer and reader, the reader being an idealisation', 'a rational mind formed by the rational body of knowledge of which the essay is a part' (Lillis 2001: 38). Furthermore, she argues that the essayist literacy serves to privilege 'the discursive routines of particular social groups while dismissing those of people who, culturally and communally, have access to and engage in a range of other practices' (ibid.: 39). These points are central in understanding the complex mechanisms by which some groups become excluded from full HE participation, even after they have secured entry to degree level study. Participation is not just about issues of access, or 'raising aspirations' but about cultural and literacy practices within higher education institutions. As Lillis states:

> The conventions surrounding the production of student academic texts are ideologically inscribed in at least two powerful ways: by working towards the exclusion of students from social groups who have historically been excluded from the conservative-liberal project of HE in the UK and by regulating directly and indirectly what student-writers can mean, and who they can be.
>
> (2001: 39)

Lillis illuminates through her study the ways that the essayist literacy practice serves to exclude certain social groups at both the ontological and the epistemological levels. The essayist literacy, upheld in universities, positions the writer in specifically classed, gendered and racialised ways as the masculine, white and middle-class subject who is objective, decontextualised and neutral and who is reflecting rather than constructing reality and truth through rational and scientific methods. The relations by which knowledge gets produced are perceived as apolitical and/or irrelevant in such practices and other ways of writing are not recognised as legitimate or valuable. If we consider this in relation to attempts to widen participation in higher education, and acknowledge the different ontological and epistemological perspectives students bring to their studies, then we might be able to understand why this issue is so central to developing strategies within universities for equality, inclusion and social justice.

This draws attention to the major strategy currently adopted within higher education for 'widening participation students': study skills provision.

Study skills conceptualises academic conventions as sets of mechanical skills (that widening participation students are seen to lack), which are disconnected from wider struggles around disciplinary knowledge, epistemological debates and ontological positions (Burke and Hermerschmidt 2005). As a result, students constructed as 'traditional' (i.e. those 18–19-year-olds coming through A-level routes) are seen as not needing specialist instruction with their writing, because they are constructed as coming to university with the 'right' knowledge, skills and competencies and also as capable of self-regulation within the acceptable academic framework of essayist literacy. Students constructed as 'non-traditional', on the other hand, are seen, and see themselves, as needing special help with their writing as well as other kinds of 'communication skills'. For example, Paul says:

> I have trouble with it coming out of my mouth. That's why we are actually doing communications as well. Because obviously, if you are going to be a teacher you've got to get up in front of a class or an assembly and you've got to talk. You've got to talk . . . well, I don't talk fluent, but you've got to make sure you get your view across to them kids so they know what you are talking about and they also understand what they are going to write down.
>
> (Paul, interviewed in 2004)

Although it is understandable that study skills provision is seen as a useful support strategy, it is crucial to widening access and participation that such provision is significantly re-conceptualised to draw attention to the different epistemological frameworks available to student writers, which plays a central role in the production of knowledge. Different epistemological frameworks are tied in with particular cultural/social histories (e.g. colonialism, racism, (hetero)sexism, etc.) and this needs to be exposed as part of a wider strategy to challenge inequalities. Furthermore, all students need to be involved in academic writing courses, so that the assumptions underpinning essayist literacy can be deconstructed and problematised. This would give all students the opportunity to carefully consider the kind of contribution to meaning-making they want to make through their writing at university and could also contribute to challenging hegemonic academic practices within universities that serve to maintain privilege and exclusion. Such an approach would put ontology and epistemology at the centre of focus, moving away from a concern with individuals who are seen to lack the right skills, cultural capital and aspirations. How and what we write is recognised as tied to complex questions of methodology. Reconceptualising writing as a social practice places ontological issues (e.g. the ways that selves are (re)authorised through written texts) and epistemological questions (e.g. the construction of meaning through texts) at the centre of concern. Techniques and skills can still be addressed but not as the main, or only, issue for academic writing and writers.

In considering how an academic literacies approach might work in practice, I will draw on Lillis and Ramsey's (1997) concept of the 'orchestration of voices, which highlights that referencing is a social practice. This concept helps to critique conventional study skills approaches to teaching 'referencing', which emphasise the mechanics of compiling a bibliography. The concept of 'orchestration of voices' extends the focus to include the complex selective and intellectual processes that readers and writers experience when trying to bring together the different voices from the field in order to construct their own authorial voice in their writing (Burke and Hermerschmidt 2005). It highlights that referencing involves much deeper concerns about making connections between concepts and theories in the field as writers struggle to give authority to their writing. In working with this concept in the classroom, students recognise that there are power relations at play when citing different authors, some of whom have more status than others. It highlights that referencing involves subjective processes of selection and exclusion and that referencing is about positioning yourself within or outside of heterogeneous academic communities. The concept of 'orchestration of voices' reveals the relationship between subjectivity, power, authorial voices in the literature and the ways in which students position themselves in their reading and writing (ibid.). In this way, the focus shifts away from 'special students with special problems' to the implications of particular practices and conventions for access to meaning-making and knowledge.

Conclusion

In this chapter, I have deconstructed two key hegemonic discourses around widening participation policy and practice. I have interrogated the taken-for-granted assumptions around 'raising aspirations' and 'fair access' that locate the problem in individuals from 'deficit cultural backgrounds', thus hiding the mechanisms by which exclusions in higher education are reproduced at the cultural, discursive, institutional and structural level.

Drawing on New Literacy Studies, which conceptualises academic literacies as social practices, I have also argued that study skills approaches reproduce the construction of 'widening participation students' as an identifiable, homogenous group with special needs. The discursively constructed problems of these students are tied to their perceived deficit cultural backgrounds, including their participation in access courses, which are seen as inferior to A-level courses. As a result, 'widening participation students' are offered study skills provision, which is institutionally separated from disciplinary teaching and constructed as 'remedial' and skills-based (Burke and Hermerschmidt 2005).

My central argument in exploring these discourses and practices is that widening participation needs attention at the level of epistemologies and pedagogical practices within higher education institutions and in relation to complex gender relations. The deficit discourses that locate the problem at the individual level not only hides the workings of privilege within the academy but serves as a mechanism of exclusion. The discourse keeps certain assumptions in place, for example, that the British higher education system is underpinned by principles of fairness and that identifying talented individuals from 'disadvantaged' backgrounds is a straightforward process that involves professionals making fair decisions based on neutral and apolitical sets of admissions criteria. It conceals the re-privileging of particular values and cultures that are discursively constructed as universal 'goods' but are heavily invested in complex colonial, patriarchal and racist histories and epistemologies. Even the study skills provision, that is seen to support students, operates to re-privilege essayist literacies that Lillis (2001) argues governs what students can mean in their writing and who can write/know. Widening participation policy and practice must move away from deficit discourses and perspectives that hide the complex power relations tied to certain values to developing policies and practices that begin to challenge deeply embedded inequalities and exclusion in higher education.

Part III

Experiences of lifelong learning

Chapter 7

Community education

Participation, risk and desire

Lyn Tett

Introduction

It is in response to immediate problems that people often get their first desire to engage in learning, but the way in which these problems are conceptualised is guided by gendered, 'raced' and classed assumptions of what is possible. Similarly, different educational traditions and gendered assumptions guide people's ideas about what learning is, what its focus should be and how it should be done. Traditionally community education provision has focused on education's role in improving social conditions for marginalised groups and individuals, by working with people in their own communities (see Tett 2002). The community educator is seen as an agent of social change, who does not separate the process of learning from the intentions of teaching. This educational tradition involves purposeful educational intervention in the interests of social and political change: change towards more justice, equality and democracy. In this chapter I will explore the impact of gender, 'race' and class on participation by women in community-based provision within this tradition and the role played by 'risk' and desire. I will consider some of the emotional and social factors that can prevent participation in learning and education and those that might encourage it, through an analysis of interviews with students who have participated in community education programmes. My argument is that the intersections of gender, 'race' and class shape learning identities and therefore what people regard as acceptable risks, knowledge and desires. In this analysis I agree with Zmroczek who argues that the emphasis should be on moving research 'away from a preoccupation with personal identity and towards a commitment to political engagement' (1999: 4). I will illustrate how this analysis is enacted out in practice through an examination of learners in community-based literacies programmes but first an analysis of adult participation in learning and education is presented.

Participation in post-compulsory learning and education

Overall, participation in post-school education and training in the UK is a highly classed, 'raced' and gendered activity where those who leave school with few or no qualifications are unlikely to engage in learning later, even informal learning, with less than a third reporting participating in some learning during the preceding three years (Sargant and Aldridge 2003). The lowest participation figures are 'found among those outside of the labour market: retired people (48 per cent) and those unable to work due to a health problem or a disability (42 per cent)' (ibid.: 15). So, it appears that if you do not succeed in education in the first place, then you will not want to engage in learning later either. Participation is also gendered and 'raced' with White men more likely to participate in well-funded, work-based provision and White and Black women in local, community based provision that is the least well resourced.

A wide variety of governments and educational bodies recognise that these inequities in access to learning in adulthood are a problem that should be tackled. For example, there is a widespread commitment to policies that promote 'lifelong learning' that aim to develop the individual's capacity for learning over the life span. There is also an encouragement to the providers of learning programmes to widen opportunities in order to enable learning to take place in many different ways and contexts (e.g. DfEE 1998; CEC 2000d; Scottish Executive 2000). However, in most of these supply and demand side policies there is a strong emphasis on economic skills development and individual learning. For example, a European Union policy paper argued that the aims of lifelong learning 'are dependent on [citizens] having adequate and up-to-date knowledge and skills to take part in and make a contribution to economic and social life' (CEC 2000d: 5). The British Prime Minister has similarly argued that 'Education is the best economic policy we have' (Blair 1998) and the Scottish Executive (2001: 7) suggests 'in an increasingly globalised economy, Scotland's future prosperity depends on building up the skills of her existing workforce and improving the employability of those seeking work.' These policies also emphasise the association of lifelong learning with skills, individual motivation and economic survival. Permeating the lifelong learning discourse, then, is an emphasis on the individual, isolated learner and the main aim is to focus on increasing people's skills and employability. This emphasis can exclude the very people it is hoped will re-engage in learning as they see themselves condemned, as Field (2000b) has argued, to a life sentence of undesirable and unwanted education and training.

This association of economic skills with learning has a strong effect on women with children, particularly as their domestic work makes it difficult to distinguish 'love' from 'labour'. Although society plays lip service to qualities associated with care giving – sensitivity, patience, empathy and compassion – these habits of mind are relegated to what Wendy Luttrell calls the 'ontological basement of different ways of knowing' (1997: 31). Gendered views of knowledge – that is, splits between intellect and emotion, affect and cognition, autonomy and relatedness – fragment the knowledge people feel able to claim for themselves. Many people incorporate these splits into their 'common-sense' views of comprehending the world and its workings as familiar and knowable. In this sense, it is 'self and identity forming [and it] contains a paradox. It is both a self-destructive, and an enabling, understanding imposed by gender, "race" and class relations' (Luttrell 1997: 26).

The judgements and emotions that are generated about how successfully or otherwise people meet the demands of school have a particular effect on the decision to participate in post-school education and learning. The myth of meritocracy implies that anyone who is brought up properly, who is supported enough by caring parents, who is loved and feels good about themselves, will rise above the hardships imposed by poverty, sexism and racism (see Tett 2002). This myth permeates common-sense understandings of what returning to learning implies because failing to meet the demands of schooling is seen as an individual problem. As Mohanty (1994: 147) points out:

> Education represents both a struggle for meaning and a struggle over power relations. Thus education becomes a central terrain where power and politics operate out of the lived culture of individuals and groups situated in asymmetrical social and political positions.

For all these reasons, returning to learning and education is a very risky business for working-class women, particularly those who had to stifle the development of some aspects of themselves for the sake of others both while they were at school and subsequently. In order to explore these issues, the rest of this chapter will focus on the experience of women who were participating in community education programmes concerned with learning literacies in terms of their abilities to take risks, make choices and have their desires fulfilled.

Literacies, risks and returning to learning

Because the discourse surrounding adult literacy and numeracy tends to focus on what people lack rather than what they have and emphasises their deficits not their strengths, 'admitting' to having difficulties is seen as an unacceptable risk, a fear of how learners might be labelled by others. Literacy in particular is seen as something that everyone should have and surveys, such as the International Adult Literacy Survey (IALS) (OECD 2000), that identify people as lacking these kinds of knowledge and skills emphasise deficits and the negative consequences of the lack of literacy. Hamilton and Barton (2000) have argued that these surveys fit well with the globalising project of capitalism because they justify a vision of literacy that fits in with the projected needs of an ideal, consumer-oriented citizen who is responsive to new economic contexts for literacy use. Such surveys also justify a skewed vision of what literacy should be, rather than it being based on people's lived experiences. The findings from IALS that are publicised treat people who have literacy and numeracy difficulties as shameful to the nation's educational system and they also position individuals as people who have somehow failed to learn. The emphasis of the discourse is on individual failure, not on the circumstances and structures that might make learning difficult.

For all these reasons, participating in literacy provision as an adult is a particularly risky business. This is compounded by the issue that the essence of risk is about what *might be* happening rather than what *is* happening because anticipating what is risky only suggests what should *not* be done, not what *should* be done (Adam *et al.* 2000). This means they are about anticipating something that has not yet happened. What it is possible to anticipate, however, is based on a set of gendered and classed assumptions that are taken for granted and unconscious, and, as a result, structure experiences in ways that are hidden from view. The modern social order is one characterised by constant and ubiquitous change, but with no clear direction for development or response. Individuals are confronted not only by a variety of ways of doing things, but also by a host of uncertainties about what counts as the correct way of doing them. Uncertainty can lead to dependence on others to provide guidance about what is the best way of doing things. It leads to pessimism about people's power to act, so they are increasingly seen as victims of fate who cannot help themselves or work out their own responses to problems. In turn, this creates an insidious dependence on experts to 'help' people deal with experiences 'appropriately' and this dependence can fuel mistrust of other sources of support such as peers, family and local communities. Belief in the power of fate, and doubts about people's ability to cope with life, undermine personal autonomy and responsibility while leading us to accept closer state regulation of behaviour because this is seen as another form of authoritative knowledge that is 'good for us' (see Furedi 1997: 150). As Usher and Edwards point out, 'The most effective forms of power are those which are not recognised as powerful because they are cloaked in the esoteric "objective" knowledge of expertise and the humanistic discourse of helping and empowerment' (1998: 217).

Generally, then, risk is avoided and this in turn leads to trying to remain in situations that are comfortable. Being in an environment where people see themselves as 'different' often exposes them to unacceptable levels of emotional and social risk as they try to reconcile themselves to losing their normal confidence. These risks are borne by individuals even though their cause is often a failure of social and educational policy to provide appropriate support. In addition, the dominant discourse of literacy, of 'deficit' individuals who lack skills and knowledge, adds to the difficulties that individuals face in life and in learning.

The research on which this chapter is based involved asking literacies learners about their pathways into community-based provision (see Maclachlan and Tett 2005). Our respondents were twenty women, all working class, taking part in a variety of community settings. Eighteen were White and two were Black and all were able-bodied. The interviews with the women illuminate how gender, 'race' and class intersect to impact on a decision to participate, with the meanings and effects of class changing 'across, time/space, "race" and gender' (Archer 2003a: 18). This impact is particularly strong in relation to unhappy memories of school days when institutional, social and economic factors and inequalities interacted in complex ways with multiple identities to render particular routes 'unthinkable' for a diverse range of people. For example, one student suggested that 'I thought it would be like school and I hated it but I didn't want my kids to go through the same things at school that I did either.' Another, who took part in a workplace literacy programme, reflected, 'They are bad memories, and it puts you off learning because it makes you feel such a failure, and you don't want that again.'

So, for many people, there is both the risk of participation and also the risks associated with the possibility of change. For example, one student said, 'My mother expected me to leave school and get a job although my brother was expected to stay on because he would have a career. It took a long time for me to see myself as anything else than a wife and mother.' Another said that gearing herself up to go along to a group 'was torture because I thought they would look down on me. I already looked down on myself but I had to do something to change for the sake of the children.' Later she was able to see herself as a competent learner but the emotions associated with the risk of that first step still remained with her. Another who successfully completed a course said:

> I wouldn't go on a course by myself . . . If a few were going together from work, then that'd be different, you'd feel OK, and if one of us is stupid and can't do it, you can always ask the others . . . and if they don't know, then I'm no[t] stupid on my own. We can have a giggle about being thick together.

The women that we interviewed described their return to the literacies programmes mainly in terms of meeting the needs of others through fulfilling responsibilities to their families, particularly their children. Doing this, moreover, was often described in terms of encouragement or persuasion from their partners and rarely framed in terms of a right to have an education for themselves. The reasons for participating in provision were couched in terms of 'being able to help the children with their homework', or 'being more confident with my parents', 'being able to shop better for the family', 'being able to help my husband with his work', not about the differences it would make in their own personal lives. The students also described fitting in their studies into the limited time they had available. For example, one student commented:

> In my community it is a responsibility of the family to look after the elders. Husbands have long hours of work so they can't share household

responsibilities. Women do not have time for themselves, looking after young children and their husbands, providing help to the elderly. The one woman in the house performs all these jobs.

This shows how the material constraints experienced by working-class women and the ways these are stratified by 'race' and gender interact in constraining their attempts to engage in reading and writing more generally (see Mace 1998). Stealing time, as Lillis points out in the context of her study of women in Higher Education, also 'involves taking something from others, which is their right, not yours. Therefore guilt is a common theme in the women's talk: guilt about using time on themselves, rather than with their families, and especially with their children' (2001: 112). Unlike participating in Higher Education, however, learning literacy and numeracy skills has long been regarded as an acceptable form of education for working-class women within the discourse of illiteracy as a lack that needs to be remedied for the good of society (see Hamilton 1996). In accord with this tradition, when we interviewed women near the beginning of their programmes they described their participation in terms of being able to do things for others, particularly their families. So, as long as their studies did not interfere with their domestic and family lives, their guilt was kept at bay. This also reflects dominant notions of gender, which suggest that a good mother should be an educated mother and that a working-class woman has a right to study if it is for the benefit of her family. Participating in these forms of education, then, may be just another way of fulfilling social gender norms rather than transgressing them.

Hope and desire

So far this chapter has concentrated on risk but the other side of risk is hope and desire. To hope is to revitalise the present by undermining the sense that the way things are currently is inevitable and immutable (Halpin 2003) and to foster desire means presenting alternative visions of what could be. In terms of education and learning, this vision is about fostering a desire to know more, and a belief, however tenuous, in the possibility of doing so. It is about education that moves away from inequitable, individualised, deficit models of learners and brings about change in understanding of both self and society. Engaging with others in mutual learning is both a source of and potential outcome of hope, and hope is closely bound up with the willingness to experiment, to make choices, to be adventurous. So hope and desire have creative roles in encouraging the development of imaginative and transgressive solutions to seemingly intractable difficulties.

The nature of the women's desires about education was not fixed but changed over time depending on the support from family and partners and on economic circumstances. Knowledge is not neutral, and what counts as knowledge is determined by those who have the power to create and uphold dominant discourses and means that people need to have their own experience acknowledged and valued. So it is vital to challenge what is seen as acceptable to learn because, as Lillis points out:

> literacies that are considered to be functional, meeting basic needs, and romantic, reading heterosexual romance stories, are not seen as transgressing local structural norms. They were not seen as a bid by women to engage in another kind of life.
>
> (2001: 112)

Therefore, the agenda for developing literacies has to be informed by issues of social justice for all, equality, and democracy in everyday life, if an alternative model of learning that places the emphasis on how adults can and want to use literacy is to be developed. This would mean that the focus moves to what people have, rather than what they lack, what motivates them rather than what is seen as something they need. Approaches are required that open up, expose and counteract the institutional processes and professional mystique whereby dominant forms of literacy are placed beyond question. They have to challenge the way what are seen as acceptable forms of literacies are classed, 'raced' and gendered. The learning and teaching process needs to be reconstructed so that students are seen as equal in social and political terms. This involves using the literacy practices of everyday life in the curriculum so that the home and community life of participants is both valued and challenged. This is because:

> Many of the most intimate dramas, the deepest malaises, the most singular suffering that women and men can experience find their roots in the objective contradictions, constraints and double binds inscribed in the structures of the labour and housing markets, in the merciless sanctions of the school systems, or in mechanisms of economic and social inheritance.
>
> (Bourdieu and Wacquant 1992: 201)

If learners are positioned as experienced and knowledgeable social actors, then they become active players rather than passive recipients of education. Learning then becomes a shared endeavour between tutors and students, a two-way, rather than a one-way, process (see Thompson 2001). Within this paradigm people's classed, 'raced' and gendered experiences would be seen as a learning resource to be used, rather than a deficiency to be rectified. Learning to be literate therefore involves understanding the way in which power is distributed unequally within the social structure, so that the practices of some are marginalised while others are privileged (see Tett 2004). The adoption of the literacy practices of privileged groups in society reinforces the identity and confidence of such groups. The reverse also occurs: negative views about literacies are internalised and this has consequences for how people see themselves and thus

...dermine their own self-esteem. Having been encouraged to ...opment of some aspects of themselves for the sake of others, ...omen in our study returned to learning and went on to regain the ...es and autonomy denied to them at school. This, however, was nearly a... a tentative unfolding of the desire for something different as they recovered from their earlier negative experiences of schooling.

Many of the learners we interviewed talked about both the emotional and social turning points in their lives that caused them to reassess the risks of engaging in learning in the first place. They also talked about the realisation, once they were part of a learning group, that others shared the same issues of poverty, lack of time, and guilt about only being a 'good enough' mother. This type of collective learning involves the active engagement of people in the construction, interpretation, and, often, the re-shaping of their own social identity and social reality so they see themselves in a different light. This can involve huge emotional and social risks and so this awakened desire to re-engage with formal learning must be met by tuned-in and receptive educational systems. This is a pedagogical challenge but it also concerns equity and social justice because participation in education brings a range of social, economic and personal benefits that should be available to *all* people. Our interviewees talked about the changes they experienced in their self-esteem, their experiences at work and in their ability to take action.

In terms of self-esteem, the women talked about how their perceptions of what they could do had changed. For example, one suggested, 'It's making me realise that I'm not stupid.' Another said, 'It made a whole lot of difference to how I feel about myself since I learned to read better. You feel better when you learn to do a lot of things for yourself you know.' Others talked about how they were more able to take decisions and be their own person after many years of focusing on the needs of others. For example, one suggested, 'It helped me to realise things about myself, be more mature, make up my own mind.' Another said, 'I'm not afraid to voice my opinion now, even if I'm wrong. I speak up a lot more now. Before I came to the programme I would never have done that because I didn't want to make trouble.' Others commented on how they were taken more seriously by others, for example, 'I'm being taken more seriously at work now. I'm not just a woman who left school and then had lots of kids.' 'I want to become something now – before I just thought I was a nobody.' Another suggested, 'I basically know what I'm talking about now. I'm confident and capable and know I can achieve things.' In some cases people participated in programmes in order to avoid negative changes such as 'feeling at a loose end when the children left home and not wanting to vegetate'. While another said, 'I have agoraphobia and coming to the course has helped me get out of the house.' Perhaps the issues raised by the literacies programmes are best summed up by the quote from one learner. She said, 'I'm giving something back to my community now I can read and write better. But if you want people to succeed then you have to have the structures in place. That means more resources, more flexibility, more support.' The women saw the programmes as very valuable but the resources available were always limited and insufficient to provide the support necessary to help make participants' desires a reality.

Conclusion

The importance of recognising the intersections of class, 'race' and gender in community education provision is that knowledge is seen as something that is used, tested, questioned and produced rather than as something that has to be accumulated and assessed through qualifications that signify possession of it. Communities in civic society are often seen as needing knowledge that others possess. However, if, rather than dichotomising the act of acquiring already existing knowledge from the activity of producing new knowledge, it is seen that these two aspects of knowledge are dialectical, then these relations can be transformed (see Martin 2001). From this perspective, learning is essentially about creating knowledge, skills and understanding that makes sense of the world and helps people to act upon it collectively, in order to change it for the better. The curriculum always represents 'selections from a culture' (Williams 1961) so knowledge is never neutral or value-free, and what counts as worth knowing reflects those particular social and political interests that have the power to make it count. Power and politics operate out of the lived culture of individuals and groups who are situated in unequal social and political positions. Knowledge should be actively constructed in the creative encounter between the expertise of the tutor and the experience of the learners, with each role conferring a distinctive kind of authority if change is to occur (see Tett 2003).

Learners are embedded in different social realities, where power manifests itself concretely and specifically, and educational practices need to take these particularities and differences into account. Community educators thus have an important role in making sure that the complexity of the intellectual, emotional, practical, pleasurable and political possibilities of learning is not reduced to the apparent simplicity of targets, standards and skills (see Thompson 2000). Finding a voice to do this can happen through being part of a social, mutually supportive group that is engaged in learning. Such learning is a political, as well as an educational, activity because spaces are opened up for the public discussion of the issues with which people are concerned. Active groups can force into the public domain aspects of social conduct such as violence against women in the home that previously were not discussed or were settled by traditional practices. This means that their voices 'help to contest the traditional, the official, the patriarchal, the privileged and the academic view of things' (ibid.: 143).

An emphasis on whose experiences count, and how they are interpreted and understood, helps us to challenge the 'common sense' of everyday assumptions about experience and its relationship to knowledge production. This allows new claims to be made for the legitimacy of reflexive experience leading to 'really useful knowledge' (see Johnson 1988) for those who are involved in generating it. In questioning the discourses that frame the ways of thinking, problems and practices that are regarded as legitimate, it begins to be possible for people to open up new ways of reflexively thinking about the social construction of their experiences. When people create their own knowledge and have their voices heard, narrow definitions of what is thought to be 'educated knowledge' and who it is that makes it, are thrown into question. In this way, the experiences and stories that have been excluded, and the mystification caused by 'expert' knowledge, can be interrogated as a way of articulating views that come from below rather than above:

> This is important because, in identifying and making spaces where alternative ways of thinking and being can be worked up, such practices increase the possibilities of knowledge – that is knowledge that is useful to those who generate it.
>
> (Barr 1999: 82)

A popular curriculum that addresses the concerns of women and actively draws upon their experience as a resource for educational work in communities increases the possibilities of developing knowledge that is useful to those who generate it. Approaching education and learning in this way would not be new but would involve revisiting much earlier debates over the role of education, as Margaret Davies argued in 1913:

> Even a little knowledge is a dangerous thing. It causes a smouldering discontent, which may flame into active rebellion against a low level of life, and produces a demand, however stammering, for more interests and chances. Where we see ferment, there has been some of the yeast of education.
>
> (Quoted in Scott 1998: 56)

This 'yeast of education' will need to be applied to work in literacies learning through ensuring that women's lives and concerns are put at the centre, which means focusing on issues such as violence against women, women's economic, physical, and mental health needs; recognising the importance of childcare and transportation; and organising learning in ways that do not further isolate women from each other. Perhaps by tapping into learners' urge to 'tell it like it is', community educators can serve as a community of supportive listeners for new and revised stories, and this, in turn, can lead to political action. But in the final sense for working-class women to be visible and valuable and to learn to speak in a unique and authentic voice, women need to create their own knowledge. Doing this is risky because it requires courage and spirited conviction for students to learn and tutors to teach against the view that some people and some kinds of knowledge are worth more than others. This means, as Wendy Luttrell argues, refusing to accept or promote schooling as a badge of honour, a way to command respect or authority. Credentials are not answers to social inequalities, but acting on the desire to 'be somebody' – to be seen, heard, and taken seriously as a citizen – is a necessary step towards change.

(1997: 126)

Chapter 8

From childcare practitioner to FE tutor

Biography, identity and lifelong learning

Helen Colley

Introduction

There has recently been considerable growth of interest in theoretical perspectives that view lifelong learning as a process of social participation in communities of practice, rather than as one of cognitive acquisition. Lave and Wenger's seminal work on situated learning throws the spotlight upon the relationship between learning, biography and identity:

> [S]ocial communities are in part systems of relations among persons. The person is defined by as well as defines these relations. Learning thus implies becoming a different person with respect to the possibilities enabled by these systems of relations. To ignore this aspect of learning is to overlook the fact that *learning involves the construction of identities* . . . identity, knowing and social membership entail one another.
>
> (Lave and Wenger 1991: 53, emphasis added)

Some work within the project 'Transforming Learning Cultures in Further Education' (TLC), in the ESRC's Teaching and Learning Research Programme, has explored this process of 'learning as becoming' for students on further education (FE) courses in childcare, healthcare and engineering (Colley *et al.* 2003; Colley 2006). It investigated the interplay of students' existing classed and gendered predispositions and the dispositions demanded by occupational cultures, as mediated by vocational education and training (VET). This illuminated learning as an embodied process, and focused on its emotional, as well as cognitive and physical, aspects.

This chapter also draws upon the TLC project, but focuses upon the biography and lifelong learning of one of the seventeen FE tutors who participated in it. It presents an account of her life history and evolving career, as she moved from being a senior childcare professional to becoming an FE tutor. In doing so, it reflects feminist insights (Eckert and McConnell-Ginet 1999) that entrants to a community of practice often bring with them previous lifewide as well as lifelong biographies. They bring, too, existing knowledges, identities, practices and values established elsewhere. This does not undermine the view that learning entails 'becoming a different person'. However, it does suggest that the process is more complex than tends to be assumed, and may involve elements of both enduring identity and 'unbecoming'.

Studying teachers' biographies and identities

There has long existed a body of literature drawing on school teachers' biographies and accounts of their own practice to explore their learning (e.g. Lacey 1977; Goodson 1992; Clandinin and Connelly 1995), with some specifically focusing on the role of gender (e.g. Nias 1989; Sikes 1998). However, there is little research on the life histories of FE tutors.

In contrast with schools, FE is an under-researched sector of education, despite its centrality to the current dominant agenda of lifelong learning. Tutors' trajectories into teaching also tend to be very different from those of school teachers, especially in vocational subject areas, where tutors' occupations prior to teaching may continue to underpin their identities in powerful ways (Robson 1998). While a number of studies have allowed FE teachers' experiences of managerial restructuring their sector to be heard (e.g. Ainley and Bailey 1996; Shain and Gleeson 1999; Viskovic and Robson 2001; Bathmaker and Avis 2005), these have not explored the inter-relationship of individuals' life histories and their professional culture, practice and identities. This chapter makes a contribution to overcoming this gap in knowledge, through one tutor's account of her lifelong learning in terms of her evolving identities. Her narrative is explored from a critical feminist perspective in relation to the learning site in which she teaches, the vocational culture of childcare, and deep-rooted social structures of class and gender.

Case studies such as this, drawing on the particular experiences of learners or teachers, have been criticised as inherently individualised and de-politicising (Avis, in press). These accusations, however, conflate the starting point of an investigation with its explanatory end point. The latter integrates a critical theoretical analysis of society as capitalist and patriarchal (as well as racialised). Individual studies of identity represent a powerful tool for feminist researchers, and for all those concerned also with class, race, disability, and other categories of subordination: 'The fact that gender is co-constructed with other aspects of identity is not just noise . . . such a focus may be the only way to uncover and begin to explain many important general patterns' (Eckert and McConnell-Ginet 1999: 190). Not only do such studies reveal the day-to-day micro-practices which constitute the operation of gendered (and other oppressive) social relations. Through each one of those unique 'close-up' experiences, they also offer a fractal expression of the whole set of social relations constituted by capitalist patriarchal society and its 'relations of ruling' (Smith 1997) which are all too often distorted or invisible at larger scales of analysis (Gorman 2005). A focus on activity and interactions helps to go beyond explanations of difference limited to early gender socialisation, and to illuminate the dynamics of 'people's active engagement in the reproduction of or resistance to gender arrangements in their communities' (Holmes and Meyerhoff 1999: 180).

The study

This chapter draws on data from the first phase of TLC, a four-year longitudinal research project which started in 2001. TLC had three key aims: (1) to deepen understanding of the complexities of learning; (2) to identify, implement and evaluate strategies for the improvement of learning; and (3) to enhance research capacity among FE practitioners. The case study presented here illustrates the general approach of the project, as a partnership between researchers based in four universities and four FE colleges, across seventeen different learning sites. The detailed methodology can be found elsewhere (Hodkinson and James 2003), but in brief, the core data were generated through: repeated semi-structured interviews with the tutor in each site and a sample of six students in each cohort during the length of the project; a questionnaire survey of all students in each site; researcher observations; and reflective journals kept by the tutors. This chapter draws upon the early interviews conducted with the tutor, where we focused on her own life history and her career in FE, and other data from the first two years of fieldwork. The data were transformed using heuristic methods of narrative synthesis (Moustakas 1990), which are particularly helpful for producing critical explanations, rather than just representations, of complex data (Josselson 1995; Richardson 1998). The biographical narrative thus constructed was shared with the tutor, and her permission was obtained to use it. I now briefly introduce the tutor and her learning site, before moving on to her life history.[1]

Joanne Lowe and the childcare learning site

Joanne Lowe's main responsibility is as tutor for the full-time, two-year CACHE[2] Diploma, a Level 3 vocational education course in childcare, primarily for school-leavers. This is a long-established and universally recognised training course in nursery nursing, a registered occupation in the UK. Half of the course is taught in college, and half consists of a series of work placements for the students in schools and nurseries, where they care for babies and small children up to the age of 7 years. The CACHE teaching team are all female, as are the vast majority of students, reflecting the traditional gender stereotyping of childcare work. The students are also predominantly white and working class, although this college is located in a major city with a large minority ethnic population.

Many of these students have not performed well at school or in Intermediate level courses taken at sixth forms or college, and the CACHE Diploma has lower entry requirements than other Level 3 courses. College policies to maximise recruitment meant that some students did not even meet these requirements. Despite the difficulties of such an intake for a Level 3 course, teaching in the learning site has achieved excellent ratings in inspections, and is held in high regard by the CACHE national examination board and by local employers.

Joanne herself is in her mid-thirties. She is a former nursery nurse and nursery manager, and made the transition to become a full-time FE lecturer five years before this research began. She has a dynamic and extrovert personality, and provides charismatic and authoritative leadership within the site. When I shared this reconstruction of her narrative with her, she described it as her 'classic "working-class girl made good" tale about my life'.

Joanne's history

The company of women

Joanne's early life was marked by poverty and hardship, but supported by the efforts of her mother and grandmother at the head of the household:

> My mum and dad split up when I was very young, so I don't really remember them being together. So, ever since I can remember, it's been me, our Kelly, and my mum, and my nana. My nana was your traditional, you know, looked after us when mum was at work, single parent working and all the rest. My mum has always worked, I don't remember a time when she hasn't worked. We were exceptionally poor.
>
> My mum wasn't an educated person, I don't think she even came out of school with anything, but she always had this very strong belief that you should provide for your family. I've always had immense respect for my mum because of how hard she tried to look after us and provide for us. Her attitude to our education was always: 'You must get an education, you must go to school.' She was very positive about that, even though life must have been very, very difficult for her. My mum worked in the retail trade, she started off on the tills. She worked her way up through training, and then she did her personnel degree and went into personnel, and now she works at the university and she teaches courses there, equal opps and ethics. She's always been really dedicated to whatever she does workwise, which is where I think I get it from. She's my inspiration and role model really.

Overcoming academic failure

Despite doing well at school, Joanne 'got in with a bad crowd' and lost interest in studying for a period before her final-year examinations. She regretted this bitterly when she got disappointing results, but her efforts to get back onto an academic track in the school sixth form did not work out:

So I went to careers, and I always wanted to be a teacher, and they said, 'Well, why don't you do nursery nursing?', which they still do, and it's really annoying, you know: 'You're failing at everything else, go be a nursery nurse.' So I applied to college, and that's how I got into nursery nursing.

In her own family and community, this was not seen as a setback but as cause for celebration, and Joanne's re-engagement with learning became a lifelong one:

> I remember going to college, everybody was so proud: 'Wow, Joanne's going to college!', and I was so proud, 'cause I was the first person in our family to ever go to college. At one point I was going to jack it in, and my mum was just mortified, she was like: 'Don't jack it in, this is your chance, and you know you'll really regret it,' and I ended up going back. I don't think I've had a year in my history since then that I haven't, either through work or through myself, done something to do with either training or a qualification, and I think I'll always be like that. I've done my Cert. Ed. [teaching qualification], and now I'm doing my degree part-time at university.

A public service ethos

Joanne enjoyed working with children and felt she was intuitively good at it. Even so, during her first college course, spending time with her 'inseparable' best friends, earning money through part-time work, and 'getting by' with minimal studying were her main priorities. After qualifying, she went to Canada to work as a nanny for a couple of years, but came back because she missed her family. When she returned, getting a job in public nursery provision, and being promoted rapidly, provided another formative experience.

> It was just such a sense of pride that I'd got there, and I had this post and I did it well, and I'd only been there 6 months when I got offered to act up as the manager. I loved my job, I loved the balance of being able to go into a room and work with the kids and the staff, and having that responsibility, 'I'm the deputy manager'. It was very much also the council-run early years centre, which is one of the highest quality provisions they have in the country. I have got so much respect for the organisation, the policies, the work, the principles, what they think about looking after children, the team and all that kind of ethos.

When Joanne moved with her boyfriend to London, she was faced with a stark decision. She very much wanted to continue working in childcare, but nearly all nursery provision there was private and, in her opinion, of lower quality – conditions she was not prepared to accept. Seeing an advertisement by an FE college for a childcare lecturer, she applied and was 'gobsmacked' to be offered the job. She later found out that her experience in public service provision, with its reputation for high quality, had been the deciding factor in her appointment. Her re-entry to the academic world again provoked conflicting feelings:

> I didn't even know what I was going to be doing, so that absolutely terrified me then, and I thought, 'Oh my God, you're a total fraud, they're going to find you out that you're not who they thought you were!' My mum had always said: 'Whatever you want to do, you can do it if you try hard enough.' But I've never ever thought of myself as an academic. So coming from a very working-class background, it was just such an immense sense of pride that I'd got there from quite a difficult upbringing, and my mum was so proud of me.

An emotional commitment to work

When Joanne moved back to her home city, she obtained her current post in FE. Unusually, the majority of the teaching team there are former nursery nurses rather than qualified teachers or health workers, and Joanne emphasised the strong bond between them, both in work and in their social life: 'the four of us are really, really close'. She still felt deeply committed to her work:

> Childcare is a subject I'm really passionate about anyway. I loved working with kids, I think it's a fantastic job. It's poorly paid, which is a downside of being a nursery nurse. But I know what the students are going to be doing inside-out, because I've done it, and I've done it in lots of different capacities, so I can be enthusiastic with them.
>
> I couldn't go into that classroom and do half a job with the students, because I'd feel I'd be letting them down. If it means I have to take up all my free periods seeing them because they want to talk to me or they don't understand something, I'll do it. People in the office say, 'You know, you shouldn't do that, they've got a tutorial, or they should sort it out themselves.' But if they want me to support them, I'll do it, that's what I see my job as, and I've got no qualms about doing extra than I'm supposed to.

This is reflected in the emotional bond she described between herself and her students, in a course where relatively high numbers tend to drop out during their first year:

> The 16–19-year-olds, they're nearly all girls, and we have such a banter in the classroom! My second years, I love every minute teaching with them, and we've got some right characters in there. We get on really well, we do the work. You know, I kept every single one of them that I started with. We've got really good relationships, and it's not difficult to go in and teach them. They're respectful, but we have a laugh as well.

Such, then, was Joanne's account of her life and career to date. Let us move on to consider how that life history connects with the learning site and the broader cultural and social practices of childcare.

A vocational culture of emotional labour

Lave and Wenger (1991) argue that learning begins with legitimate but peripheral participation in a community of practice, in which newcomers and the existing community interact:

> Legitimate peripheral participation refers both to the development of knowledgeably skilled identities in practice and to the reproduction and transformation of communities of practice. It concerns the latter insofar as communities of practice consist of and depend on a membership, including its characteristic biographies/trajectories, relationships and practices.
>
> (ibid.: 55)

While novices may transform the community they enter, there is nevertheless the potential for the community itself to exert a conservative, reproductive effect if it has a strong vocational culture.

In trying to understand how Joanne's biography intersects with the culture of childcare, and with her own role as tutor in facilitating students' participation in that community of practice, there are two key questions we need to consider. Is there a 'different kind of person' that a nursery nurse has to become and if so, what kind of person is that? Related to this formation of new identity, are there 'characteristic biographies' that provide some people with the disposition and predisposition to construct that identity appropriately for full membership of the childcare community?

Notions of quality in childcare seem well defined and widely accepted:

> There is an extraordinary international consensus among child-care researchers and practitioners about what quality child-care is: it is warm, supportive interactions with adults in a safe, healthy, and stimulating environment, where early education and trusting relationships combine to support individual children's physical, social, emotional and intellectual development.
>
> (Scarr 1998: 102)

The emotional dispositions and identity of nursery nurses are held to be of major importance (Blau 1999). One internationally used quality measure, the Caregiver Interaction Scale (CIS), focuses on personal attributes that should be developed in the nursery nurse: sensitivity, gentleness, enthusiasm, effort, and enjoyment of children, with harshness and detachment taken as contra-indications of quality (Tietze *et al.* 1996). This establishes a norm for the kind of person that one has to become to enter the community of childcare practice.

Through the emphasis on 'warmth', 'supportive and trusting relationships' and on the emotional development of the child alongside other aspects, it is clear that the deployment of emotion by the worker herself is central to this view of caring for children. I have given a detailed account elsewhere of how students on the CACHE Diploma encountered and learned to do such emotional labour (Colley 2006). In their work placements, they had to deal with tasks they found embarrassing or unpleasant (taking little boys to the toilet, being soiled with urine or vomit), and with situations they found stressful (tears, tantrums, aggression, disobedience and provocations). In group tutorials discussing their workplace experiences, Joanne taught them how they should cope with this: 'Don't forget, you've got to stay cool and say, [nonchalant tone] "Oh, that's not a very nice thing to do, is it?", and keep your own feelings under control.'

By the end of their first year, the management of feeling had become a central theme in students' accounts of their learning. It gave them a sense of new-found maturity, and demanded leaving behind their former identity as a child and childish desires for play in the nursery. It entailed a complex emotional orientation to their work: they had to engage more intensely with children, but with a purposeful, detached objectivity at the same time. These are examples of learning as 'becoming a different person' in learning to do emotional labour.

In many respects, Joanne's account of herself reveals how thoroughly she has engaged with this caring identity and vocational culture. We have seen from her narrative how she is proud of her practitioner background in childcare itself (FE colleges tend to employ qualified teachers and health workers as lecturers in this subject), and she frequently shares her own experiences of nursery nursing practice with students. She talks of her tendency to develop close personal bonds with others – family, friends, colleagues and students – and how important these are to her. These bonds often seem to have shared experience and identity as their basis. As a 'working-class girl made good', she believes strongly in the importance of early years education to combat disadvantage, and feels the responsibility of supporting her working-class students to 'make good' too. Joanne herself notes how her dedication transcends normal work-role boundaries, and involves a degree of self-sacrifice, and her students recognise this too:

> She's great, is Joanne. She'll help you do anything. She'll sort stuff out for you, she does anything. I'll go and ask her if this is right, she goes, 'Yeah, but you could do this to make it better, and you need to put more of that in, more of this in, describe this more.' It's just how she pushes me along.

> Joanne sorted things out for me, which I think is nice, 'cos then it's not the

awkward situation of me having to go to the teachers and say 'Please can I?', you know. You feel that if you needed to talk to her about anything, she's there, you could talk to her about stuff if you needed to.

She refused to risk compromising the public service ethos which informs her core values, even though this meant quitting the job she had loved so much. Moving into FE has been a way for her to maintain that ethos, not only in her own individual practice as a tutor, but also because it is shared by her colleagues, and supported by their links with the CACHE examining board. However, once again, this returns us to the point about care as self-sacrifice. That ethos may be seen as underpinned by the progressivist ideology that has long dominated primary and early years education. As Walkerdine (1992) has argued, progressivism also plays a role in constructing the identity of the (female) professional as self-denying carer of the child.

Joanne's account of her own history can be seen, then, as one of the 'characteristic biographies' (Lave and Wenger 1991) for entry into childcare. She locates her upbringing in an all-female household with strong matriarchal figures at its head, and in a poorer section of the working class, where she learned from her mother and grandmother the need for self-sacrifice, and witnessed the 'ancient tapestry of female tasks' (Bates 1991) as they cared for her. She also internalised a profound working-class work ethic from them. Combined with her own disposition to enjoy working with children, these deep predispositions of class and gender may have suited her well for the feminised culture of the nursery, and may in turn have been reinforced by her immersion in that culture. As Skeggs (1997) also notes, nursery nursing is seen as an occupation offering respectability to working-class girls, a point echoed by Joanne's and her family's pride in her career.

This is not to suggest that there is anything uniquely personal to Joanne, nor essentially 'natural' to women, about this capacity for caring. Along with other feminist authors (Hochschild 1983; Gilligan 1995; Hughes 2001), I have argued that the division of labour which allocates caring work overwhelmingly to women does not derive from some innate female ability to express emotion more or better than men, but is part of their oppressed and subordinate position in patriarchal capitalist society (Colley 2003). In contrast with the idealised version of quality childcare which sees sensitivity and detachment as unproblematic opposites, Hochschild demonstrates that emotional labour combines emotional sensitivity and engagement with detachment, since it 'requires one to induce or suppress feeling in order to sustain the outward countenance that produces the proper state of mind in others' (1983: 7). Caring in this way, however, demands a high level of devotion and self-sacrifice, which in turn bear costs for the carer. I turn now to look at how Joanne experienced the impact of those costs in her work as an FE tutor, and the subsequent transformations of practice and identity this provoked.

Transforming practice and identity

In spite of Joanne's enthusiasm and dedication to her work, there were critical incidents during the year which arose as she did 'extra than I'm supposed to'. One theme that arose frequently in interviews and in her reflective journal was the difficulty of working at Level 3 with students who had not succeeded academically at school:

> I seem to be getting frustrated very much this term, I don't know if I need a break, I'm very conscious of the fact that my fuse is shorter at the moment. There are a couple of students that are getting to me. Things that frustrate me are where I've got students that constantly talk in class, or that don't, you know, give you eye contact or seem to be paying attention.

She struggled with her desire to bond emotionally with them, and protect them from the harsh realities of studying at this level, alongside the demands of supporting them in their studies and ensure their achievement on the course:

> I have tried so hard to support the 'weak' group, and it doesn't seem to *bother* them that they are so behind with their assessed work. It is just a third of the group, but they are such a drain on my resources. Sheena, in particular, seems to take no responsibility for her own learning. She is happy to blame everyone else. I had a disciplinary meeting with her, which she requested, so I could give her exact deadlines! As I thought about it, I realised I was making a rod for my own back! I support her more, spell everything out to her, so she has to take even less responsibility?! I was feeling so frustrated with them that we weren't having fun any more.

Hochschild (1983) argues that those who put their 'heart and soul' into their job risk stress and burn-out, and this possibility is certainly suggested by the evidence above. Women in caring roles, including teaching, often assume too much responsibility for those in their charge (Gilligan 1995; Hughes 2001). This responsibility, expressed through self-sacrifice, then becomes 'despotic', and undermines the possibility of genuinely close relationships. Such a scenario seemed to be unfolding for Joanne in the first term of the year. Not only were some students failing to get on with their academic work, but this was threatening her relationship with the whole group. It was creating an untenable level of stress, and damaging her relationships with colleagues. However, participation in the TLC project provided her with space for reflection, as she noted in her journal:

> I have been incredibly stressed lately about work and did question whether the project itself was making me question my role too much? It's good to get it down on paper actually. As for the question of whether the research

makes it worse – I don't care. If I can change the challenging parts of my role/personality, then it's all for the good.

She came to realise that her workload was unsustainable on a personal level, and by the end of the year, she had also developed the view that this approach was pedagogically weak:

The students don't develop those skills for themselves, because they know I'll do it. They know they can sit back and, I mean, what has traditionally happened in the past, if they're struggling they'll sit back, they'll ignore it, because they know I'll deal with it in the end.

Through the research project and discussions with her colleagues, Joanne developed a more manageable strategy the following year:

I am still developing this thing of making the students take more responsibility for what they're doing than me, and I think that has really changed this year and I want to carry on with that, not just for me, but for them: it makes them think about what they're doing so much more. It has been a really big thing for me, and it's been great, and I think it has come about from doing the research that I am stepping back from my students, and I hope I can develop in that professional way through next year as well.

In this last interview, two years into the research, Joanne's voice seemed to have become far more that of a teacher. Although she continues to identify herself with pride as an experienced nursery nurse, and has brought to the role of FE tutor many of the attributes central to that former identity, something seemed to have been left behind in the initial years of her transition to teaching. Her narrative of becoming an FE tutor focused solely on those attributes related to sensitivity and engagement with others. It represented bonding with her students, emphasising her shared experiences with them, and offering them unstinting support as professional goods, with detachment as their opposite. This stance was reinforced by the added pressures of college and course policies to take on greater numbers of students, including those with low levels of academic achievement. It mirrored the idealised representation of the vocational culture enshrined in childcare quality measures. It also may have mirrored what Joanne learning in her family during her own early years, about social expectations of female caring.

Joanne's later narratives suggest that she had (re)discovered that detachment is also required in the realised role of FE tutor. She welcomes her return to this realised, rather than idealised, form of emotional labour as a protection for herself. It is both a becoming and an unbecoming. Yet Hochschild (1983) warns that such self-protective moves may still entail their own costs. One danger is that the tutor may feel she is not doing her job 'to the best of her ability' –

something that is clearly very important to Joanne – and may suffer low self-esteem for holding back from fuller engagement with her students. The other is the risk of eventual cynicism and guilt through the deliberate separation of personal and professional identities. This may be particularly pertinent in the current masculinist managerial regimes of FE, where femininities are marginalised or dismissed (Leathwood 2005b).

Conclusion

The recent vogue for collecting teachers' stories entails certain seductive dangers, particularly in a context of managerial restructuring of educational systems, institutions, and professional practice: 'A voice and a story which celebrate only practice create a valuable covering noise, an apparently quite emancipatory noise, while that very practice is narrowed and technicized' (Goodson 1995: 56). All too often, a naïve focus on the personal and practical can result in disembedding teachers' stories from the wider context in which they are constructed and enacted.

The analysis of Joanne's story offered here is one that has been concerned with the interconnections of personal and professional identities with the cultural, social and political conditions in which those identities are formed and continue to evolve. It suggests that this process of career transition and identity (re)formation is not a purely individual one. Although choice and agency are certainly part of Joanne's story, we can see how some of this at least resonates with Bourdieu's (1986) notion of 'the choice of the necessary'. Institutional factors and social structures also play their part. Class and gender in particular can be seen to imbue this tutor's experience lifelong learning. Her evolving personal and professional identities cannot be understood without locating them in the deeply feminised vocational culture of childcare.

The implications for teaching and learning in FE are twofold. First, there is a need to recognise that improving teaching and learning in this site was not primarily a technical question of developing new skills and competencies. The pedagogical changes that Joanne made to her practice – part of her lifelong learning as a teacher – were as a result of changing *herself*. From a feminist perspective, however, such changes may not be sustainable in the long term if teaching continues to be framed by *feminine* values, or located within a sectoral culture that is *masculinist*.

Second, if – as the TLC project suggests – improving teaching and learning is a question of transforming learning cultures, any such efforts need to take into account the weight and durability of the vocational cultures with which VET courses such as the CACHE Diploma are associated. There is a need for space in FE, in which tutors like Joanne, along with their students, can critically understand the way that social structures such as gender and class deeply influence their lifelong learning. They might then be empowered to go beyond feminine ways to conform, and find feminist ways to resist.

Acknowledgements

Transforming Learning Cultures in Further Education is part of the ESRC Teaching Learning Research Programme, Project No. L139251025. I am grateful for this support as well as for the contribution of the entire TLC team to discussions on the development of the analysis presented here.

My heartfelt thanks are due to Joanne Lowe for her partnership in generating the data presented, and her permission to use it. Her dedication to this research project was yet another example of her willingness to go beyond the call of duty, and her collaboration and trust were valued gifts.

Notes

1   All names and locations have been anonymised to preserve confidentiality.
2   Council for Awards in Childcare and Education, the awarding body for the qualification.

Chapter 9

Disability, gender and identity

The experiences of disabled students in higher education

Sheila Riddell

Introduction

This chapter explores the way in which disabled students negotiate their identity in higher education in relation to gender, social class and disability. It is argued that in order to capture the complexity of identity formation, it is important to understand both the inter-relationship of a range of social variables as well as the negotiation of individual identity in specific contexts. Throughout the chapter, I point up the tensions which may arise between these two approaches, the one emphasising the broad brush picture and the other emphasising individual variation and complexity. Case studies are used to explore the way in which women and men from different social class backgrounds and with different types of impairment negotiate identity, placing different meanings on disability in the construction of self. The position of dyslexic students in higher education is explored, since this group makes up a large and growing component of the disabled student population.

The research project

Data presented in this project are drawn from an ESRC-funded study (*Disabled Students and Multiple Policy Innovations in Higher Education* R000239069) conducted jointly by researchers at the Universities of Edinburgh and Glasgow between 2000 and 2003. The research used a range of methods including analysis of HESA data on undergraduate students in UK higher education institutions (HEIs) for 1999/2000; a questionnaire survey of institutional policies and practices in relation to disabled students; and in-depth case studies of forty-eight students in eight higher education institutions in England and Scotland. Case studies involved interviews with students, lecturers and support staff and observation of the type of adjustments made in a range of learning environments. Full details of the research are available in Riddell *et al.* (2005).

Social categories and individual identity

Since the election of a New Labour government in 1997, there has been a growing emphasis on the promotion and monitoring of equality within civil society. The Race Relations (Amendment) Act 2000 placed a duty on public bodies to actively promote equality and to monitor progress. A similar duty has been established under the terms of the Disability Act 2005, and the Equality Bill, being debated in the House of Lords at the time of writing, will establish this duty in relation to gender. The European Employment Directives require member states to ensure equal treatment in employment to individuals in relation to six strands (race, disability, gender, religion/belief, sexual orientation and age). The devolved governments of Scotland and Wales also emphasise the duty to positively promote equality on a range of grounds. This new emphasis on equality in the public sphere requires a much greater degree of monitoring and target-setting, and tends to assume that, in each sphere of equality, an individual's identity can readily be categorised. Complications immediately arise in relation to the categories employed, for example, in the area of ethnicity, a growing number of children are of mixed heritage, and may choose to prioritise one aspect of their identity over another. Disability, too, is a slippery category, since only a small proportion of individuals are born with an impairment, the majority developing an impairment during the course of a lifetime. Individuals with an impairment may choose to identify as disabled for reasons associated with identity or administrative convenience, but may also choose to 'pass' as 'normal', partly as a result of experiencing discrimination and stigma (Watson 2002). Tensions also arise in relation to the policy of mainstreaming, which assumes that equality should permeate all aspects of the everyday work of government, and that all aspects of equality should be reflected equally in all policies. This generic approach to equality does not sit easily with monitoring systems, which tend to address one particular aspect of equality at a time.

There continue to be debates with regard to the relative emphasis which should be placed on individual identity or social structures in understanding the forces which shape individual lives. Within social science, there is currently much interest in the ways in which individuals develop and negotiate their sense of self over the life course. In contrast with earlier accounts which saw identity as a stable expression of an individual's position within wider economic and social structures, theorists of late modernity (e.g. Beck 1992; Lash and Urry 1993) have questioned the notion of an essential self, emphasising instead the self as a social construct, constantly defined and redefined in a range of social contexts. These views have been criticised for placing too much weight on individual agency, although Beck has emphasised that poorer people face 'an abundance of risk', whereas the socially advantaged may use their resources to protect themselves from some of the dangers which form part of the backcloth of working-class lives.

Within gender studies, such debates are also taking place, sometimes located within debates over the politics of redistribution and the politics of identity (Young 1990; Fraser 1997; Phillips 1997). Writers such Butler (1990) maintain that biological sex is no longer particularly salient in terms of men's and women's identity. Rather, gender should be seen as a spectrum of behaviours, attitudes and predilections, with men and women free to choose from a smorgasbord of qualities in assembling a gendered identity to suit their particular taste. Skeggs (1997), on the other hand, maintains that for working-class women, social class as well as gender continue to be powerful foundational categories. The ability to select from a range of possible identity options is a possibility only for a privileged few who have access to a wide range of economic and personal resources.

Such debates are also current in disability studies. Writers like Oliver (1990) and Abberley (1987) recognised that disability was socially relational, since impairment is always experienced in a specific economic, cultural and political environment. The result of this is that the extent to which a given impairment is perceived and experienced as disabling is context-specific. A basic example of this is that the presence or absence of an elevator either facilitates or denies access to a wheelchair user. Despite the fact that the social model of disability is built on a foundation of social relativism, there was a tendency of early writers within the disability movement to assume a binary divide between disabled and non-disabled people (e.g. Barnes 1991). Recently, there has been a growing challenge to the idea of disability as a fixed and unitary category (see Corker and Shakespeare 2002; Riddell and Watson 2003). Contributors to the Corker and Shakespeare collection reflect on the implications of post-modernity for the disability movement. The editors conclude that it is no longer feasible to adhere to the idea that disability represents some sort of essential characteristic. Rather, it should be seen as something which may be used for strategic and political goals, and juggled with other competing identities such as those associated with gender, social class and ethnicity.

Within many spheres of social policy, including higher education, tensions are emerging between different aspects of equality and identity. On the one hand, equality audits require accounting and monitoring using simple categories which, it is assumed, will have salience to the individuals concerned. On the other hand, some social scientists argue that fixed notions of identity are fairly meaningless, and the type of categories employed in equality monitoring are misleading and without foundation. Like Archer and colleagues (2003), the research described here was based on the assumption that it is important to take account of both social categories and individual identity in understanding the way in which individuals understand and negotiate their lives. Neither the study of broad patterns nor individualised understanding is sufficient in itself, but in combination these approaches can provide a rich account of the social context in which individuals live their lives.

The social profile of disabled students in higher education

Despite persistent gender divisions in the curriculum, higher education has become an increasingly female-dominated arena, in which women outnumber men and perform better, particularly in the pre-1992 institutions. Disabled students provide an interesting counter-example, since within this group men outnumber women, particularly in the area of dyslexia (see Figure 9.1). While the proportion of disabled students in higher education increased significantly between 1995 and 2000, this growth was largely accounted for by the rapid increase in the number of students disclosing dyslexia (see Table 9.1). Disabled students are more likely to come from middle-class backgrounds than other students (see Table 9.2), and this is also explained by the preponderance of men categorised as dyslexic, who are particularly likely to be middle class. They are also more likely to be white than non-disabled students (see Figure 9.2). Subject studied also varies by disability; dyslexic students, predominantly male, are particularly likely to be taking creative arts and design courses, which in general tend to be studied by women rather than men (see Table 9.3). Clearly, questions arise as to why more students are identifying themselves as disabled, why dyslexia is the most rapidly growing category, and why this group is pre-dominantly male and middle class. As indicated earlier in this chapter, while quantitative analysis is very helpful in revealing broad patterns, it does not pro-vide insight into the way in which individuals make sense of their experiences. In the following section, case study data are used to explore the various ways in which disabled students negotiate their identity within higher education, specifically in relation to disability, gender and social class.

The case of dyslexia

The use of the term dyslexia is now commonplace in education, and its origins may be traced to the growth of the profession of educational psychology in the mid-twentieth century. However, there continues to be a lack of scientific consensus around the topic. Rice and Brooks (2004) conducted a systematic review of the evidence on the nature, incidence, diagnosis and treatment of dyslexia in adults and concluded that the condition was poorly defined and methods for judging the outcome of 'treatments' were unreliable. Fundamental research on dyslexia, it was concluded, must be regarded as 'tentative, speculative and controversial' and diagnosis procedures must be regarded as unreliable, since 'the standard diagnostic criteria for diagnosing dyslexia cast much too wide a net'.

The review noted major design flaws in many studies, particularly in relation to the use of control groups. In order to test the hypothesis that dyslexic pupils or adults are different from other groups with reading difficulties, two control groups are needed: one made up of people in the 'normal' population and one

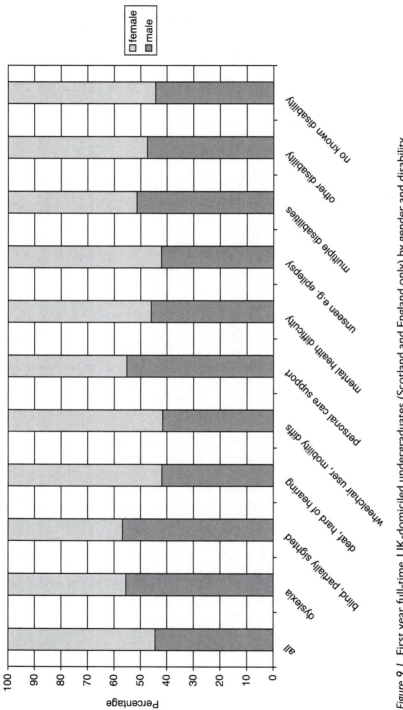

Figure 9.1 First year, full-time, UK-domiciled undergraduates (Scotland and England only) by gender and disability.

Table 9.1 First year, UK-domiciled undergraduates known to have a disability by type of impairment, 1995–2000

	1995–96	1996–97	1997–98	1998–99	1999–2000
Total known to have a disability	15,754	19,337	20,486	22,469	22,290
Dyslexia	17.9%	19.9%	23.1%	25.5%	32.7%
Unseen disability	48.6%	42.8%	45.1%	39%	29.7%
Blind/partially sighted	3.9%	3.8%	3.4%	3.3%	3.5%
Deaf/hard of hearing	7.1%	6.4%	5.9%	5.8%	5.8%
Wheelchair user/ mobility impaired	4.9%	7.1%	4.1%	4.6%	4.4%
Personal care support	0.2%	0.2%	0.3%	0.2%	0.3%
Mental health difficulties	1.8%	2.5%	2.2%	2.8%	3.3%
Multiple disabilities	3.6%	4.9%	5.1%	6.7%	7.3%
Other disability	11.9%	12.4%	10.7%	12.1%	13%
Total first year undergraduates	448,199	491,474	479,329	522,887	525,140
Not known/sought	56,517 (12.6%)	29,746 (6%)	20,970 (4.4%)	17,829 (3.4%)	31,860 (6%)

Source: HESA.

made up of people with reading difficulties who have not been diagnosed with dyslexia. However, the vast majority of studies, including those which posit neurological, physiological and genetic routes of causality, are inconclusive. Voluntary organisations such as the British Dyslexia Association and the Dyslexia Institute promote definitions based on physiological differences, while the British Psychological Society (BPS) adopts the following more inclusive definition: 'Dyslexia is evident when accurate and fluent word reading and/or spelling develops incompletely or with great difficulty' (BPS, 1999). The above definition, however, has been criticised on the grounds that it fails to discriminate between people with generic learning difficulties and those with dyslexia. A fundamental aspect of the many definitions of dyslexia is that it is qualitatively different from 'common or garden' learning difficulties (see, for example, Riddell *et al.*'s 1994 study of the contested terrain of dyslexia in school).

To summarise, there continue to be major and unresolved debates in relation to what dyslexia is, whether it is caused by single or multiple factors, how it is to be diagnosed and how educators should respond. Given the requirement of the DDA that reasonable adjustments be made for accredited disabled students,

Table 9.2 First year, full-time, UK-domiciled undergraduates (Scotland and England) by disability, social class and type of institution

	Pre-1992			Post-1992			Non-university HEIs		
	No known disability	Known disability	All	No known disability	Known disability	All	No known disability	Known disability	All
N	67,713	2,816	70,529	40,691	2,273	42,964	15,850	1,046	16,896
Professional	21	22	21	11	13	11	10	13	11
Managerial, Technical	47	48	47	41	41	41	43	47	43
Skilled-non manual	12	12	12	15	15	15	15	15	15
Skilled-manual	12	12	12	20	17	19	19	15	19
Partly skilled	6	6	6	11	11	11	10	9	10
Unskilled	1	1	1	3	3	3	2	2	2

Note: Columns do not sum up to 100 because of rounding errors.

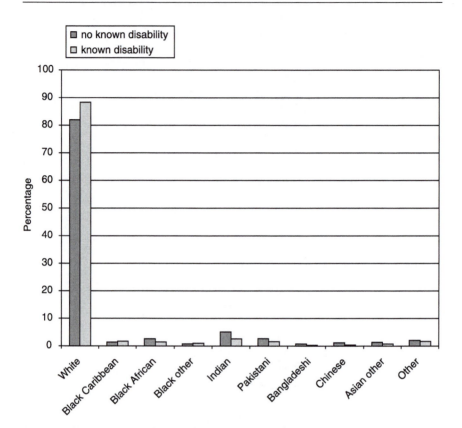

Figure 9.2 First year, full-time, UK-domiciled undergraduates (England only) by disability and ethnic background.

Note: N = 221,376.

there is growing concern about the variability of the criteria and assessments used to identify dyslexia in higher education at a time when there is a major increase in the number of students with a diagnosis of dyslexia.

Given the survival of fundamental academic disputes around the condition of dyslexia, it is unsurprising that students themselves struggle with its meaning, and how it relates to other aspects of their identity. This is illustrated through the case studies presented below.

Liam: dyslexic student at an ancient Scottish university

At the time of the research, Liam was a fourth year student at an ancient Scottish university. Dyslexia was not diagnosed until the start of his third year as a result of an intervention by a lecturer in media studies, who recognised a discrepancy between his performance in seminars and in written assignments. Referral to

Table 9.3 Subject studied by type of impairment (undergraduates only)

	No known disability	Dyslexia	Blind, partially sighted	Deaf, hard of hearing	Mobility difficulty	Mental health	Unseen	Multiple disabilities	Other disability
Medicine/dentistry	2.3	1.1	1.6	1.2	–	–	2	–	1.2
Allied to medicine	13.4	7.6	6.4	10	4.3	4.6	10.2	5.6	7
Biological sciences	5.3	6	4.5	4.2	4.7	5.8	6.9	5.5	5.8
Veterinary sciences	0.3	0.2	–	–	0	0	0.1	0	–
Agriculture and related	0.8	2	–	0.7	0.9	–	1.4	–	0.9
Physical sciences	4	5.5	4.4	4.2	2.6	3.6	5.2	4.8	4.6
Mathematical	1.2	0.7	1.3	1.1	–	–	1.5	–	1.1
Computer science	5.6	6.3	7.6	6.1	7.9	5.1	5.2	7.3	5.8
Engineering and technology	7.3	9.2	6.7	5.6	3.5	5	6.8	7.3	5.9
Architecture, building and planning	2.4	3.1	1.6	1.8	1.7	–	2.2	1.6	2.2
Social, economic, political	7.3	8.5	10	8.4	12.1	7.5	7.5	11.1	9.7
Law	3.2	1.3	3.7	2.4	4.2	2.9	3.6	4	3.7
Business and admin	11.8	8.9	10.4	7.5	6.7	3.8	9.7	9.5	9.3
Librarianship and info sciences	1.4	1.4	1.2	1.2	1.7	–	1.9	2.3	1.7
Languages	5.8	2.2	5.7	5.6	6.1	9.1	5.9	3.7	5.6
Humanities	3.4	4.4	4	5.6	6.1	8.3	3.9	6	5.9
Creative arts and design	6.6	17.6	6.5	8.7	7.2	11.8	8.8	10.6	8.9
Education	4.6	3.5	3.5	4.2	2.7	–	4.8	2.5	3.4
Combined/invalid code	13.2	10.3	20.3	21.3	26.1	25.8	12.5	16.4	17.2

the disabled students' adviser led to a psychological assessment. According to Liam, he was assured by the adviser before the assessment was conducted that it was almost certain to be positive:

> I think you have to pay £200, but the disability officer said, 'You can get that back if you are dyslexic and we haven't had anyone yet who has been tested who hasn't been and I'm pretty confident you will get it back', so I never ever had to pay the £200.

Liam was delighted to receive the diagnosis, but was advised by the disability officer to be 'as diplomatic in the scenario as possible'. He expected his English tutors to respond by giving him support with his assignments, and was shocked by the lecturers' reaction:

> You know, I went to one guy, in fact, the first guy I saw, and said, 'Look, I've been diagnosed as having dyslexia' and I was about to say, 'Who can I go to discuss essays with?' and he said, 'Oh, you know, in my experience dyslexics don't spell any worse than the other students.' Afterwards, when I left, and this says everything about the guy, he just said, 'Don't hassle me.' I thought, this guy, he's supposed to be teaching English Literature and doesn't even have a basic grasp of what dyslexia is.

Another lecturer was reported as saying: 'Well, I taught students at Oxford who are much more dyslexic than you, you're only moderate.'

Liam's experience with a media studies tutor was very different. The tutor was aware of Liam's uneven performance, and as someone whose first language was not English, had considerable sympathy. He was also aware that Liam was producing up to fifty drafts of an assignment. He therefore suggested that Liam should limit himself to three drafts before submission, on the understanding that he would be able to re-submit if it was not up to the required standard. In addition, the tutor made special allowances when marking:

> You know, if there was an essay from a dyslexic student I tend to try and ignore the kind of structural difficulties and try and see what they are saying and so I tend to mark them on the ideas rather than the actual presentation. But that's totally improvised, that's not because of anything.

In addition to his awareness that the allowances he made were 'improvised' rather than based on sound principles, the tutor also felt uneasy because the support given to dyslexic students was based on the demands they made rather than some more objective judgement of their relative need:

> I felt that in a sense Liam was disadvantaged by his dyslexia but also he was getting all this kind of special attention which I was happy to give. I don't

think it was proportional to the attention I had given to other students with dyslexia. So I feel quite uneasy about that as well.

Overall, the tutor felt that Liam had been treated unfairly by the exam system and should have sought an alternative form of assessment, since the only compensation made, additional time, was unlikely to be helpful in overcoming the barriers faced:

> The overall degree he got (an upper second) was not a reflection of his abilities at all as I came to know him. In his exams he was getting a 2.2 and all of his coursework was first class. So even the fact that he had extra time, I don't think that was adequate compensation. So I felt really strongly after that – that here we are assessing a student within a system of assessment that is obviously not giving him a fair deal because he can't really demonstrate what he knows and what he is capable of.

The tutor asked for his concerns to be minuted at the examiners' meeting, but compensatory action was not possible at that point. Liam felt that the award of a 2.1 degree represented a major injustice:

> I applied for funding from the Students Awards Agency for Scotland for a PhD and they said, 'Sorry, you don't get funding because you didn't get a first.' And I'm thinking, 'If I was black, this would be racism, blatant racism, but I've possibly missed out on £20,000 worth of funding which everyone says I'm capable of because the system was weighted against me and I was misinformed at the time.'

Maurice: dyslexic student at an ancient Scottish university

Maurice was a second year medical student who had previously completed a degree in Physiology and Sports Science. His parents were both teachers, but his dyslexia was not formally diagnosed until the second year of his first degree. At school, he was regarded as 'a bit slow':

> I went through school – everything was never fine – I was always slow. Always from the start of primary school, my mother and father would have been brought in because my reading wasn't very good, my reading was always very slow. Both my parents were teachers, so I think what really happened was that they sort of worked with me a bit. Nothing was ever diagnosed except that 'Maurice's a bit slow', do you know what I mean, and I must have just muddled through school, to be honest. English was never a strong point and I don't know if that was why I went down the science route, because it wasn't structured essays, factual

learning. It was understanding, and I was always better with diagrams and thing like that.

Maurice was prompted to go to the disabled students adviser for a diagnosis because of the problems which emerged in his second year with assignment writing. A lecturer noted the discrepancy between his oral and written performance:

> He stood out from the very beginning in class. He usually led the questioning and in all oral interchange he was outstanding . . . but it wasn't coming through in his written work, that similar ability to construct concepts, to critically handle them.

Just as he had been labelled 'slow' at school, university staff began to see him as a lazy, disorganised student. When he asked why he had been given a poor grade for an assignment, he would be told: 'Well, Maurice, it just doesn't look – it looks like you've done it the night before . . . It doesn't flow, there is no structure to the essay.'

Following a visit to an educational psychologist, Maurice was told that he was dyslexic, and described a feeling of relief at being able to exchange a negative identity for a more positive one:

> Initially my diagnosis was 'You are dyslexic' and at that time that was a relief to me. I didn't take it to heart, I didn't think I was retarded or something like that. I think some people do take it to heart. I thought, 'Well, that's quite a relief' and I was quite happy with the position that the university was going to give me some extra time in exams and I thought, 'Oh, that's good, it will take a bit of the pressure off me a bit more in writing essays.'

In reality, the extra time in exams was experienced as a mixed blessing, but the sense of release from blame meant that Maurice was able to finish his first degree and embark on a second.

However, the negotiation of identity with significant others was ongoing. When he enquired about entering medicine, he received a slightly frosty response from the medical faculty:

> I came to enquire about it and they were a bit standoffish about the whole dyslexic thing . . . Their point of view is that they see it as an excuse and they say, 'Why do you want extra time in an exam? You wouldn't get extra time during a surgery or extra time in resuss.'

Fellow students were also likely to look down on anyone who might be regarded as less able: 'I know it is better being dyslexic, I can feel my medical friends saying "And how did you fail that test, Maurice?" There are a few people think that.'

While having the diagnosis of dyslexia was important to Maurice in bolstering his self-esteem, he was reluctant to discuss this with other students:

> There's about three other people in my year who are dyslexic in medicine and I've bumped into them as we've arrived at the exam hall 25 minutes early, you can work it out, but that's the only way. Sometimes it comes up in the conversation, 'Where were you?' 'Seeing the special needs adviser.' 'Oh, what's that about?' It never gets brought up in conversation with any academic members of staff.

Maurice continued to struggle with the idea that he shared a common identity with someone with more significant impairments:

> I don't like thinking of myself as disabled, I don't even like, when you started talking, I don't even like that you almost put me in the category with someone in a wheelchair. I almost find that offensive. No. I mean, God, I'm glad I'm not and it's almost a relief that I don't have to deal with a physical or other disability. I really don't like holding it up or shouting about it at all. I like that it's been identified and I'm not stupid, I rather look on it like that.

Despite his ambivalence about the category of dyslexia, Maurice maintained a sense of himself as a person who was discriminated against by the university assessment system, which prioritised mastery of the written word and 'tested my weakness'. Rather than extra time in exams, Maurice considered that an alternative form of assessment based on oral work should be permitted. At the very least, he felt that 'People who are marking my exam scripts or marking my course work should know that I am dyslexic, so that allowances could be made.'

Sheena: dyslexic student at a post-1992 English university

Sheena was a 32-year-old mature student studying for an MPhil in Psychology following a first degree in Psychology at an English post-1992 university. She had initially embarked on a PhD, but had been told at the end of her first year that this was not realistic due to her difficulties in writing. This had been a severe blow and she felt that she had suffered an injustice. Sheena's early education involved many changes of school, since her father was in the armed forces. Like Maurice, she grew up with a sense of herself as slow and un-coordinated, although dyslexia was not diagnosed formally until much later:

> No, I didn't know that I had it. I've always had a sense of feeling different. I

was the last kid, for example, in my class to move out of pumps because I couldn't tie my bloody laces. I was sixteen before I could use a normal clock. I always knew there were things I couldn't do that other people could, but I always thought I must be horrendously stupid and that. I was also one of three and I was the only daughter to fail my 11 plus and that kind of reinforced the whole idea that I must just be incredibly stupid . . . I did think, 'Well, why am I good at this and why am I crap at that and why am I so clumsy all the time?'

Sheena managed to get through her first degree without major difficulties as a result of 'over-learning', but 'there were a few times that they had to re-read my exam scripts as my writing is absolutely appalling and for my tutors to allow me to do that was very nice'. At the start of her working life, literacy problems with spelling and organisation became more apparent and she eventually went to a chartered psychologist for assessment. The diagnosis of dyslexia had a profound impact on her sense of self:

> You know you have these problems and you suspect that you have these problems but you spend your whole life covering up and compensating for them and you get to a point when you wonder if it's just your paranoia and then somebody goes, 'Yes, you were right, you do have a learning disability or learning difficulty or whatever' and it's like all of those things that you quite suspected but weren't quite sure. All of those things that you thought made you slightly more cracked up than everybody else is true and that was the hard part. I think that was the hard part for me getting the diagnosis and feeling different as well, and all of a sudden I had a legitimate reason.

However, during the first year of her MPhil, disclosure became a major issue. It transpired that her supervisor had discussed the possibility of dyslexia with other people, including the disabled students' adviser, without including Sheena in the conversation. As a result, Sheena experienced a sense of betrayal and loss of control over the management of her own identity:

> If you disclose something to one tutor, . . . it then becomes public know-ledge and at some point I think it did. That worried me hugely because it does undermine your confidence in the institution where you study. But, yeah, I think there was an element of control there, I don't mind admitting that control is important because control allows you to predict what's going to happen next and give you structure and it gives you some certainty at least.

For Sheena, the diagnosis of dyslexia did not imply an acceptance of disability as an essential part of identity:

I don't see myself as disabled. I ask myself the question, 'Has it stopped me from doing anything?' and the answer is 'No'. My only worry is that if I had known earlier it would have become self-limiting so I'm very pleased that I didn't find out that I had it before I went off and did things that I found challenging.

Learning difficulties, on the other hand, was a term which Sheena found less antagonistic:

I don't identify with the notion of disability, I do identify with the notion of difficulty. Because difficulties can be overcome. Disability, I think it feels much more like a life sentence, do you know what I mean, it seems much worse to have a disability than to have a difficulty that you have some kind of notion, some capacity for overcoming. I don't think of myself as disabled.

One reason for Sheena's rejection of the idea of herself as a disabled person was that it conflicted with her self-image as a determined and competent individual:

It [being identified as someone with a learning difficulty] just makes me proud or stubborn but I don't want people to kind of think, 'Poor you', because you get on with it, don't you? You don't make a drama out of a crisis, you just get on with it.

Sheena believed that some people in the university continued to have doubts about the validity of a diagnosis of dyslexia. Ultimately, her own ambivalence about dyslexia and disability was reflected in uncertainty about whether to disclose a disability in a job application. Initially, she decided not to identify herself as a disabled person, but subsequently she realised she needed the protection which would flow from this:

I wouldn't, I would not tick the disabled box – I think maybe I did actually rein in my pride and tick the disability box and I rang them and said, 'I'm dyslexic and if I'm coming to your centre then I need access to a word processor.' So, yeah, I think in that instance I made it work for me and then I thought, well, damn it, why should I handicap myself? In other instances I haven't because I'm very suspicious, despite the fact that the Disability Discrimination Act exists. I'm very very suspicious of people making a judgement about who you are depending on whether you tick a box or you don't. Because I think people don't understand that you can have dyslexia and be completely, perfectly affable, perfectly bright person who just has a few problems in these areas over here.

Conclusion

In this chapter, we noted that disabled students have different social character-istics compared with non-disabled students on a variety of dimensions. Because of the predominance of dyslexic students, disabled students as a group are more likely to be male, middle class and studying creative arts and design. This raises question about the use of dyslexia by different groups of students. Furedi (2004) has suggested that disability is increasingly used in order to obtain additional support for those whose difficulties might previously have been attributed to lack of academic ability. Clearly, university is seen as almost inevitable for middle-class students (Reay 2002), and it is therefore plausible that those who have difficulty in meeting the required standard might look for ways of obtaining additional support.

Case study data suggest a rather more complex picture. It is evident that disabled students are engaged in an intense period of identity-negotiation as they enter higher education, and gender, disability and social class are all key elements to be fitted into a plausible whole. All the dyslexic students who featured in our case studies made clear that the difficulties they experienced were very real, but they still rejected the idea of themselves as a disabled person. Maurice and Liam conformed to the profile of the 'typical' dyslexic student, being male, middle class and highly ambitious, and both made significant demands on the institution to compensate for their difficulties. Shona, on the other hand, from a less socially advantaged background, appeared to manage negotiations for additional resources less effectively and was unable, like Maurice and Liam, to argue for special arrangements.

In many ways, the strategies surrounding the use of disability, and, more specifically, dyslexia, exemplify the arguments of the early social model theorists. Clearly, disability is socially relational and is experienced and enacted differently by individuals in varied social contexts. This is particularly evident in middle-class students' strategic use of dyslexia as a non-normative and relatively non-stigmatised condition. With regard to the policy implications of this work, it is clear that there is a need not simply to monitor equality categories such as disability, social class and gender, but to combine this with an understanding of their dynamic and socially constructed nature, allowing them to be used by different individuals and institutions for varying ends.

Acknowledgements

I would like to thank my colleagues who worked with me on this study. Alastair Wilson is now a senior research fellow in the Faculty of Education, Strathclyde University, and Teresa Tinklin is now a freelance researcher, living and working in Sheffield.

Chapter 10

The in/visible journey

Black women's lifelong lessons in higher education

Heidi Safia Mirza

> Young black women set off into the white world carrying expectations of mythic proportions . . . their odysseys, they believe will transform their lives . . . but separated from their cultural communities these young women's passages turn out to be isolated individual journeys . . . 'into the heart of whiteness'.
>
> (Casey 1993: 132)

Introduction

Higher education in Britain remains a 'hideously white'[1] place, rarely open to critical gaze (Back 2004). It is not a place you expect to find many 'black bodies'.[2] Being a body 'out of place' (Puwar 2001) in white institutions has emotional and psychological costs to the bearer of that difference. Simmonds, a black woman academic writes, 'The world I inhabit as an academic is a white world . . . in this white world I am a fresh water fish that swims in sea water. I feel the weight of the water on my body' (1997: 227).

In this chapter I wish to explore the personal costs of the position of marginality for black women in higher education. Lifelong learning is about the profound experiences you have when moving between 'worlds' of difference. We need to ask questions about what shapes these worlds and how are we implicated through our inclusion, exclusion, choice and participation in reproducing it, for as Casey describes in her poignant passage above, black women's innocent expectations and eager quest for knowledge can take them on an unexpected journey 'to another place' where they are transformed, but are also transforming.

There is a paradox concerning black women in higher education. On the one hand, they are almost invisible in the higher and senior levels of the academe – a state that has persisted in the twenty-five years I have been teaching and researching in higher education. Recent figures suggest there are only ten black women professors in the UK (THES 2004). Black and minority ethnic staff, 92 per cent of whom are on low grade less senior posts, make up 2.5 per cent of those working in higher education, and of these only

1.6 per cent are female (Carter *et al.* 1999). On the other hand, black women are present in new universities as students in significant numbers, a phenomenon that I have seen grow over the same time (Modood and Acland 1998; Connor *et al.* 2004).

Though ethnic minorities make up 6 per cent of the working population in the UK, they make up 15 per cent of all students. Young black people of African and Asian origin are nearly three times more likely to be in university than their white counter-parts. If we look at the percentages of young people under 21 on full-time undergraduate courses, black and minority ethnic women are the highest participants of all. As a proportion of the average 18–19-year-old population, we find 59 per cent of young black women going to university to do a degree, as are 48 per cent of young black men.[3] I am intrigued by this invisibility/visibility split between staff and students, and the significance it has in terms of understanding the experience of black women in higher education.

The duality of invisibility/visibility characterises black women's appearance and disappearance more generally in our telling of our social (his)story.[4] But I am not concerned with a simple disappearance and appearance of the physical – 'now you see black women, now you don't' – I am more concerned with the shifting constructions of their messy complicated 'otherness' in our changing troubled higher educational institutions.

Outsiders within

I first began to think about the invisibility/visibility couplet when I was asked to give a keynote address at the centenary celebration of women's first admission to Trinity College Dublin in 1904.[5] Trinity College was a grand place, and as I walked through the cobbled court yards, dined in the Commons and gazed at the grand vaulted Old Library I saw that young women now moved with seeming ease and authority in these ancient and 'hallowed' spaces. I wondered what it was like 100 years ago to be Alice Oldham, the first female in an all-male college. Women were seen as being a 'danger to the men', and as the College Board cautioned, they had to be watched: 'If a female had once passed the gate it would be practically impossible to watch what buildings or chambers she might enter, or how long she might remain there' (Parkes 2004: 2).

But what must it have been like for the first woman of colour in an elite white male university in Britain? Preparing for my paper at Dublin I did some research and to my surprise I found a hidden genealogy of black women's presence in higher education in England that began before the admission of white women in Ireland.

Cornelia Sorabji, who was Indian, went to Somerville Hall Oxford in 1889. She was the first woman ever to study Law in a British university (Visram 2002).[6] Continuing my search I stumbled upon a small crumpled photograph tucked away in the corner of a dark display cabinet on the suffragettes at the back of the 'World City Gallery' at the Museum of London. The photograph was of the Indian Suffragettes at the 1911 Women's Coronation Procession.[7] The procession was a huge rally organised by the suffragettes to highlight their struggle during the coronation celebrations of George V. There were 60,000 women, 1,000 banners and the column of marchers snaked for seven miles. Under a banner with their emblem of an elephant were assembled several Indian women suffragettes (ibid.). I learnt that one of the most active Indian suffragettes was Sophia Duleep Singh, whose sisters Bamba and Catherine (daughters of Maharaja of the Punjab) also went to Somerville College in 1890.

I never knew Indian suffragettes existed. Indian women remain largely outside the historiography of British suffragettes (ibid.). Excavating such erasure of black women's genealogy in British academia exposes a 'counter-memory' which tells a different 'truth'. Similarly, our collective amnesia about black women's presence in higher education exemplifies the continuous battle for the reappropriation of cultural difference in the constantly shifting and changing hegemonic war against racism. Spivak (1988) calls such conscious negation of black women from discourse a form of 'epistemic violence'. I had always thought the struggle for a space in higher education was a 'white woman's history' – as indeed I thought that the suffragette movement was a white woman's movement. But I have been learning[8] that history is about what is chosen to be revealed by whom and when. Mohanty writes against a hastily derived notion of 'universal sisterhood' that assumes a commonality of gender experience across race and national lines: 'I have tried to demonstrate that this [feminist] scholarship inadvertently produces Western women as the only legitimate subjects of struggle, while Third world women are heard as fragmented, inarticulate voices in (and from) the dark' (1993: 42).

Embodying difference

I was, however, excited by the excavation of Indian women as activists, scholars and writers. Women like me, in demonstrations back then, in a time when we were not even supposed to have an existence (Spivak 1988)! However, for me, the question in this instance of revelation is, as Mohanty suggests, not just acknowledging their 'difference', but rather the more difficult question of the *kind of difference that is acknowledged* and engaged (Mohanty 1993). But the kind of difference I found should not have surprised me. The Indian women at the procession were described by a governor of an Indian province in terms of their 'oriental' appearance as: 'Particularly striking and picturesque . . . in beautiful dress . . . the most significant feature of the whole procession, as they demonstrated the "women's" question was without race, or creed, or boundary' (Visram 2002: 164).

In contrast to the staunch, serious, defeminised white middle-class suffragettes, these 'strange and exotic creatures' were described as non-threatening in their ability to bring about change through their harmonious multicultural 'otherness'. A spectacle to be gazed upon, it was as if these Indian women were 'known better than they know themselves' (Mirza 1997a: 20). Simmonds discusses how racial knowledge is constructed about the other and the experience of being a 'curiosity': 'Adorned and unadorned I cannot escape the fantasies of the western imagination . . . this desire for colonized bodies as spectacle . . . is essentially an extension of the "desiring machine" of capital' (1997: 232).

Similarly, Cornelia Sorabji who was by no means a feminist or a radical (she was pro British rule and against Gandhi's independence movement for India) talks of her special treatment at Somerville. She was introduced into influential literary and political circles and always wore a sari. She was given special privileges (a fire to dress in the morning) and was chaperoned to lectures. Though she was never later allowed to practise as a solicitor in Britain, she demanded and got special dispensation to sit her law exams as a woman in college. She writes that the men students were so kind, giving up a book if the librarian said she wanted it. This special treatment exasperated her and she said of her tutor, 'I wish he would treat me like a man and not make gallant speeches about my intellect and quickness of perception' (Visram 2002: 95). For black women it is impossible to escape the body and its reconstructions as we daily negotiate our embodied social situations. Cornelia returned to India and championed the property rights of the Purdahnashin (veiled women confined to the private domain by religious practice), but lived her final years in England in an asylum where she died in 1954 (Vadgama 2004). Such sad revelation makes me wonder about the 'weight' of living a non-white existence in a consuming white world.

Being a curiosity, a special case, 'one in a million', can be an emotional and professional burden to black women in the academy. To be an exotic token, an institutional symbol, a mentor and confidant, and a 'natural' expert of all things to do with 'race', is something that many black women academics recount in their careers in the academe (Williams 1991; Spivak 1993; hooks 1994; Mirza 1995; Simmonds 1997; Razack 1998; Essed 2000). But we need to be careful in how we situate these 'tales of women with dark skin', for as Bhattacharyya (1998) eloquently argues, such heroic 'new' stories in themselves do not counter invisibility and the negative stereotypes deeply embedded in our thinking.

By telling the stories of Sophia and Cornelia I am not advocating the 'black women were there too', as some sort of a triumph, that numbers and presence are all. This would be to invoke a benign multiculturalism that suggests that diversity in and of itself – that is, mere presence of black women – signals the attainment of equality. I tell the stories of these lost and invisible pioneers because as Mohanty explains:

> The challenge of race resides in a fundamental reconceptualization of our categories of analysis so that differences can be historically specified and understood as part of larger political processes and systems . . . difference seen as benign variation (diversity), for instance rather than as conflict,

struggle or threat of disruption, by-passes power as well as history to suggest a harmonious, empty pluralism.

(1993: 42)

For black women, existence is not just about physical space, it is also about the power to occupy a historical space.

Is diversity desirable?

The visibility/invisibility distinction that characterises black women's presence in higher education must be contextualised within the pervasive, all-consuming discourse of 'diversity in higher education' (Law *et al.* 2004). The question here is 'What has diversity done to open up (or close down) possibilities for black women as students and teachers in higher education?' In the context of policies on widening participation in higher education, and the media exposure of the continued lack of equity in access, particularly for working-class black and white young people, 'diversity' has become an all-consuming discourse that no right-minded university, old or new,[9] would dare be without as a intrinsic part of its identity and image. However, as the Higher Education Funding Council for England (HEFCE) declares in its policy statement, *diversity* is less about equity and more about diversity of HE provision so as to secure the 'best fit' to meet the diverse needs of students, the economy, and society: 'Diversity is widely agreed to be a desirable feature in higher education . . . the goal must be to secure the pattern of diversity that most cost-effectively meets the needs and aspirations of the greatest number of stakeholders' (HEFCE 2000: 3–4).

Diversity as a discourse of social inclusion is based on the philosophy of 'getting the right people for the job on merit' and the 'business benefits of a more diverse workforce to reach a wider market' (Cabinet Office 2001: 18). Government strategy overtly claims diversity is about good public relations, and 'inclusivity' as good for business. The ministerial Foreword to the official guidance for the higher education sector embraces the business principle, stating:

> It is vital for the continuing health of the higher education sector that it should recruit from a wide and diverse human resource pool. This is not only on the grounds of equity, but equally sound for business reasons.
>
> (ECU and JNCHES 2003: 2)

The driver for change comes from a pragmatic recognition of demographic changes with a projected ageing population and reduced fertility in Britain. This has led to a concern about underutilised labour and the need for black and 'ethnic minority' groups to be included in an expanding service sector in a global economy (Metcalf and Forth 2000). The employment of these groups, it is argued, will bring added benefits since they will increase access to certain customer groups. Public changes on ethical and social responsibility have persuaded companies that a 'rights'-based approach may also be good for business (Fredman 2002).

Unmasking diversity and difference

The discourse on 'diversity and difference' which emerged in the 1980s evolved in response to the recognition that equality is not simply about sameness, but about inclusive difference. Calls for the recognition of the difference age, gender, sexuality, disability, ethnicity, culture and religion make signalled an important and liberating time for many silenced minorities. The black feminist critique was a destabilising force for the modernist epistemological standpoint of white feminism which had failed to embrace the diversity of women's experiences across class and race lines (Collins 1991; Mirza 1997b). The assumption, as Chandra Talpade Mohanty explains, is that 'feminist studies discursively present Third world women as a homogenous, undifferentiated group leading truncated lives, victimized by the combined weight of "their" traditions, cultures and beliefs, and "our" (Eurocentric) history' (1993: 42).

However, while postmodern notions of 'difference and diversity' were important for hearing marginalised voices, they also led to fragmentation which not only dissolved the notion of a universal subject, but in so doing undermined the basis for collective political projects along the old modernist lines such as in the civil rights and feminist movements of the 1960s.

Kenan Malik has delivered a sharp critique of the shift from equality to diversity. Diversity, he suggests, evolved from the identity politics of the 1980s where the politics of recognition gave voice to hitherto silenced minorities such as those who were black, gay or female: 'where once I wanted to be treated the same as everybody else despite my skin colour, now activists want to be treated differently because of it' (Malik 2003). Malik has a point. This new-found focus on 'difference' is not innocent – it obscures the nature of racism, as Stuart Hall explains: 'The Black subject and Black experience are constructed historically, culturally; politically . . . the grounding of ethnicity in difference is deployed, in the discourse on racism, as a means of disavowing the realities of racism and repression' (1992: 257).

Why does diversity get 'stuck'?

In higher education many diversity action plans and equality statements have been produced by universities to meet the requirements of positively promoting racial equality required by the Race Relations (Amendment) Act (2000). Armies of consultants and professionals have been recruited to produce complex bureaucratic target-led, glossy action plans and strategies which are underpinned by the notion of 'respecting diversity in order to achieve equality' (Bhavnani et al. 2005). However, despite these action plans, endemic racialised class and gender divisions show little sign of abating (Connor et al. 2004;

Blanden *et al.* 2005; Reay *et al.* 2005). The question then becomes, why is there such little real diversity on the ground when we talk so much but achieving the goal of diversity as a moral and social good at the top? How can so much 'diversity talk' engender so much 'diversity paralysis'?

Sara Ahmed (2005) argues diversity does not simply bring about institutional change. The question we must ask is 'what work does "diversity" do in education?' Ahmed suggests institutional 'speech acts', such as a university making a commitment to diversity, or admission that they are non-racist and 'for equality', are 'non-perfomatives' – that is such speech acts 'work precisely by *not* bringing about the effects they name'. Thus, she explains, having a good race equality policy gets translated into *being good at race equality* – 'as if saying is doing'.

> Declaring a commitment to opposing racism might function as a form of organization pride . . . the university now says: if we are committed to antiracism (and we have said we are), then how can we be racists? . . . the work of such speech acts seems precisely how they function to block rather than enable action.
>
> (ibid.: 8)

Thus, as Ahmed argues, newer universities which are seen as 'diversity led' (as they have many students from ethnic minorities and lower socio-economic backgrounds) present themselves as 'being diverse' without having to do anything. Simply 'being diverse' means such new universities need not commit to 'doing diversity'. On the other hand, the 'ideal' research-led 'sandstone' universities are elite precisely because they have an image that is not diversity led. They use the language of globalisation and internationalism where diversity for them means appealing to a wide variety of diverse people across cultures. Ahmed explains, diversity here is not associated with challenging disadvantage, but becomes another way of 'doing advantage'.

To explain why diversity remains 'undone' in higher education, Ahmed explains while the term diversity may 'circulate', its documents and statements get 'stuck', 'cut off from histories of struggle which expose inequalities' (ibid.: 19).

Counting the costs of 'just being' in higher education

But what happens to those who come to represent 'diversity' in higher education – the black and minority ethnic groups targeted to increase the institutions' thirst for global markets? Higher education research shows black and female staff are likely to be concentrated in lower status universities, be on lower pay and more likely to be on short-term contracts (Carter *et al.* 1999; NAO 2002). Similarly, students are to be found in lower status new universities and concentrated in particular subject areas. Particularly those of African origin are more likely to be performing on the 'lower tail end' of attainment (Modood and Acland 1998; Connor *et al.* 2004). However, despite these endemic inequalities, black women persist in their desire for education as social transformation (Mirza 2005). Levels of participation in further and higher education are as high for women of black African, Caribbean and Indian origin as among white women, both 23 per cent (WEU 2002).[10] The questions here are: 'Why does this persistence prevail in such hostile places?' and 'What is the cost of just being there?'

Black women and the politics of containment

Black women are increasingly visible in public spaces as professionals in previously race/gendered homogenous places such as universities, the judiciary and the media. The black feminist writer Patricia Hill Collins suggests this shift in the positioning of race and gender and class through changing power relations and privatisation has led to reconfigured patterns of institutionalised racism. In what Collins calls the 'new politics of containment', surveillance strategies become increasingly important when middle-class black women enter institutional spaces of whiteness in the increasingly devalued public sphere from which they were hitherto barred. She explains:

> Whereas racial segregation was designed to keep blacks as a group or class outside centers of power, surveillance now aims to control black individuals inside centers of power when they enter the white spaces of the public and private spheres.
>
> (Collins 1998: 20)

Collins argues black women are watched in desegregated work environments to ensure they remain 'unraced' and assimilated (ibid.: 39). Being seen to be assimilated is important as standing out can invoke deep feelings of need, rejection and anxiety within the 'white other' (Ahmed 2004). To be unassimilated or 'stand out' invites a certain type of surveillance that appears benign but can be deeply distressing for black women.

For example, surveillance means being accountable and having more attention than others heaped up upon you. A black female professor related when she was first appointed with fanfare and excitement. She was a 'special case'; one in 'a million'; a black female trophy. She was in the university news (front page and the web) and she was invited to many high profile functions and events. Though it was not her job, in the first week she had to publicly present a detailed plan for delivering equal opportunities and race equality for the next five years to the senior managers and executives of the university. In three months she had been required to write five reports on her targets, attainments, and strategies and also found herself accountable to three different line managers (as it could not be decided to whom she should report, the executive, academic area, or the faculty). Their 'kind and supportive' attention was all-consuming but she received no real support for her academic research and teaching. Finally she became ill. No other professor had received this exhausting and intense level of scrutiny or expectation in such a short space of time.

There is an irony to heightened visibility for the 'invisible' in our polite and gentle corridors of higher education. A national survey of ethnic minorities in higher education found black women were more likely than any other group to report being the victim of sexual harassment and discrimination at work (Carter et al. 1999). This raises many questions about the safety of black women in public spaces. The case of Anita Hill, the African-American woman whose high profile case against the African-American Supreme Court Justice Clarence Thomas demonstrates how sexual harassment can be racialised within an institutional context. Anita Hill lost her case and it is argued this happened because of the way the 'black woman' is constructed and given meaning in the public discourse on 'race' (Morrison 1993; Collins 1998). Anita Hill did not fit any of the stereotypes of 'the black woman' (i.e. she was not an 'overachiever', 'welfare mother', etc.), thus she could not be easily understood and received no sympathy in the public mind. She was not seen as a credible defendant and was labelled as a 'traitor-to-the-race', because of her public denouncement of a senior black male colleague. As Collins points out, the 'black woman' is predetermined by an already written script: 'surveillance seems designed to produce particular effects – black women remain visible yet silenced; their bodies become written by other texts, yet they remain powerless to speak for themselves' (1998: 38).

Black women's journeys into higher education, as Kathleen Casey writes in the epigraph to this chapter, are journeys into the 'heart of whiteness' where a homogenous identity, 'the black woman', is created by 'a white gaze which perceives her as a mute visible object' (Casey 1993: 111). Being a 'mute visible object' is something that consumes your very being and, as bell hooks argues, black women need healing strategies and healing words to enable them to deal with the anguish that sexism and sexist oppression create in their daily life. She suggests black women need to theorise from a 'place of pain . . . which enables us to remember and recover ourselves' (1994: 74). She explains such a location is experienced and shared by those who are 'aware' of the personal and collective struggle that all forms of domination, such as homophobia, class exploitation, racism, sexism and imperialism engender. She suggests courageously exposing the 'wounds' of struggle which will teach and guide us on new theoretical journeys which challenge and renew the inclusive feminist struggle.

Such a 'place of pain' manifests itself in many ways. Recently I attended an equal opportunities workshop where we were asked to identify experiences of institutional racism. A young Iranian woman, a graduate student, recounted how her husband, a qualified medical doctor was experiencing racial discrimination when trying to get a placement in the NHS (National Health Service). A white male member of the group, an established academic piped up and said, 'Don't worry, love . . . it wouldn't happen to you as you are so attractive.' In that one moment all the black women in the group were reduced to no more than their embodied 'otherness' – mute visible objects. His unthinking comment was made possible by the unspoken power of his authorative gaze.

Patricia Williams, an eminent African-American professor, talks of the collective trauma such everyday incursions into your self-hood engender:

> There are moments in my life when I feel as though part of me is missing. There are days when I feel so invisible that I can't remember the day of the week it is, when I feel so manipulated that I can't remember my own name, when I feel so lost and angry that I can't speak a civil word to the people who love me best. These are times I catch sight of my reflection in store windows and I am surprised to see the whole person looking back . . . I have to close my eyes at such times and remember myself, draw an internal pattern that is smooth and whole.
>
> (Williams 1991, quoted in hooks 1994: 74)

Excluding practices

There are costs to 'just being there' in higher education. Many black and minority students are more likely to leave university before completing the course. As Connor *et al.* (2004) argue, the most influential reasons are unmet expectations about the HE. While financial and family difficulties, institutional factors, such as poor teaching, and wrong subject choice also feature, ethnic minority people also reported 'the feeling of isolation or hostility in academic culture' (ibid.: 60). These are worrying findings as it signals the fact that many black students do not feel they 'belong'. The findings of Diane Reay, Miriam David and Stephan Ball (2005) have shed some light on the process of exclusion 'felt' by young working-class and ethnic minority people seeking to enter higher education. Reay *et al.* suggest young people can engage in a process of self-exclusion when making university choices. Drawing on Bourdieu, they write that processes of exclusion work through having 'a sense of one's place which leads one to exclude oneself from places from which one is excluded' (ibid.: 91). As one working-class student in their study says about going to an elite university, 'What's a person like me doing in a place like that?' Reay *et al.* state: 'Choosing to go to university . . . for the working classes is about being different people in different places, about who they might be but also what they must give up' (ibid.: 161)

Processes of exclusion in higher education are difficult to unpack as they are underscored by the complex dynamics of class, gender and race. Experiences are complex and relational and are located at the intersection of structure, culture and agency (Brah 1996). For some students, university can be a positive experience. As Shirin Housee demonstrates, South Asian young women can find a space at university to express assertive, independent, personas which enable them to freely express their religious identity. In opposition to the stereotype of Asian women as victims and recipients of patriarchal culture, they were 'fighting back . . . and were not going to accept racism, sexism or any other -ism' (2004: 69).

However, while spaces of opposition can and do open up, Back (2004) suggests there are two antagonistic forces at play in higher education. One that moves unconsciously and haphazardly towards what Hall (2000) has called 'multicultural drift', and the other remains the 'sheer weight of whiteness' (Back 2004: 1). With regard to the latter, in some institutions the 'sheer weight of whiteness' is overt and almost impenetrable. Research looking at the University of Cambridge shows how elite culture is self-reinforcing. It was seen by others as a white, male, 'tough and macho' culture that was 'secretive, intimidating and insular'. It was assumed by those at Cambridge that those in privileged positions were there because of their ability and merit. However, over 70 per cent of readers and professors had a degree from Cambridge and a third of academics had no experience of any other university, the majority being there for over twenty years (Schneider-Ross 2001).

Puwar draws on the social theorists Bourdieu and Foucault to explain how cultures of exclusion operate within contested social spaces such as universities:

> Social spaces are not blank and open for any body to occupy. Over time, through processes of historical sedimentation, certain types of bodies are designated as being the 'natural' occupants of specific spaces . . . Some bodies have the right to belong in certain locations, while others are marked out as trespassers who are in accordance with how both spaces and bodies are imagined, politically, historically and conceptually circumscribed as being 'out of place'.
>
> (2004: 51)

Puwar suggests black bodies out of place are 'space invaders'. She argues there are several ways in which black bodies are constructed when they do not represent the 'racial somatic norm' within white institutions (Puwar 2001, 2004). First, there is 'disorientation', a double-take as you enter a room, as you are not supposed to be there. You are noticed and it is uncomfortable. Like walking into a pub in a town where you don't live. There is confusion as you are not the 'natural expected occupant of that position'. I know this well, in many meetings even though I am a professor, I have been mistaken for the coffee lady! Even students do a double-take when they see you are the social theory lecturer.

Second, there is 'infantalisation': here you are not only pigeon-holed into being 'just a race expert', but black lecturers are seen as less capable of being in authority. This can mean black staff are assumed to be more junior than they are (I have been told to stop using the photocopier as it is not for administrators). There is a constant doubt about your skills, which can affect career progression. Third, there is the 'burden of invisibility', or hyper-surveillance. Here you are viewed suspiciously and any mistakes are picked up and seen as a sign of misplaced authority. You have to work harder for recognition outside of the confines of stereotypical expectations, and can suffer disciplinary measures and disappointment if you do not meet expectations in your work performance.

Sometimes I am shocked by the deeply racist comments I hear in everyday life in the higher echelons of our 'civilised' universities. Recently I was on search committee for the appointment of a chair in a prestigious university. I was sent an email by a senior white male academic about the applications. He stated there had been several, who were described in terms of their research (they were not racialised), and one application from a 'not very credible Indian'. Why was 'the Indian' racialised and none of the others? What difference did it make that he was Indian? What was I being 'told' in this coded message? Was it, 'all Indians want to come to England and will try anything'? Or that other trope that 'Indian qualifications are not very good, and anyway an Indian can never be as good as a white (British) academic'? Why did the white *male* academic who sent the email not think about what he was saying to me – a women of Indo-Caribbean heritage? Was it because even though I am one of them (an Indian), I am now 'one of us' (i.e. an honorary 'white' who can speak their language)? Why did he say it at all? Maybe because he could.

Franz Fanon's timeless prose can help us understand the personal costs of the racialised phenomenon of 'a not very credible Indian':

> 'We have a Senegalese teacher. He is quite bright . . . Our doctor is coloured. He is very gentle'. It was always the Negro teacher, the Negro doctor . . . I knew, for instance that if the physician made a mistake it would be the end of him and all those who came after him. What could one expect after all, from a Negro physician? As long as everything went well he was praised to the skies. But look out, no nonsense under any conditions . . . I tell you I was walled in; no exception was made for my fine manners, or my knowledge of literature, or my understanding of quantum theory.
>
> (Fanon 1986: 117)

Relocating the self

From the diaries of Cornelia Sorabji (Visram 2002) and the eloquent lectures of Patricia Williams (Williams 1997) we can begin to open up and understand the complex multidimensional world black women inhabit on the margins of white institutions. Moreover, we need to understand black women's agency and subjectivity in relation to their space on the margin. Marginality, as bell hooks argues, can be a radical location in which black women can situate themselves in relation to the dominant group through 'other ways of knowing'. hooks recounts her own story of leaving home and going to university and becoming a successful academic:

When I left that concrete space on the margins, I kept alive in my heart ways of knowing reality . . . [I was] sustained by remembrance of the past, which includes recollections of broken tongues that decolonize our minds, our very beings.

(1991: 150)

bell hooks argues that we should reclaim the word 'margin' from its traditional use as a marker of exclusion and see it as an act of positive appropriation for black women:

Marginality is a central location for the production of a counter hegemonic discourse – it is found in the words, habits and the way one lives . . . It is a site one clings to even when moving to the centre . . . it nourishes our capacity to resist . . . It is an inclusive space where we recover ourselves, where we move in solidarity to erase the category coloniser/colonised.

(ibid.: 149–50)

Black women appear to occupy parallel discursive spheres in what Diane Reay and I have called a 'third space' (Mirza and Reay 2000). Nancy Fraser calls this third space, 'hidden counter public' spheres which are arenas where 'members of subordinated social groups invent and circulate counter discourses, which in turn permit them to formulate oppositional interpretations of their identities, interests and needs' (1994: 84).

In our research on African-Caribbean women educators working in black community schools (sometimes called supplementary or Saturday schools), Diane Reay and I found black women working alongside the dominant educational discourse. In their space on the margin, with their quiet and subversive acts of care and 'other ways of knowing', these women:

operate within, between, under and alongside the mainstream educational and labour market structures, subverting, renaming and reclaiming opportunities for their children through the transformative pedagogy of 'raising the race' – a radical pedagogy, that ironically appears conservative on the surface with its focus on inclusion and dialogue with the mainstream.

(Mirza 1997b: 274)

Black women appear to seek social transformation through educational change. The African-Caribbean women teachers in black supplementary schools, as indeed those working and studying in universities and schools, struggle for educational inclusion in order to transform opportunities for themselves and their children. In covert and quiet ways (unlike street riots which signal masculine social change), these women work to keep alive the black communities' collective desire for self-knowledge and a belief in the power of schooling to militate against racial barriers (Fordham 1996: 63). As Casey writes, education acquires a different meaning in the context of racist oppression:

> In a racist society . . . to become educated is to contradict the whole system of racist signification . . . to succeed in studying white knowledge is to undo the system itself . . . to refute its reproduction of black inferiority materially and symbolically.
>
> (1993: 123)

For African-Caribbean women, educational institutions were not just mechanisms through which individuals are unconsciously subjected to the dominant ideological system but rather, as Freire (2004) argues, education is the terrain on which they acquire consciousness of their position and struggle. Just as the black women educators had developed through their experience a strategic rationalisation of their situation and opportunities, so too have black women in higher education developed a sense of their space on the margin through self-actualisation and self-definition.

Conclusion

> The black woman's critique of history has not only involved us coming to terms with absences: we have also been outraged by the ways in which it has made us visible, when it has chosen to see us . . . we cannot hope to constitute ourselves in all our ill conceived presences that invade herstory from history, but we do wish to bear witness to our own herstories.
>
> (Carby 1997: 45)

Black women have been virtually invisible in higher education as professional lecturers, researchers and teachers. In tiny numbers they are often the only black member of staff in a department, and often in part-time work and in lower less stable contracts (Carter *et al.* 1999). On the other hand, they are visible in large numbers in certain new universities as students. For example, in the university where I teach, black women can make up as much as 65 per cent of the students on health and social science courses. But by flagging up this paradox of invisibility/visibility it is not just the numbers I am concerned with here. It is the construction of the invisibility/visibility split in terms of black women's embodied experience as black bodies 'out of place' in higher education.

Diversity documents in our higher education institutions highlight gender, race (or sometimes socio-economic class) numbers to show how successful (or not) they are at achieving equality. Black women are highly visible when our bodies help higher education institutions achieve their wider moral and ethical goals, and help them appeal to a wider global market. But this is not true representation or equality. In our universities, 'diversity' is 'skin deep'. Black people are celebrated in colourful brochures with smiling 'brown' faces – like a box of chocolates, there is one from every continent and one of every colour – Chinese, African, Indian. Objectified and commercialised, no one asks, 'How do they feel about that?' They find themselves appropriated, their bodies comodified, 'for the desiring machine of capital' (Young 1995, in Simmonds 1997: 232).

However, black women slip into invisibility in the site that matters the most – how they are valued and embraced in everyday practice and the transforming difference that they bring to their institutions. Such absences are not simply a silence, a forgotten oversight, but an erasure of their very being. With the new-found 'fetish for difference' that diversity brings, black women have become 'hot' property in the academy in terms of research projects and teaching, once they stay in their place as 'natives in the academy' (Puwar 2004). In universities black women struggle daily against

> [the] presumption that scholars of colour are narrowly focused or lacking in intellectual depth . . . whatever our history, whatever our record, whatever our validations, whatever our accomplishments, by and large we are perceived as one-dimensional and treated accordingly . . . fit for addressing the marginal subjects of race, but not subjects in the core curriculum.
>
> (Madrid, in Lopez 1993: 127)

Paulo Freire, the visionary Brazilian educationalist, argued that education is the struggle over meaning as well as power relations (Freire 2004). For black women, universities are not simply a place to get qualifications and pass exams in an increasingly instrumentalist market-driven educational culture (Giroux and Giroux 2004). As Mohanty argues, for black women:

> Educational sites represent accommodations and contestations over knowledge by differently empowered social constituencies . . . thus education is a central terrain where power and politics operate out of the lived culture of individuals and groups situated in asymmetrical social and political positions.
>
> (1993: 43–4)

Manuel Castells (2004) argues universities are global elite information networks that are important to sustain because, with encroaching neo-liberal market forces, the university is the last remaining space of freedom. However, as we have seen here, within these precious places of freedom, academic institutions still create paradigms and knowledges that transcribe race and gender power relations. If we are to transform our academic institutions into truly democratic inclusive spaces, we need to be ever vigilant of excluding practices as we journey through higher education.

Notes

1 The BBC was called 'hideously white' by Greg Dyke, the Director General of the BBC in 2001, for being 98 per cent white. With less than 1.3 per cent of black and minority ethnic staff in higher education in UK (THES 2004; Carter *et al.* 1999), it too can be called hideously white.

2 Black is used here to mean women of visible difference, this includes women of colour such as those of African and Asian origin unless otherwise specified (Mirza 1997a; Brah 1992; Sudbury 2001). Terms such as 'minority ethnic' and 'black and minority ethnic' are used when studies cited have used these categories.

3 This is compared to 31 per cent of young white women and 28 per cent of young white men aged 18–19 in full-time undergraduate degree courses (NAO 2002: 6).

4 Phoenix (1996) suggests that research on black women and mothering is character-ised by the 'normative absence/pathological presence' couplet. Black women are absent from studies on 'normative' mothering but are constructed as deviant others, i.e. single mothers, teenage pregnancy, etc., when they do appear.

5 This chapter is a reworking of a keynote address given at Trinity College, Dublin, 12 May 2004, for the symposium entitled 'Reshaping the Intellectual Landscape: Women in the Academe', to celebrate a century since women's admission to the college in 1904.

6 For an image of Cornelia Sorabji, see the National Portrait Gallery website http://www.npg.org.uk/live/search/person.asp?LinkID=mp61443

7 For an image of the Indian women suffragettes, see Museum of London website http://www.museumoflondon.org.uk/MOLsite/piclib/pages/ bigpicture.asp?id=1032

8 I was a commissioner on the Mayor's Commission for African and Asian Heritage (MACCH) 2003–5. During this time we took evidence as to the 'forgotten' contri-bution of minority communities to the historical wealth of Great Britain and the institutional and organisational shortcomings in recognising and displaying this contribution (GLA 2005).

9 In the UK we have a distinction of 'old' and 'new' universities – old are the established traditional elite 'sandstone' and 'redbrick' research-based universities such as Oxford and Cambridge. The new universities are sometimes referred to as the 'post-1992' universities when polytechnics and HE colleges merged and gained university status in a new rationalisation and expansion of HE.

10 However, only 7 per cent of Pakistani and Bangladeshi origin women have further and higher educational qualifications (Dale *et al.* 2002).

Chapter 11

Older women as lifelong learners

Barbara Kamler

Introduction

This chapter examines the experiences of older women aged 60–85 who were participants in a collaborative research project called 'Stories of Ageing'.[1] This three-year longitudinal study was designed to counter the invisibility of older women and the purveying of ageist images about growing older. Using principles based on Haug's (1987) memory work and Walkerdine's (Lucey *et al.* 1996) video diary methodologies, forty women explored their own life stories by engaging in critical processes of writing, filming, talking and performance. The processes of producing visual and verbal texts had powerful effects on these older learners and challenged the idea that creativity and cognitive ability necessarily decline with age or that ageing itself is necessarily a 'problem'. The project was successful both in documenting change in the lives of older women, and in developing a pedagogic model of lifelong learning which produced change.

The 'Stories of Ageing' project presents a number of challenges to current conceptions of lifelong learning. In recent years there has been a proliferation of excellent learning spaces for older women and men sponsored by bodies such as the Council of Adult Education, the University of the Third Age and a variety of community-based groups committed to agendas of positive ageing. Typically, however, these spaces are described as Third Age education, for the young–old, or Fourth Age education – for the old–old. They are not included as part of the larger project of lifelong learning.

This is a curious phenomenon, given the OECD definition of lifelong learning as creating a society of individuals who are motivated to continue learning throughout their lives, both formally and informally (OECD 1996). In practice, however, 'throughout their lives' appears to mean 'working lives'. There may well be an urgent need to promote the widest possible participation in education and training for all age groups, as Morris (2001) and others argue. But individuals who are post-work, or in the 60–85 demographic of the women in our study, are presently excluded from the vision of lifelong learning.

This exclusion is evident in the language of educational policy-makers, such as Australian David Kemp, when he was Minister for Education, Training and Youth Affairs.

> There is little doubt that the nations which will succeed in the 21st century will be knowledge societies – societies rich in human capital, effective in their capacity to utilise and deploy their human resources productively and successful in the creation and commercialisation of new knowledge. In such a world there will need to be greater opportunities than ever before for lifelong learning and for preparation not just for the first job but for succeeding jobs.
>
> (Kemp 1999)

It is also evident in the 1998 Australian Bureau of Statistics survey, which concluded that Australian participation in lifelong learning was high, with 72.4 per cent of the population between 15 and 64 years taking part (Watson 1999). Amazingly, however, those in the over-64 years category were not 'counted' in the survey, presumably because they were *too old* for lifelong learning. In many university lifelong learning policies, we find a similar focus on participation in education and training for work, on upgrading professional skills and qualifications. The goal is to create a disposition to learning in *younger* students which continues post-university, rather than develop multi-age learning communities that genuinely span the lifecourse.

A focus on employability, jobs and working lives is perhaps not surprising in light of rapid economic changes and increased levels of global competition. Yet an economic or narrow developmental approach to lifelong learning creates a number of significant exclusions. It is at odds with more inclusive goals, such as widening participation to groups of people previously excluded from taking up learning opportunities due to social, economic or geographical constraints (NIACE 2004). And it excludes learners who are post-work.

So to be provocative I'd ask: Do we see the post-work years as the end of productive learning and contributing? Is there an age when we think intellectual capacity ceases? And how old do we think the lifelong learner can be? As old as 60 or 70? What about age 80? Or 90? To explore such questions, I examine the vigorous, intellectual work accomplished by one community of older Australian women. I argue that we need to design new spaces of lifelong learning that foster growth and change, rather than 'keeping mum busy'; and that older women need to be taken seriously as learners and positioned as producers of knowledge.

My aim in this chapter is to use the 'Stories of Ageing' project to rethink what it means to learn until the *end* of our lives. I analyse both the pedagogy of the writing, video and performance workshops and the stories produced by the women to illustrate how the process of text production fostered a remaking and rewriting of self. Excerpts from a final group interview are selected to highlight how the women's participation over three years in challenging narrative communities affected their lives outside the workshops. I conclude by reflecting on the potential of such work for recasting lifelong learning as cross generational learning with wide social and cultural, as well as personal benefits.

The research project

The 'Stories of Ageing' project was designed to examine ageing as change, rather than decline or deterioration. Arber and Ginn (1995) argue that while gender and ageing are inextricably intertwined in social life and personal biography, they have not been integrated in sociological theory and have rarely been researched in terms of their intersections. Further, there have been few adequate paradigms for integrating research on the biological dimensions of life with the social and cultural features (Turner 1984).

Our study of older women called on more coherent approaches to ageing which have begun to develop in recent years. These include the recent preoccupation in social gerontology with positive ageing and the deconstruction of negative images of ageing. We have drawn on lifecourse perspectives developed in the sociology of ageing, in particular what Bury (1995) refers to as dynamic approaches (e.g. Arber and Evandrou 1993). And we share postmodern views of ageing (e.g. Featherstone *et al.* 1991) and feminist poststructuralist perspectives on ageism and ageing (Laws 1995; Ray 1996).

Our research design was innovative in at least three ways:

- its focus on women, because they not only live longer than men, but have been marginalised in mainstream research, with men being the normative standard;
- its longitudinal, three-year design which anticipated growth and change in the lives of older women. While it is common to examine change in the lives of young people, so entrenched is the cultural expectation that age is about decline or death, that longitudinal studies of the social and cultural aspects of ageing are rare;
- its critical and interdisciplinary focus on cultural stories and representation. These provide different lenses on ageing outside a biomedical focus.

Our focus on women's own stories and visual representations of themselves was pivotal. We believed these could effect change in both theoretical representations of ageing and in the lived realities of ageing women. For us, the relation between lived and imagined stories is significant. The stories we tell provide the frameworks through which we act (Lyotard 1984). Stories are interpretive resources for dealing with the everyday world and for taking ourselves up within the cultural story lines available to us (Gilbert 1993; Davies 1994). Such notions allow us to theorise the ageing woman as positioned within the categories our available cultural narratives have provided (Kamler and Feldman 1995). But we also see her as capable of taking up discourses through which she is shaped and through which she may reshape herself. This is the case whether the story she produces is a verbal text, like those produced in the writing workshops, or a performance of everyday life, like those filmed in the video workshops of this project.

For three years we worked with forty women, aged 60–85, living in their communities to produce stories that captured the complexity and diversity of growing older. The women brought a mix of personal and professional histories and came from a range of heritages, including Eastern European, Anglo-Celtic, Philippina and Vietnamese. We took the women seriously as learners and offered them the opportunity to learn new skills – in writing and video production and later in theatre performance. They, in turn, offered their stories and insights so that we, as younger researchers could gain more complex understandings of ageing from their filming and writing. From the outset, this was a cross-generational learning exchange; older women from the community and younger researchers from the university working together, using our different knowledges and experience to produce new understandings of ageing together.

Workshops spaces for lifelong learning

We constructed the 'Stories of Ageing' workshops as sites of pedagogy and data production. The challenge of the project was to create a pedagogic space that would allow women to rewrite the narrow range of cultural narratives that define ageing as loss and deterioration. We regarded the forty older women participants as collaborative partners in the investigation, rather than research subjects and developed strategies to position them as knowledgeable text producers.

In the writing workshops we used principles based on Frigga Haug's (1987) memory work to develop a pedagogy which was collective and deconstructive. Stories were drafted, revised and developed as part of the group process. Typically, we met weekly for two hours with two groups of ten to twelve women over an eight-week period each year of the project. Each week the women wrote at home on a topic we designated. They brought their texts to the workshop to read aloud to one another for comment and critique. These texts always promoted much discussion and raucous laughter. At the end of each workshop we set a topic for the following week, usually emerging from our discussion.

While some of the women had previously attended creative writing workshops, our approach was different in its critical orientation. We shared a political agenda with the women – to rewrite negative and diminishing narratives of ageing. Together we were committed to developing richer and more complex perspectives about what it means to grow older. We encouraged the women to attend to the detail of what appeared to them at first to be boring. We gave them tools to ask critical questions about the writing and treat it as clay (Kamler

2001b). They wrote and rewrote, they looked at what they had not said as well as what they had. They developed other endings, other ways of thinking about their experience as older women in ordinary spaces (Kamler 1999).

In the video workshops, we developed a similar pedagogy of writing, discussion and critique to help women produce video diaries of their lives. We used the video diary methodology developed by Valerie Walkerdine and her colleagues (Lucey *et al.* 1996) to access the stories of young working-class women. Their agenda too had been feminist and they used video on the assumption it was a technology which would somehow access reality more directly and in less mediated ways than language and writing. This was an assumption we modified as we came to realise that video images were no less mediated by our influence in the workshops than the written stories.

In the first year of the study we worked with a group of predominantly Anglo-Australian women; in the second year, we worked with the Australian-Vietnamese Womens' Welfare Association in Melbourne to form a second video workshop of Vietnamese women using an interpreter. As none of the researchers spoke Vietnamese and the Vietnamese women speak little English, we needed to negotiate complex processes of translation and interpretation and effect cross-cultural dialogue without a common language (Kamler and Threadgold 2003). We offered the women camera skills and engaged in critical analyses of visual and televisual images. The women made videos in their own homes and communities and we viewed, discussed and edited these in the workshops. Learning techniques of story-boarding, narrative and editing extended the women's technical expertise. These new skills gave them technological credibility with their grandchildren and made them more critical viewers of visual representations of older women.

In the third year of the project women from the writing and video workshops came together to produce and perform a multimedia performance script 'We're Not Nice Little Old Ladies' (Stories of Ageing Project 1999). This was an exciting collaboration between the research team and a local Melbourne Council to commemorate the 1999 International Year of Older Persons. The Glen Eira City Council donated a theatre space and the services of a professional writer and director to convert the women's research stories into a public performance. Importantly, the idea for the performance came from the older women, not the research team. As the women came to believe in the collective power of their stories to teach others, they asked for more direct involvement in moving their stories from our workshops into the community at large.

What eventuated was a seven-stage, twelve-month project plan, including script development and theatre skills, culminating in two public performances by the women in November 1999 and the publication of a script. The director used a team of theatre artists to take workshops and involve the women throughout the decision-making process to develop a wide range of skills and sense of ownership. The women were guided through an exploration of staging ideas, the use of props, movement, vocal work, sound effects and visual images.

They made decisions on publication format and artwork, marketing and publicity. They were directly involved in all aspects of backstage, stage and front-of-house management.

This was intensive, demanding work. The older women's creativity, energy and good humour over the three years were inspiring to younger researchers trying to re-imagine the later years of our own lives. Their critical writing and video work and extraordinary stamina in the rehearsal and performance process provide a significant challenge to notions of lifelong learning that exclude older learners. In the process of making these texts, the women began to create other positions outside stereotypes of ageing. Making stories became a powerful way to reflect on the past but also to create new understandings of ageing and themselves.

Home sweet home

Over the three years of the project the women produced a rich array of cultural products in the form of video diaries, written stories, interviews and a theatrical, multimedia performance script. Collectively their stories capture the diversity of growing older. They tell of older women's sexuality, courtship and solitude. They explore relationships with family and friends, experiences of migration and homebuilding and death. They deal with negotiating the challenges of daily life as the women actively confront the emotional and physical changes that accompany ageing.

Some of their richest stories focus on the ordinary topic of 'home'. Home is typically thought to be one of the boundaries that constrains an older woman's life and keeps her isolated and lonely. Home is also the space where women labour to look after others and nurture them. The women, however, told other stories about what it means to make a home at the end of one's life. Unsentimental stories of being contented and alone, of being alone and part of a community, of growth and change. Phillipa writes about the anticipation and pleasures of the garden she has created:

> I came here in 1975 and it was the planting and laying out of the garden that first endeared me to unit living and on my own for the first time in my life. Come and we'll walk around the garden.
>
> These pots of primula and polyanthus add colour and a welcome at the front door. Things are starting to bloom, the wattles, westringia and correa. This green flowering correa picks up the light of the night sky and becomes as fairy lights. The casuarina and kangaroo paw give much pleasure still, they being the first planting all those years ago. This fairly dense planting remains a joy as well as providing privacy from an overlooking unit. There are five units with each owner responsible for their own garden.
>
> This plot was a herb garden until the heat and dry of last summer dried

all the plants. I now have it filled with bulbs, freesia and daffodil. Since the rain, the herbs are breaking through, which the bulbs will cope with.

This picket fence and gate I recently had built so as to close off my back garden, now awaits a coat of paint. Through the gate we come across my latest endeavour – three metres of a new brick path which extends an existing path to the new fence. With family all interstate no-one has yet said what a fine job I did. Yes, it does look professional and I know they will say the same. It was the sweeping of the sand to fill between the pavers that gave the right finish . . .

Enjoying a cup of coffee while standing at the kitchen window, I see a stream of light and colour across the grasses of the closing day, the bird sounds echo in the distance.

The pleasure of Phillipa's text lies in its invitation to the reader to enter a space we rarely see. It is a space Phillipa has made for herself, a riot of colour, scent and sound, pleasuring all of the bodily senses. This is a place where she is quite literally 'at home', where the older woman asserts her right to make her freedom. It is a place where things dry up and die and struggle to live again.

This is the first place Phillipa ever lived alone and she lives in peace, fully connected to the world around her. Her writing brings a different understanding into existence. Ageing need not bring loss of sensual pleasure. Ageing bodies remain active and fulfilled – planting, laying out a garden, making a path – inviting to others. The rhythms of Phillipa's prose hold the traces of her body at work, labouring to produce growth and change, pausing in a quiet moment to enjoy a stream of light at day's end.

Other women in the workshops constructed lively images of living alone. Some women wrote about finding new freedom and independence later in life. Some worried over the challenges of leaving the family home for a seniors' community, others over the pain of moving house so frequently or of their children behaving badly. Rich images from the video diaries show Vietnamese women meditating in serene, early morning domestic spaces; praying in temples with their communities; exercising with diligence and humour; singing while chopping vegetables, creating rhythms of food preparation and giving to community and family. A scene from the performance script 'We're not Nice Little Old Ladies' creates a collage of verbal and performed images about home at the end of one's life.

Dramatis personae: Four women between the ages of 70 and 85
Scene: Melbourne, Australia
[Two women are sitting centre-stage with a tea pot, two cups and a cake plate on the table before them. One woman is standing stage-left placing flowers into a vase. Another woman is sitting at a desk stage-right with a photo album and a pack of cards.]
Table woman: Home now is my garden and my bed. It's the place where I

properly belong and where I find rest, refuge and satisfaction. When I've been out all day and am 'fair done-in' I can't wait to get home, go inside, lock the door, ignore the winks of the telephone machine, pour myself a drink and flop into a chair from which I survey my back garden.

Desk woman: We started to think about moving to a unit or village but I loved my little home. We had built it straight after World War II – in a paddock – with no road, electricity, gas or sewerage. How could I leave this home? Every corner had history, every shrub and tree planted and nurtured. How could I leave all this?

Table woman: I just think I will live a little longer here . . . and enjoy tomorrow's walk up the hill as the sun sets, and the wonderful golden light with the clouds in the still cold evenings – and the deep blue of the mountains. Yes, I will stay a little longer.

Desk woman: I'm having pangs about moving away. I know it's something I need to do, and part of me looks forward to the new challenge. But another part of me cries out – this is not the same as any other of many previous departures.

Flower woman: Although some of us have trouble adjusting to old age on our own after our partner has died, many women find – maybe unexpectedly – that this is a truly liberating time. No longer does one have to tidy away things that might offend the partner; or have meals at regular specified times; or sleep at night or shut all the windows – or open them. One can feel free to just sit if one feels so inclined. One can choose for one's self.

(Kamler 2001a: 232)

The audience of grandchildren, sons and daughters, friends, university professors and members of the community who watched the older women perform their stories and ageing bodies under the spotlight were mesmerised. This was a rare cultural space where older women became authorised teachers. They quietly insisted that their younger audience think past the stereotypes of ageing and imagine what it might mean to make a home at the end of our lives.

Collectively, their stories refuse 'home sweet home' images of stability. They represent 'making home' as a lifelong process of change, of remaking and rebuilding after divorce or the death of a child or spouse; after war, or marriage, or migration to Australia; or ill health. Such stories have a great deal to teach a culture obsessed with youth and fearful of ageing. They pose important challenges to a public policy tradition which tends to regard older women as a homogeneous group and imagine them as passive recipients of government services, while older women construct themselves as lively contributors to their communities.

Ageing as change

The 'Stories of Ageing' project was successful in developing a pedagogic model of lifelong learning that documented and produced change in the older women's lives. Meeting together in the workshops the women found a community of survivors, a space of friendship and laughter and a place to be taken seriously as learners. But the narrative work also had significant material effects on the older women's sense of well-being and survival. Through the process of physically remaking stories of ageing in film, writing and performance, many women began to rewrite themselves as well as their texts.

This is evident in the final group interview evaluation of the project, where the women reflected on the changes they experienced. Here Connie, the writer and producer of a highly polished video diary titled 'Step by Step', reflects on her renewed confidence and pleasure in learning to control the technologies of 'young people'.

CONNIE THE SKITE

Muriel: Did it change you in any way, Connie

Connie: Yes, I'm a skite now.

All: [laughter]

Jo: Is that what your family call you?

Connie: No, not really. But it used to be I didn't want to tell anybody I was making a video because you know what most people are like your own age. They just look at you to think 'What on earth is she up to?' Especially the video because that seems to be for young people, doesn't it? Getting around with cameras and everything and tripods and all this sort of thing. But anyway, now I don't mind telling them and they seen me on TV the other night and they got a different view of me and I've got a different view of them, too.

All: [laughter and commentary]

Connie: Yeah, but I do a bit of public speaking and it has given me more confidence, you know, sort of thing. That's what I've found about it and I just loved every minute of it. And as for that performance and everything, how it all come together was just marvellous. It just seemed to be bits and pieces and this and that and then all of a sudden we've got a lovely book, a book launch, a beautiful show everyone is raving about it and it's on television. What a time we've had!

Beryl was a participant in the writing workshops. Like Connie, she speaks of validation and an enhanced sense of agency from her participation in the project. But most unexpectedly, her engagement in textual production also helped her find the courage to put herself back in the workplace arena she still longed for.

BERYL GOES BACK TO WORK

Beryl: I cheated coming here because I came late, you were supposed to be 70 and I was 65.

All: [laughter] Woooooooo . . .

Beryl: I did the writing and I didn't want to do the performance and I didn't. All my life I have conformed. And if anyone said jump, all I ever said was 'How high?' And since I've been coming here I don't want to. But when I came I was 65, and I was sick, really sick. And I was telling everybody I was like an 85 year old. Until I came here and I saw some 85 year olds and I reviewed that to 105. And then walking through the city one day, I don't know if it was the topic of the week or what, but I was walking and all the workers were out at their lunch hour and I had this overwhelming grief. 'I want to go back to work. I want to be part of all that.' And I have.

Barbara: So what did you do? How did you do it?

Beryl: With a lot of encouragement from Pat I went to an employment thing and found a young woman who said, 'You're only 66.' And I think with all the writing we did about me, I was able to write away letters and tell people how good I was, with this young woman pushing me from behind. And I got a job and it's just what I want. I mean it's only two afternoons a week, it's not a big deal, but to me it is. And it was that day that I walked through the streets coming here. I'm a staff support person and counsellor at Mobil House. And I'm back in the big corporate world you know and I don't have enough clothes to wear, but I couldn't have done it without all this. First, all the discipline of focusing on a subject and then being listened to and validated which was so powerful.

The workshops were clearly a significant learning space for Connie, Beryl, and other older women in the project, but two features stand out in relation to rethinking the project of lifelong learning. The first is that we regarded ageing as a process of change, rather than decline. The second is that we designed the pedagogic spaces of the workshops to position the women as knowledgeable producers of text and foster their intellectual growth. We treated older participants as both teachers and learners. We provided opportunities for reciprocal mentoring and recycling what they learned back into their communities. The older women learned new skills and technologies from younger people, but these were mobilised to produce new understandings of their own. The younger generation, in turn, became their audience – their students – challenged by what these older women had to say.

Our work was small scale – forty women over three years – but it is suggestive of an approach to lifelong learning that is less ageist and more gender-inclusive than current conceptions. Such an approach emphasises teaching and learning across generations, rather than updating skills for the workforce. It positions older learners as knowledge producers, not simply consumers. It invites older people to make new knowledge, rather than just keep up to date with the latest ideas and trends of younger people. It seriously addresses the question: How do we use the knowledge accumulated over a lifetime in ways that benefit not only the learner – the older person – but the society in which they have lived during their lifetime? If we could imagine this kind of learning opportunity on a larger scale, then perhaps we'd all look forward to growing older ourselves.

Note

1   The 'Stories of Ageing' project was made possible by a three-year Australian Research Council Grant (1997–1999) entitled *Stories of Ageing: A Longitudinal Study of Women's Self-representation*. The chief investigators were Barbara Kamler (Deakin University), Terry Threadgold (Monash University, now relocated at Cardiff University), and Susan Feldman (Melbourne University, now relocated at Victoria University).

Chapter 12

War and diaspora as lifelong learning contexts for immigrant women

Shahrzad Mojab

This chapter presents a critical feminist reading of lifelong learning. The two emerging notions of lifelong learning, one which is concerned with job training and recurrent education, and that aimed at social transformation, will be interrogated in the context of immigrant women's struggles for learning, working, and transforming their lives in diaspora. In particular, the chapter draws on the results of my research project entitled *War, Diaspora, and Learning: Kurdish Women in Canada, Britain, and Sweden.*[1] One of the objectives of this project was to study the impact of war and displacement on Kurdish women's learning. There are about 25 to 30 million Kurds who, since the latter part of twentieth century, have been subjected to 'transnationalization' as a result of war, displacement, and re-constitution of nation and ethnicity in the diaspora (Mojab and Hassanpour 2004). Kurdish women face enormous challenges in the process of resettlement and gaining full citizenship rights in their adopted countries. They have to learn about a whole universe that differs from their previous world – learning to live in different economic and social systems, acquiring different languages, and integrating into different legal and political regimes.

My approach is a critical feminism rooted in historical materialism and informed by dialectics. It has much in common with Chandra Talpade Mohanty's notion of transnational feminist theory:

> [C]ross-cultural feminist work must be attentive to the micropolitics of context, subjectivity, and struggle, as well as to the macropolitics of global economic and political systems and processes [the challenge is] to do this kind of multilayered, contextual analysis to reveal how the particular is often universally significant – without using the universal to erase the particular or positing an unbridgeable gulf between the two terms. Implicit in this analysis [is] the use of historical materialism as a basic framework and a definition of material reality in both its local and micro, as well as, global, systemic dimensions.
>
> (2002: 501)

I will begin with a brief review of the existing critical literature on lifelong learning as a way of framing my methodological and theoretical framework. This will be followed by mapping out the experience of Kurdish women in Europe as 'citizen' learners, and by way of conclusion, I will argue that we can unravel ideological and social relations embedded in '*lifelong* learning' when we engage in a multilevel analysis of this concept through the lived experiences of learners, in particular marginalized women.

Lifelong learning as contested terrain

The political and economic upheavals of the 1990s have left their mark on education. A major source of change is the globalization of the capitalist economy and its restructuring, which make extraordinary demands on education in general and adult education in particular. The changing economy calls for the reorganization of adult education into a training/learning/skilling enterprise fully responsive to the requirements of the market. Within this political and economic context, lifelong learning has been deployed in two ways: first, it is a central concept in the hegemonic claim that lack of skill causes unemployment; it supposes that constant retraining prepares workers to be ultimately adaptable, and always ready to acquire new skills as the needs of capital dictate. Second, lifelong learning has been deployed as an ideological concept in two ways: (1) the concept has become an ideological distraction that shifts the burden of increasing adaptability onto the worker; and (2) it is also a ray of hope for a more democratic and engaged citizenry.

My questions are: why is lifelong learning being enthusiastically endorsed by some adult educators, policy-makers, the business community, and others? Should we cautiously welcome it or resist it? It is noteworthy that in the past decade international adult education declarations were drafted in the context of lifelong learning ideology; these documents generally promote a democratic or ambitious vision by tying learning and learners to citizenship, participation, justice, gender equality, peace, economic development, civil society, indigenous peoples and minorities' rights. Let me quote at length from the Hamburg Declaration:[2]

> [Adult education] becomes more than a right; it is a key to the twenty-first century. It is both a consequence of active citizenship and a condition for full participation in society. It is a powerful concept for fostering ecologically sustainable development, for promoting democracy, justice, gender equity, and scientific, social and economic development, and for building a world in which violent conflict is replaced by dialogue and a culture of peace based on justice. Adult learning can shape identity and give meaning to life. Learning throughout life implies a rethinking of content to reflect such factors as age, gender equality, disability, language, culture and economic disparities.
>
> Adult education denotes the entire body of ongoing learning processes,

formal or otherwise, whereby people regarded as adults by the society to which they belong develop their abilities, enrich their knowledge, and improve their technical or professional qualifications or turn them in a new direction to meet their own needs and those of their society. Adult learning encompasses both formal and continuing education, non-formal learning and the spectrum of informal and incidental learning available in a multi-cultural learning society, where theory- and practice-based approaches are recognized.

There are, however, serious constraints on making the link between social and cultural rights and the economic and political imperatives. It is in explaining these constraints that we face contesting, contradictory, and, most often partial, theoretical explanation. In other words, despite the knowledge explosion on lifelong learning, I still find the most comprehensive critic in Frank Coffield's important article 'Breaking the consensus: lifelong learning as social control' (Coffield 1999).

Coffield notes that, despite all the debates, there is a consensus which has developed over the past thirty years to the effect that lifelong learning, on its own, will solve a wide range of educational, social and political ills. He states that this consensus is naïve, limited, deficient, dangerous, and diversionary. Coffield asks: 'If the thesis is so poor why it is so popular?' (ibid.: 479). He provides an answer by arguing: 'It legitimates increased expenditure on education.' 'It provides politicians with the pretext for action.' 'It deflects attention from the need for economic and social reform.' And 'It offers the comforting illusion that for every complex problem there is one simple solution' (ibid.: 486). He calls this policy response to market demands 'compulsory emancipation' through lifelong learning (ibid.: 489). Nonetheless, Coffield's alternative proposal is framed in notions of liberal democracy that avoid a deeper analysis of capitalist relations of power. It is important to note that a similar critique was provided by Ivar Berg two decades earlier (Berg 1970).

A number of British educators use Marxist theoretical and epistemological frames of analysis to explain constraints on lifelong learning policy and its democratic aspirations (see, among others, Cole 1998; Rikowski 1999, 2001; Colley and Hodkinson 2001; Colley 2004; Hill 2002). Their main arguments are: (1) the current policy environment for education is 'anti-egalitarian' and this should be contextualized in the national ideological and policy context as well as the global context (Hill 2002: 1). Hill also argues that the capitalist class has a 'Business Plan *for* Education and a Business Plan *in* Education'; (2) contrary to its claims about the 'withering away of the state', neo-liberalism demands a strong state to promote its interests; a strong interventionist state is needed by advanced capitalism particularly in the field of education and training – in the field of producing an ideologically compliant and technically skilled workforce; and (3) 'labour-power' is the single most fundamental commodity on which the whole capitalist system rests. In an important study of mentoring,

Helen Colley argues that the learning/training mentoring model for youth is indeed further 'promoting the brutal commodification of the very humanity to which it appeals' (2004: 100).

What is lacking, however, is an attempt to integrate an analysis of race, gender, class, and learning in a Marxist dialectical sense. An inquiry into 'learning', not in terms of its forms, that is formal, non-formal, and informal, but learning as class consciousness will require a merging of Marxist methodology and anti-oppression frameworks. While class consciousness can be thought of in terms of the distance between subjective and objective interests, this does not mean that the goal is to move a group toward a static set of objective interests. Paula Allman argues that '[T]he human condition is not only riddled with injustice and oppressive division, it is illogical' (1999: 1). She advocates 'authentic social transformation' as a process 'through which people can change not only their circumstances but themselves' (ibid.: 1–2). This entails a lifelong learning process, as Allman would suggest, where human consciousness and questions such as 'how it is constituted' and 'how it can be rendered more critical' are at its core. To put it differently, the reading of lifelong learning as a nexus of citizen/worker/learner is a mechanism of individualization through which learners are turned into portable learning units and where no attention has been paid to the dynamics of change through consciousness. The context of immigrant women's lives can illuminate this theoretical claim.

Kurdish women as the 'learner' in lifelong learning

I begin with personal experiences. My intellectual and political growth is intertwined with the struggle of Kurdish women. Over more than two decades, I have learned about their aspiration for homeland, pleading for speaking their own language, and desire to exhibit their cultural practices and political values. As the fourth largest ethnic people in the Middle East, Kurdish women have been involved in one of the longest nationalist projects of the twentieth century. Their homeland, Kurdistan, was forcibly divided among four neighbouring nation-states of Iran, Iraq, Turkey and Syria, which have used violence against Kurdish demands for self-rule. This has turned the idea of a unified homeland, the greater Kurdistan, into a national dream.

Since the early twentieth century, Kurdish women have also experienced modes of life under the rule of colonial powers, imperialism, and local dictatorial regimes. They have also experienced a range of oppositional politics ranging from nationalism, to Marxism, socialism, communism, and recently, political Islam. Despite this range of political activism and struggle, certain hegemonic social relations, that is, patriarchal domination, in its feudal, religious, nationalist, and modernist forms, encompass Kurdish women's lives. Over decades, the function and intensity of this domination have been shifting as the internal and external forces in the region have changed. It is beyond the scope and the focus of this chapter to further elaborate on all these complexities;

however, I try to read Kurdish women's lives and experiences as an evolving site of historical tensions and contradictions. Through this dialectical and materialist historicization we can understand the sigh of a Kurdish woman *peshmerge* (guerrilla, freedom fighter) living in Sweden when she says, 'If only these people [Swedes] knew! If only they knew who I am or was, what I have done, what I can offer them today.' Shilan is lamenting her life today in Sweden where she is only being constructed, as she puts it,

> as this pathetic refugee woman who only needs their empathy. While in fact what I need is a forum, a space, to tell them as an illiterate woman, under the condition of suppression of my government, how I mobilized, gathered women, recruited them for the national cause; how I self-taught myself reading and writing in order to be able to read the political literature; how I learn to manage a large community of youth, support them, give them hope in life, and inspire them for a better life in future. Here in Sweden, they think I know nothing, I have no skills, they only push me to learn the language, but for what?[3]

The Kurds of Iraq experienced a massive dispersal following the Gulf War in 1991. Europe, in particular, Sweden, received a large number of Kurdish refugees (for statistical information, see Mojab and Hassanpour 2004). Displacement on such a large scale can often drain the educational resources of a nation-state, in so far as learning is a crucial factor in the process of successful re-settling and re-rooting. However, theories of learning do not account for the contexts and contingencies of learning, their diverse forms, and the creativity of the learners in moving beyond the confines of formal and informal learning. This is in part the case because the past is present in the lives of Kurdish women, and shapes their learning and living in the diaspora. Their past constitutes histories of war, conflict, forced assimilation, ethnocide, and linguicide in the states of Turkey, Iran, Iraq, and Syria that rule over them. This constant presence of overt violence is in sharp contrast with life in the West, where new, unfamiliar, and often invisible forms of conflict and violence pose new challenges.

My research revealed five ways through which Kurdish women's learning in Sweden is experienced. It has been lived as a process of (1) detaching women's learning from their past and present experience; (2) separating learning from the daily struggle of Kurdish women in the context of Sweden; as well as a mechanism of (3) disjuncture between women's learning needs and desires and the Swedish political agenda in creating new citizens; (4) disjuncture between immigrant women's learning needs and the context of closer state and market relations; and (5) as a circular process of closure in possibilities for involvement in feminist activism. I call this complex process the 'Closure, Opening, Closure Syndrome'. It is not possible to treat each of these instances separately; it is the totality of all that pushes us to rethink some of our assumptions about learning and lifelong learning. To elaborate, I will draw on moments in the research where these relations, processes, or mechanisms became visible.

During the data collection, I noted that when participants were asked about their learning and life in diaspora, they would invariably begin by explaining the history that led to their exile. Each woman would recount up to twenty years of history of political organizing and resisting state repression, leading to flight and/or imprisonment, and ultimately exile. The women revealed that they were still intimately tied to these political struggles, but in different ways. In September 2002, I attended the first anniversary celebration of the Kurdish women's radio programme in Stockholm, Sweden. More than 300 women, men, and children participated in a festive celebration of the first Kurdish women's radio programme in diaspora. A few weeks after this successful event I arranged a meeting with eight Kurdish women activists who were instrumental in managing and running this radio programme. We began our day-long discussion with the question of why a radio programme and why and how it has become so successful. The immediate response was related to the particular ways that patriarchy is reproduced within the nationalist organizations, and the impact of this patriarchal nationalism on the reproduction of unequal gender relations in the Kurdish diaspora community. One woman suggested that 'nationalism has grown stronger in exile. Thus we had to turn to ourselves.' The 'turning to ourselves' meant to distance themselves from multiple sources of patriarchy and/or colonialism: Kurdish political parties in Sweden, Kurdish community as a totality with strong ties to traditional forces of power in homeland and hostland; Swedish government sources of funding; Swedish feminist organizations; and other immigrant feminist groups. Most of the women active in the radio programme in Sweden are utilizing their experience with radio broadcasting during their struggles in the mountains and camps on the border of Iran and Iraq. The harsh condition of war forced these women into a certain creativity and ingenuity. For instance, women were engaged in instant training to become radio technicians, nurses, primary health-care providers, social workers, and community organizers. Much of the training was done in the context of daily analysis of the situation of war and the longer political strategy for winning the war. Thus, literacy and acquiring good reading skills were undertaken in the context of training as broadcasters. We can see that embedded in this model of learning are several critical elements of *learning for life*: (1) *groundedness*, that is, learning which is located in material condition of life; (2) *practice*, that is, learning which materially can be assessed and transformed into higher level of consciousness; and (3) *survival*, that is, learning with lasting impact on life[4] (Mojab and McDonald forthcoming).

Kurdish women who were trained in health care or community organizing during their camp life on mountains, are the ones who are keen to become teachers, nurses, or social workers. In pursuit of this 'learning ambition', as Sahar called it, Kurdish women who attempted to stand outside the normative boxes of learning faced multiple barriers from a number of forces. Sahar was trying to establish a feminist Kurdish women's group. Her insistence on the notion of 'feminism' stemmed from her frustration with Kurdish political parties, the Swedish government, and Swedish feminist activism. Sahar said,

> Kurdish political parties still look at women as an auxiliary women's group with the responsibility for cooking for festive events and for putting on their colourful cloth to represent Kurdish culture in Sweden. The ones that are more progressive, have good rhetoric, but in practice they are the same. When I approached the Swedish government for funding, they referred me back to the Kurdish Federation,[5] exactly the source that I wanted to avoid. It is difficult to build an alliance with Swedish feminist groups, they think ethnic minority women are politically incapable of developing a critical feminist platform. I decided the only funding chance that I might have is to create an organization for immigrant women where Kurdish women could be one of the groups. Through this process, I have been ostracized by the community, I have been threatened, and I feel abandoned by everyone: my community, my hostland, and feminists.

Listening to Kurdish women's narratives of contestation in learning and living in Sweden, urged me to take their grievances to the Swedish government officials.[6] I met a group of Integration Board policy-makers and presented a succinct summary of the result of my research. At this point my goal was to instil in the consciousness of policy-makers that stories of Kurdish women's experience living in Sweden are not the cries of helpless women for government hand-outs. Rather, these narrations should be seen as advocacy tools to change, develop and improve public policy. Briefly, what I presented were the following points: (1) Kurdish women have experienced multiple forced displacements before arriving in Europe or Canada; (2) Kurdish women are not a homogeneous group; there is a great deal of diversity among them based on class, education, religion, rural/urban background, and language. These differences are exacerbated by other factors such as political affiliation and citizenship in the dominant nation-states of Iraq, Iran, Turkey, and Syria; (3) Kurdish women demonstrate a high level of political and social consciousness on issues of patriarchy, equality, and social justice; (4) the experience of war, multiple forced displacements, and diaspora, have equipped Kurdish women with a complex learning mechanism and strategy. This includes survival, resistance, struggle, and renewed social and political learning; and (5) Kurdish women have a critical approach to the notion of 'homeland' and 'hostland' due to years of oppression by the dominant nation-states, semi-colonial domination of their homeland, Kurdistan, and the hegemonic role of Western powers in more recent histories. There is one force that pervades all these forms of domination, and that is patriarchy. It was within this context that I presented the following two recommendations which were the result of months of listening to and talking to policy-makers about Kurdish women:

1   Kurdish women are actively resisting being identified in cultural terms. Many Kurdish women who have sought asylum in Europe and North America have been active in struggles against militarism, Islamism, patriarchy and oppression. Often male-dominated, conservative cultural organizations represent neither the experiences, nor the political interests of Kurdish women. Government agencies must guard against using male-dominated cultural organizations as conduits for assessing the concerns and interests of the Kurdish community.

2   As part of their process of integration into Swedish society, Kurdish women are eager to be understood as autonomous, civically-minded members of the community. Kurdish women have been overshadowed in the public perception by the concerns and attitudes of culturally and religiously conservative men. Many women are eager for opportunities to reconstruct their histories from a feminist perspective. Projects that enable Kurdish women to produce photo exhibitions, community theatre projects, and autobiographical writing, will help to counter the recent overemphasis on Islam, nationalism and traditionalism in Swedish media and policy.

I faced a heavy and long silence. Silences often say more than words. The political and cultural agency of Kurdish women in the above mentioned recommendations contrasted sharply with the ways in which Swedish officials apparently envisioned their agency as monolithic and passive. It is this construction of immigrant women which alienates and isolates them and leaves them little choice but to limit their struggle to the comfort zone of known antagonism, that is, national patriarchy. Thus, the notion which I introduced above of *Closure*, that is, ending the traditional and limiting realm of political involvement in the national struggle into a new *Opening*, that is, expanding their knowledge and practice of feminist activism through a vast array of social engagement in Sweden such as human rights, anti-globalization, anti-war, and environmental movements. However, the ruling relations have permeated into these movements which make them another space where the patriarchal, racist, and colonial relations are reproduced, thus, once more *Closure*, where the marks of alienation and isolation are visible on the prematurely aged bodies of Kurdish women and on the loss of vibrancy and resiliency in their soul. A remarkable Kurdish woman *peshmarge* said:

> They sent me to work in a factory. The work was heavy and repetitive. I got tired soon and could not continue, but needed the government assistance. I told them about my neck and back pain, they gave me a limited sick leave and sent me to a doctor. The pills and staying at home made me very depressed. I was totally isolated, there was not even a neighbour to talk to. I saw the doctor again, this time they put me on anti-depressant drugs which made my situation even worse. Because of long absence from my job, they put me first on short-term disability and now I am on long-term disability.

These categories have many implications for me. I am limited in what I can do, I am limited in what I can learn and most importantly I don't feel good about myself.

It is heartening to read the introductory remarks of Bettina Bochynek, the Coordinator of the International Adult Learns at the UNESCO Institute for Education where she states (National Institute of Adult Continuing Education, 2005):

> The insights gained through listening to learners are at the same time very pragmatic and functional, in that they can help design policies and good quality learning provision based on the needs and aspirations of learners. On the other hand, listening to adult learners and making them partners in negotiation for both policy development and improved learning provision is imperative if we really want to achieve active citizenship and democratic cultures.

However, I have tried to argue so far that even when immigrant women loudly and clearly state their demands through the narration of stories, those with the power to make national policies still fail them in achieving their rights as a citizen. In the imagination of policy-makers, immigrant women are not constructed as 'citizens' with a desire to participate and contribute to a democratic culture. In explaining this act of exclusion, it is important to remember that this alienating construction *cannot* simply be explained by immigrant women's class location, or race and ethnicity or even their gender. It is their total subjectivity, that is, they are gendered by capital, raced by capital, and they are embodied by this relation between labour and capital. Himani Bannerji writes:

> Even forms of extraction of surplus value involve the location of certain people in the working class, and in sub-classes of the working class. And this involves the organization of patriarchy. And in Canada it involves the organization of how to read the body, the skin. In order to find your most exploitable worker you would rely on whoever is socially least valued. How else can concrete exploitation occur?
>
> (1998: 13)

Immigrant women are marginalized by capital, and we can now see that their marginalization is not a product of contingent structures, but is constitutive and necessary to the capitalist relation. We study women and come to know what particular groups of marginalized women of colour experience *learning* or *training*. We can trace policy initiatives globally such as Adult Learners' Week and identify women who are targeted as the recipients of *training* schemes from language training to literacy or to the delivery of service-related, minimum-pay, unsecured oriented jobs and we can trace women whose *learning* will be celebrated, be it new computer skills or enhancing personal communication skills. I think, it is plausible to claim that women of colour more often are considered *trainees* than *learners* (Mojab 1999, 2000). To elaborate further on this point, I will conclude this chapter by arguing that we need to interrogate the notion of lifelong learning deeper to uncover the ruling relations embedded in it.

Uncovering ruling relations in lifelong learning

The particularity of the learning/educational experience of Kurdish immigrants is rather obvious. The life histories of these new citizens of Sweden distinguish them from indigenous citizens. It is in this particularity, however, that we can detect universal trends in the educational crises we face in a rapidly changing world. It is in this micropolitics of context, subjectivity, and struggle that we can detect the macropolitics of global economic structure.

I argue that the ways in which Kurdish women experience lifelong learning in Sweden, discussed above, partially explain the disjuncture between an individual learning and training goals of lifelong learning policy in the Western world. It is partial because I need to show how these processes are linked to the underlying ideology and social relations embedded in lifelong learning. As I have tried to argue, Kurdish women, as part of their process of integration into European society, are eager to be understood as autonomous, civically-minded members of the community. Many women are eager for opportunities to reconstruct their histories and culture from a feminist-transnational perspective. However, in the practice of the lifelong learning policy, Kurdish women are isolated, racialized, and culturalized learners/workers. Their learning desire to initiate projects that enable them to produce, for example, photo exhibitions, community theatre projects and autobiographical writings, as social and collective learning projects to counter growing Islamophobia, racism, nationalism, xenophobia, and patriarchy in Europe, has not been well received by Swedish government and feminist organizations. Some urgent questions are: (1) Why does the concept of lifelong learning arise at this particular moment? (2) How does lifelong learning relate to the capitalist mode of production? (3) What are the contradictions within the concept of the lifelong learning? (4) How can these contradictions be made visible?

To answer these questions, we must consider how *learning* is deployed within capitalist relations of production where in the twenty-first century we are faced with a condition that Davis (2004) calls the era of 'surplus humanity'. The current theorization of lifelong learning, underpinned by critics of human capital theory, points out that if the life experiences and learning of marginalized workers were recognized, they could attain equality through a better paid job (Livingstone 1999b). This critique leaves the organization's ownership of workers' learning unchallenged. However, if we understand work relations in the context of capitalism, the worker cannot be confused with the idea of capital. To understand the relationship between the worker and capital, we must recognize that labour power is a commodity in the capitalist mode of production. As a commodity, labour power is subject to the law of supply and demand, and workers are in direct competition with one another to sell their commodity. In this configuration, knowledge and skill acquisition can become part of the competition. The more the concept of 'lifelong learning' becomes synonymous with market requirements, the more it becomes commodified, and alienated from the learner (Rikowski 2002).

Debates on lifelong learning focus on the differentiation of the learning process into formal, non-formal, and informal processes (for an excellent survey, see Colley *et al.* 2003). While these distinctions are useful, they offer little insight into contemporary dynamics of learning. It is not difficult to see how these forms of learning coexist in most contexts, both individual and collective. In the Kurdish case examined here, learners want to remove these distinctions. They want their informal and non-formal learning to be treated as formal education, and even continued as such. What is informal learning from the point of view of their new nation-state is, for them, more significant than any formal education they may have access to.

These learners experienced on a daily basis, in their pre-Swedish lives, traumatic events, each of which dwarfs the experience of a decade of learning in a school environment. As members of a communist movement involved in struggles against a theocratic state, they were, to borrow from a distant but similar context, 'making their own history'.[7] Having been born into the 'normal life' of a rather secular patriarchal society under Iran's monarchical regime, they experienced the rise of a modern theocracy, which targeted women as its first and most important realm of Islamization. In their struggle to turn the tide of this powerful theocracy, these women left their homes, their villages, towns and cities, joined a political party, took up arms, engaged in political and ideological training, publishing, broadcasting, organizing, and building an equal regime of gender relations in their political community. For a while, they lived in villages in 'liberated areas' of Iranian Kurdistan, where they promoted ideas of socialism and feminism. Their difficult lives, subjected to the unceasing military operations of the Islamic regime, and chemical bombing of the Ba'thist regime of Iraq, were full of successes and defeats. In these struggles, they also experienced the indifference or intervention of the capitalist West. While leading these struggles, they translated and sang the Internationale and the songs of Joe Hill, ironically a Swedish immigrant in the USA. It is difficult to imagine how the national educational system of Sweden, in spite of its social democratic history, can value or build on the experiences of these new citizens. Here the nation, and its dominant class, are in conflict with some of its citizens, their class and gender consciousness, and their internationalism, nurtured in part by the legacy of a Swedish singer.

If the nation-state is highly selective in its educational learning priorities, the market is even more restrictive in its lifelong learning vision. While the idea of lifelong learning dates back to the beginning of the twentieth century (Yeaxlee 1929), today's conceptualizations try to vindicate it by tying it to the capitalism's restlessness, a condition in which, to quote Marx, 'everything solid melts into air'. The market no longer tolerates a once-and-for-all education, and, accordingly, does not offer any such lifetime single jobs. All have already melted into air. In this almost total subservience to the dictates of the market and its jobs, there is no room for building alternative lives, communities, cultures, or societies such as the ones the Wobblies were contemplating in American factories in the early twentieth century and these Kurdish women were recreating in their mountains later in the century. There is also little space, in this market-based and nation-centred learning, for the pursuit of the democratic visions of, for instance, the Hamburg Declaration on Adult Learning (1997). It would be apparently more appropriate to call 'lifelong learning' 'market-time learning'.

Notes

1   This project was funded by the Social Science and Humanities Research Council of Canada.
2   The full text is available on http://www.unesco.org/education/uie/confintea/pdf/con5eng.pdf.
3   To protect the anonymity of Kurdish women, pseudonyms are used. The quotes are my translation.
4   There is a growing literature on the impact of war on women which alludes to some of the ways women's struggle under the condition of war potentially can turn to powerful and lasting learning for life. Among others, see Turshen (1998), Menon and Bhasin (1998), and Sideris (2001).
5   This is the Federation of Kurdish Associations in Sweden (Kurdiska Riksförbundet, Stockholm, http://www.kurdiskarf.org), which is the umbrella organization for various Kurdish community organizations.
6   On 2 October 2002, a seminar was organized at the Swedish Integration Board in Linköping where I made a presentation on the topic of 'Gender, Nation, and State Policy: Kurdish Women in Canada, Britain and Sweden'.
7   This is based on Stree Shakti Sanghatan *We Were Making History: Women and the Telangana Uprising* (1989).

Chapter 13

Conclusion

Becky Francis and Carole Leathwood

Women and lifelong learning: a troubling body of knowledge

Chapters in this book have traversed a diverse range of subjects and contexts, addressing issues as apparently varied as the education of elderly women; the experiences of black academics; and the constructions of masculinity among young non-participant working-class men. Yet across this diverse account of gender issues in lifelong learning, strong themes have emerged. The most persistent has probably been the problematisation of the encroachment by economic rationales as shaping and driving the concept of lifelong learning. Specifically, the dominance of the human capital model which (as Jacky Brine and Jill Blackmore's chapters depict) is now hegemonic across the OECD, and arguably, given the directive power of the World Bank, increasingly across the 'developing' world. In this view, the function (and we use that word deliberately) of lifelong learning is to ensure economic survival in a competitive global market place via development of a responsive, flexible and highly skilled workforce. As contributers have argued, this model can and sometimes does incorporate a liberal account of lifelong learning increasing social inclusion and well-being – this view maintains that there may be individual and social benefits simultaneous with the perpetuation of a robust national economy. But as Carole Leathwood observes, the social justice elements of lifelong learning policy (though in any case clearly subsumed to those of 'economic necessity') cause little dissonance, as both economic and 'social inclusion' narratives are equally concerned with 'inclusion into, conformity to, and the legitimation of, a starkly unequal and highly stratified society' (p. 49).

In keeping with key critics of neo-liberalism,[1] contributors to this book have drawn attention to the way in which the neo-liberal view of social and economic activity locates responsibility for economic success – both at a national level and at a personal level – with individuals, rather than with the state, or with structural factors. A neo-liberal version of subjectivity positions the self as gloriously free to determine their own trajectory, which is endlessly flexible and rich with opportunities there for the seizing. This agentic subject realises the responsibility they have, both at an individual and social level, to maximise their own potential and opportunities, and relishes embracing those aspects, skills which will help in this endeavour. Hence education becomes a further commodity in this consumerist model, with credentials to be added to the subject increasing marketablity (and, for the subject, spendability). As Jill Blackmore and others in this collection point out, this construction of what she brands the 'self-maximising self-interested individual' wantonly ignores that the self is gendered, 'raced' and 'classed' (among other structural and circumstantial aspects).

The influence of social structures versus individualised meritocracy

Hence the first of various tensions which contributors to this book have illuminated is the opposition between accounts that foreground structural or identity factors as influencing trajectories, and the discourse of individualised meritocracy perpetuated by neo-liberalism, which is hegemonic in contemporary policy. Various authors have shown how education is produced as a neutral domain, benefitting everyone equally. As Lyn Tett notes, the 'myth of meritocracy' implies that if one is 'good enough', they will be able to rise above the constraints of disadvantage – those who do not succeed fail due to individual inadequacy. This position does not recognise the unequal risks involved in uptake, which are so effectively illustrated by empirical data in several of the chapters. For example, a social construction of ability is particularly central to the discourse of meritocracy, as Sheila Riddell's discussion of the social construction and (somewhat unsystemised) allocation of the label 'dyslexia' poignantly illustrates. Her chapter shows how gender and social class (and presumably ethnicity too) mediate these associations and educational outcomes. Louise Archer and Penny Burke demonstrate how dominant neo-liberal discourses ignore the ways in which classsed and 'raced' constructions of gender interfere with the model of the 'rationale, agentic' subject. Louise's data illustrate how investments in particular (non-academic) performances of masculinity and femininity, coupled with often negative and undermining experiences of a compulsory education system that did not value their constructions and made them feel 'other' and stupid, dramatically reduce the appeal of lifelong learning for groups of working-class youth. Her chapter and that by Becky Francis also highlight the safety in particular 'gender- and class-appropriate' routes. These routes are underwritten by epistemologies that privilege some sorts of knowledge and learning over others, and by social assumptions and institutions that normalise, rather than contest, their classed, gendered and 'raced' uptake.

Authors draw on the case of women (and including analysis of social class and 'race', as well as other aspects of identity) to demolish the complicit myths of equality of choice and neutral meritocracy. Their data powerfully demonstrate the impact of embodied identities on the individual's interface with lifelong learning. This reinstatement of the social to radically challenge the notion of a-political and individualised meritocracy should not necessarily be seen as a structuralist account, as many of our contributors see identity as fluid and produced in discourse – however, they argue that material and environmental constraints are tied to different social positionings.

A masculine, middle-class white model of the lifelong learner

In chipping away the coating of neutrality that engulfs the policy presentation of lifelong learning, contributors to this book have revealed the 'unsaid' model of the lifelong learner. This model is based on masculine, Western, middle-class values, and produces white, young, middle-class men as 'normal' (hence 'othering' other learners). The chapters on policy illustrate the exclusions of women (and often of working-class and minority ethnic men) from policy. Several of the chapters analyse the ways in which middle-class norms and expectations pathologise working-class people, projecting deficit and assuming that 'remedial action' will need to be taken in order to 'bring them up to speed' (see Penny Burke's chapter). Heidi Mirza's chapter illuminates the ways in which particular subjectivities are excluded and included in the academy, with some (white, middle-class men) being more able to access and reproduce discourses of validity and authority than others. Her discussion highlights the ways in which members of this priviledged elite discursively bolster and reproduce their powerful positions. The issue of embodiment is also raised here as in other chapters. In this case, black female bodies are read as 'out of place' in the academy, but are simultaneously appropriated as 'exotic' representations of diversity for commercial ends. Minoritised embodiment is also raised in Shahrzad Mojab's chapter, which describes how the Kurdish women in her study were not heard, nor their learning recognised, by Swedish authorities (and feminists), due to their positioning in colonial and orientalist gender discourses as silent, oppressed by culture, and as uneducated (or their learning as having no validity).

Barbara Kamler's chapter illustrates how, due to the human capital rationale, the policy notion of lifelong learning is conceptualised around working lives rather than throughout lives. Clearly this model omits some groups (in this case, elderly women). Kamler uses this case to make the point that the apparently inclusive notion of 'widening participation' actually excludes certain groups.

It is recognition of the identity-laden nature of the supposedly neutral and meritocratic higher education system that deters participation for some working-class young people, Louise Archer argues. They see beyond the pompous veneer of neutrality to an upper/middle-class model that positions working-class people as Other and lacking – hence these young people see higher education as 'not for me'. Where the deficit notions evoked in programmes such as Aim Higher locate rationality in universities, and with partcipation in higher education, Louise's argument suggests that it is the working-class non-participants who have made a 'rational' choice. Hence, her chapter, and those of other authors in the later parts of the book, illustrate a point made frequently in the chapters on lifelong learning policy – how the model of subjectivity embedded in lifelong learning policy 'others' and excludes groups of people outside the model, yet covers up these exclusions and discursive 'unsaids' with seductive narratives of equal opportunity, 'choice' and meritocracy.

These arguments raise another theme threading through the book – the boundaries of the dominant policy conception of lifelong learning. Several authors elucidate the skills- and competencies-based focus of contemporary policy on lifelong learning, in keeping with the human capitalist rationale, to the exclusion of other forms of learning. Certain types of knowledge are valued, others are excluded. Several chapters, but particularly those by Sharhzad Mojab, Lynn Tett and Penny Burke, have shown how different groups of women find their knowledge and prior learning invalidated, or belittled, by the dissecting discursive knives that delineate between 'formal and informal' knowledge, 'academic and vocational', 'community and individual', 'public and private'.

So if women are excluded, and feminine-type knowledge[2] invalidated by dominant policy models, what other or resulting issues particularly face women in the current lifelong learning context? Helen Colley's chapter drew out the ways in which constructions of femininity as emotional and emotionally invested, responsible for others, and vocationally oriented, can manifest in particularly psychically charged relations with lifelong learning and teaching. Jill Blackmore also observed how the discourse of lifelong learning has an enticing appeal to women educators and managers, who have themselves been high achievers in education, and who seek to improve women's opportunities and to promote social change through lifelong learning. This point is evocative of Davies' (2003) claim that new managerial discourses on the restructuring of Higher Education in the UK and Australasia have seduced some feminists as being fairer and more inclusive to women than the previous paternalist model (she argues, of course, against both models). Jill Blackmore maintains that, 'Lifelong learning is a powerful discourse because it penetrates to the soul of educational work about self improvement, while making individuals more self-managing of their own lifelong learning' (p. 25). Yet the psychic costs of working in higher education, for black women in particular, are clearly illustrated in Heidi Mirza's chapter.

The challenge to economic models of lifelong learning from the 'voices on the margins'

The human capital model of lifelong learning is challenged by cases such as the older women participants discussed by Barbara Kamler, and indeed, as Jill Blackmore points out, the case of women generally. Jill reports that women invest more in lifelong learning than do men (and achieve highly), but are repaid less. They continue to earn less than men (and middle-class white men continue to dominate top positions in both public and private sectors), and to work in fields which are deemed less prestigious and afforded less status. And these inequaities are exaccerbated for working-class women. As Jill notes, in spite of women's success in lifelong learning courses, for particular groups of these women, the prospects of gaining secure and fulfilling employment that utilises and financially rewards their capabilities and potential are not high. This point is underlined by the experiences of the Kurdish women reported in Sharhzad Mojab's chapter.

The potential role of lifelong learning

Thus far, these themes have been highly critical and somewhat pessemistic. Sharhzad Mojab probably takes this cynicism furthest – she argued forcefully that the present model of lifelong learning is market-driven, functioning to meet the demands of capitalism. She maintains that lifelong learning is simply an ideology used to locate responsibility for failure with the individual and to offer an illusory 'ray of hope' for a more engaged citizenry. More egalitarian and emancipatory intentions and possibilities are, she (and other contributors) argue, being squeezed out by market concerns and demands. Hence Sharhzad concludes that lifelong learning should more accurately be called 'market-time learning'.

On the other hand, more optimistic positions are also represented. Lyn Tett and Barbara Kamler's chapters emphasize the positive benefits of lifelong learning to women – both for their improved self-worth and self-perception (encouraging feelings of validity, empowerment and agency), and for the social and economic benefits. Both chapters provide examples of pedagogy and learning that are 'women-friendly', reflexive, and that attempt to challenge the traditional boundaries of both of what constitutes lifelong learning, and the location of authority in the teacher rather than the learner. And both chapters recount the elation and excitment felt by some of the women engaging in these practices.

Implications

As we have seen, the neo-liberal view of the self, and the human capital view of lifelong learning which neo-liberalism embraces, have become ubiquitous in the West. Contributors to this collection have mobilised diverse theories to critique and deconstruct the dominant view – structuralism and poststructuralism, historic materialism, New Literacy Studies, radical feminism, discourse analysis. There is always a danger that while we (and other writers) are adept in critiquing neo-liberalism and deconstructing the discursive productions that it perpetuates, we struggle to imagine, or to suggest, alternatives. Indeed, this skew towards critique rather than challenge and/or revisioning has been a depressing feature of many left-leaning academic conferences and meetings we have attended recently. Contestation is of course impeded by the prevalence of neo-liberal assumptions and rationales, which naturalise the human capitalist and meritocratic model of lifelong learning to the extent that any suggested alternatives are positioned as lunacy (and as irresponsibility on both a personal and national-economic level too). Clearly we are facing the problem that economic assumptions and connected moral discourses are infecting the very notion of learning, so that learning becomes not gaining and constructing information and understanding of the world, but rather 'upskilling'. Learning becomes the signification of self-responsibility and citizenship (based on a neo-liberal model of responsible citizenship) rather than about personal pleasure, or enabling questioning and critique. But, again, most of us in the West have to some extent invested and are implicated in this model and the lifestyle it affords us. So how to go forward?

Thankfully, this book does not fall prey to what we are tempted to allude to as 'banging on about neo-liberalism without envisioning alternatives'. It includes a great many ideas and suggestions that can be drawn upon as implications for practice, and we shall endeavour to undertake this now. Obviously our intention is not to draw together a coherent and unified argument from disparate and passionately held opinions. Rather, we seek to highlight ideas emerging in particular chapters to make suggestions for policy and practice.

Implications for policy

Given the preceding critique, it is evident that if policy-makers are genuinely interested in widening participation and social justice, they need to be more attuned to the different life conditions and constraints (or facilitations) that impact on individuals' ability to participate in lifelong learning. Further, there needs to be greater awareness of the masculinised, classed and 'raced' epistemology on which the institutions supporting lifelong learning operate their practices. Such recognition might enable greater reflection on current hierarchical delineations between teachers and learners, and between different 'kinds' of knowledge (and indeed curriculum subjects). It must also facilitate avoidance of the deficit model which currently tends to be applied to 'non-traditional'[3] learners.

Concerning women particularly, policies need to facilitate and protect the family–work balance. Not simply ensuring that women have space and support for carework and so on, but also expecting that men too will need to engage in these aspects. In this sense, feminists too need to reflect on liberal feminism's increasing inculcation in viewing lifelong learning as facilitating women's equal representation and participation in the capitalist market-place, rather than challenging the values upon which this model is based, and its invalidation of other aspects of life.

Further, a far more inclusive idea of what counts as 'knowledge' needs to be embraced, along with reflection on the various hierarchies of knowledge and curriculum subjects exisiting at present. Policy-makers need to be aware of the potential benefits of lifelong learning for social as well as economic capital, and the validity of pursuing learning for purposes other than the economic.

Implications for practice

For practitioners in lifelong learning there have been several suggestions for challenging hegemonic gendered assumptions and creating more socially just practice. Key ideas include:

• *Reflection and reflexivity*. Helen Colley recommends we reflect on the gendered nature of our implication and investment in teaching and learning, and the ways in which these impact both on our practice and on our quality of life. Further practitioners might encourage student reflection, enabling students to tease out and discuss such discursive constructions and their implications. Such pedagogic practices may provide the reflective tools with which to potentially avoid their own implication in such practices. As Helen notes, 'They might then be empowered to go beyond feminine ways to conform, and find feminist ways to resist' (p. 119). Reflexivity also applies to our interactions with colleagues. Mirza has challenged academics to be 'ever vigilant of excluding practices' (p. 151) if we wish to transform our institutions into democratic, inclusive spaces.
• *Development of feminist pedagogy*. Much has been written and debated concerning the very possibility of feminist pedagogy. However, whatever position we take on this, few feminists in the current policy climate will debate the benefits of developing teaching practice that 'challenges competitive individualism, aims to change the culture of educational and other public institutions, and emphasises the importance of a liberatory education' (Leathwood, p. 52). Such practice might emphasise the intellectual, emotional, practical, pleasurable and political possibilities of learning, as opposed to reducing learning to targets, standards and skills. Interrogating the social construction of knowledge, and notions of what counts as valuable or expert knowledge would be an integral aspect of practice which hopes to 'queer' existing hierarchies.
• *Acknowledgement of 'risk'*. Educationalists need to recognise the emotional, economic and social risks for working-class women undertaking lifelong learning, and to address these issues in course design and with students.
• *Inclusive application of lifelong learning to all age groups*. Barbara Kamler's chapter provides an excellent example of the positive impact of teaching and learning across generations (as opposed to seeing learning as exclusively geared to updating skills for the workforce). Clearly an important aspect of work with older learners is their positioning as 'knowledge producers', rather than simply as consumers of knowledge.

Taken together, the chapters in this book provide a vision of collective, rather than solely individualist, constructions of learning and processes of knowledge production. The potential for the collective benefits from lifelong learning, including the possibilities of social change, is also evoked. They remind us of the need to continue to speak out against the moral and social paucity of neo-liberalism, and to continue to name and shame the inequalities it produces. They also speak volumes for the importance of a feminist analysis, and urge us to continue to subvert, re-define and reclaim educational spaces.

Notes

1   See for example, Rose (1999), Fraser (1993), Du Gay (1996), Bauman (2005) and Walkerdine (2003).
2   For example, humanities and arts, community learning, learning from the private sphere such as that relating to carework, etc.
3   'Non-traditional' being a phrase that very effectively illuminates the unspoken model of the 'normal' (traditional) learner!

Bibliography

Aalberts, T.E. (2004) 'The future of sovereignty in multilevel governance Europe: a constructivist reading', *Journal of Common Market Studies* 42(1): 23–46.

Abberley, P. (1987) 'The concept of oppression and the development of a social theory of disability', *Disability, Handicap and Society* 2: 5–19.

Adam, B., Beck, U. and Van Loon, J. (2000) *The Risk Society and Beyond: Critical Issues for Social Theory*, London: Sage.

Ahmed, S. (2004) *The Cultural Politics of Emotion*, Edinburgh: University of Edinburgh Press.

Ahmed, S. (2005) 'The non-performativity of anti-racism', paper presented at SUNY New York, 6 April.

Ainley, P. and Bailey, B. (1996) *The Business of Learning: Staff and Student Experiences of Further Education in the 1990s*, London: Cassell.

Albeit, P. (2000) 'On a contradictory way to a learning society: a critical approach', in S. Ball (ed.) *Sociology of Education: Major Themes*, vol 3, London: RoutledgeFalmer.

Allman, P. (1999) *Revolutionary Social Transformation: Democratic Hopes, Political Possibilities and Critical Education*, Westport, CT: Bergins and Garvey.

American Association of University Women (1992) *How Schools Short-change Girls*, Washington, DC: AAUW.

Angwin, J., Blackmore, J., Harrison, L. and Shacklock, G. (2001) *Job Planning Pathway: Report to Geelong City Council Youth Services*, Geelong, VIC: Deakin Centre for Education and Change.

Angwin, J., Harrison, L., Kamp, A. and Shacklock, G. (2004) *The Young Parent's Access Project: A Research Report*, Geelong, VIC: Deakin University Press.

Anthias, F. (2001) 'The concept of "social division" and theorising social stratification: looking at ethnicity and class', *Sociology* 35(4): 835–54.

AoC (2005) *AoC Briefing on Protecting Adult Learning*, February, London: Association of Colleges: http://www.aoc.co.uk/aoc/Members/comms/campaigns/adultlearning-resources/adultlearningbriefing.doc (accessed 6 December 2005).

Arber, S. and Evandrou, M. (eds) (1993) *Ageing, Independence and the Life Course*, London: Jessica Kingsley.

Arber, S. and Ginn, J. (1995) *Connecting Gender and Ageing: A Sociological Approach*, Buckingham: Open University Press.

Archer, L. (2003a) *Race, Masculinity and Schooling: Muslim Boys and Education*, Maidenhead: Open University Press.

Archer, L. (2003b) 'Social class and higher education', in L. Archer, M. Hutchings and A. Ross (eds) *Higher Education and Social Class*, London: RoutledgeFalmer.

Archer, L. (2005) 'The impossibility of girls' educational success: entanglements of gender, "race", class and sexuality in the production and problematisation of educational femininities', invited paper at ESRC Seminar Series on Girls in Education 3–16, University of Cardiff, 24 November.

Archer, L. and Francis, B. (2006) *Understanding Minority Ethnic Achievement: The Role of Race, Class, Gender and 'Success'*, London: RoutledgeFalmer.

Archer, L. and Hutchings, M. (2000) 'Bettering yourself'? Discourses of risk, cost and benefit in ethnically diverse, young working class non-participants' constructions of HE', *British Journal of Sociology of Education* 21(4): 555–74.

Archer, L. and Leathwood, C. (2003) 'Identities, inequalities and higher education', in L. Archer, M. Hutchings and A. Ross (eds) *Higher Education and Social Class: Issues of Exclusion and Inclusion*, London and New York: RoutledgeFalmer.

Archer, L. and Yamashita, H. (2003a) ' "Knowing their limits"? Identities, inequalities and inner city school leavers' post-16 aspirations', *Journal of Education Policy* 18(1): 53–69.

Archer, L. and Yamashita, H. (2003b). 'Theorising inner-city masculinities: "race", class, gender and education', *Gender and Education* 15(2): 115–32.

Archer, L., Halsall, A. and Hollingworth, S. (forthcoming, 2007) 'Class, gender, (hetero)sexuality and schooling: paradoxes within working class girls' engagement with education and post-16 aspirations', *British Journal of Sociology of Education*.

Archer, L., Halsall, A., Hollingworth, S. and Mendick, H. (2005a) *Dropping Out and Drifting Away: An Investigation of Factors Affecting Inner-City Pupils' Identities, Aspirations and Post-16 Routes*, Report for the Esmee Fairbairn Foundation, London: IPSE, London Metropolitan University.

Archer, L., Hollingworth, S. and Halsall, A. (2005b) ' "University's not for me – I'm a Nike person": Inner-city young people's negotiations of "new" class identities and educational engagement', paper presented at the British Sociological Association Annual Conference, April, University of York.

Archer, L., Hutchings, M. and Leathwood, C. (2001a) 'Engaging with commonality and difference: theoretical tensions in the analysis of working class women's educational discourses', *International Studies in Sociology of Education* 11(1): 51–71.

Archer, L., Hutchings, M., Ross, A. with Leathwood, C., Gilchrist, R. and Phillips, D. (2003) *Higher Education and Social Class: Issues of Exclusion and Inclusion*, London: RoutledgeFalmer.

Archer, L., Maylor, U., Read, B. and Osgood, J. (2004) *An Exploration of the Attitudinal, Social and Cultural Factors Impacting on Year 10 Student Progression*, Report for the Learning and Skills Council, London: IPSE, London Metropolitan University.

Archer, L., Pratt, S. and Phillips, D. (2001b) 'Working class men's constructions of masculinity and negotiations of (non)participation in higher education', *Gender and Education* 13(4): 431–49.

Arnot, M., David, M. and Weiner, G. (1999) *Closing the Gender Gap*, Cambridge: Polity Press.

Audas, R. and Dolton, P. (1999) Paper presented at Royal Economics Society Annual Conference 29 March–1 April, Nottingham.

Australian Bureau of Statistics (2004) *Labour Statistics*, Canberra: Australian Government Printing Service.

Australian Vice Chancellor's Committee (AVCC) (2004) *Summary Statistics*, Canberra: AVCC.

Avis, J. (in press) 'From reproduction to learning cultures: post-compulsory education in England', *British Journal of Sociology of Education*.

Back, L. (2004) 'Ivory towers? The academy and racism', in I. Law, D. Phillips and L. Turney (eds) *Institutional Racism in Higher Education*, Stoke-on-Trent: Trentham Books.

Ball, S. (1990) *Politics and Policy Making in Education: Explorations in Policy Sociology*, London: Routledge.

Ball, S., Maguire, M. and Macrae, S. (2000) *Choice, Pathways and Transitions Post-16: New Youth, New Economies in the Global City*, London: RoutledgeFalmer.

Ball, S. J. and Vincent, C. (1998) ' "I heard it on the grapevine": "hot" knowledge and school choice', *British Journal of Sociology of Education*, 19: 377–400.

Bannerji, H. (1998) 'Gender, race, class, and socialism', *New Socialist*, February: 13.

Barnes, C. (1991) *Disabled People in Britain and Discrimination*, London: Hurst and Co.

Barr, J. (1999) 'Women, adult education and really useful knowledge', in J. Crowther, I. Martin, and M. Shaw (eds) *Popular Education and Social Movements in Scotland Today*, Leicester: NIACE.

Bartky, S. L. (1990) *Femininity and Domination: Studies in the Phenomenology of Oppression*, New York: Routledge.

Bates, I. (1991) 'Closely observed training: an exploration of links between social structures, training and identity', *International Studies in Sociology of Education* (1): 225–43.

Bathmaker, A. M. and Avis, J. (2005) 'Becoming a lecturer in further education in England: the construction of professional identity and the role of communities of practice', *Journal of Education for Teaching* 31(1): 47–62.

Bauman, Z. (2004) *Wasted Lives: Modernity and its Outcasts*, Cambridge: Polity Press.

Bauman, Z. (2005) *Work, Consumerism and the New Poor*, 2nd edn, Buckingham: Open University Press.

Beck, U. (1992) *Risk Society: Towards a New Modernity*, London: Sage.

Bekhradnia, B. (2003) *Widening Participation and Fair Access: An Overview of the Evidence*, Oxford: Higher Education Policy Institute.

Berg, I. (1970) *Education and Jobs: The Great Training Robbery*, New York: Praeger Publishers, Center for Urban Education.

Berliner, W. (2004) 'Where have all the young men gone?' *The Guardian*, 18 May.

Bhattacharyya, G. (1998) *Tales of Dark Skinned Women: Race, Gender and Global Culture*, London: UCL Press.

Bhavnani, R., Mirza, H. S. and Meetoo, V. (2005) *Tackling the Roots of Racism: Lessons for Success*, Bristol: Policy Press.

Biggart, A. (2002) 'Attainment, gender, and minimum-aged school leavers' early routes in the labour market,' *Journal of Education and Work* 15: 145–61.

Blackmore, J. (1997) 'The gendering of skill and vocationalism in twentieth century Australian education', in A. Halsey, H. Lauder, P. Brown and A. Stuart Wells (eds) *Education, Culture, Economy and Society*, Oxford: University Press, pp. 224–39.

Blackmore, J. (2005) 'Global human rights education for women and girls: strategic feminist and educational issues', in W. Hesford and W. Kozol (eds) *Just Advocacy: Women's Human Rights, Transnational Feminisms and the Politics of Representations*, New Brunswick, NJ: Rutgers University Press.

Blackmore, J. and Angwin, J. (1997) 'Educational outworkers: the impact of restructuring upon women educators' work in post-compulsory education', *Forum of Education* 52(2): 1–23.

Blackmore, J. and Sachs, J. (2006) *Reforming and Performing Leaders: Gender, Educational Restructuring, and Organisational Change*, New York: SUNY.

Blair, T. (1998) quoted in Department for Education and Employment, *The Learning Age: A Renaissance for a New Britain*, London: Stationery Office.

Blanden, J., Gregg, P. and Machin, S. (2005) 'Intergenerational mobility in Europe and North America', London: The Sutton Trust.

Blau, D. M. (1999) 'The effect of child care characteristics on child development', *Journal of Human Resources* 34: 786–822.

Blaxter, L. and Tight, M. (1994) 'Juggling with time: how adults manage their time for lifelong education', *Studies in the Education of Adults* 26(2): 162–79.

Bourdieu, P. (1986) *Distinction: A Social Critique of the Judgement of Taste*, London: Routledge.

Bourdieu, P. (1997) 'Forms of capital', in H. Halsey, P. Lauder, P. Brown and A. S. Wells, (eds) *Education, Culture, Economy, Society*, Oxford: Oxford University Press.

Bourdieu, P. (2003) *Firing Back: Against the Tyranny of the Market 2*, London and New York: The New Press.

Bourdieu, P. and Wacquant, L. (1992) *An Invitation to Reflexive Sociology*, Oxford: Polity Press.

Bowl, M. (2003). *Non-Traditional Entrants to Higher Education: 'They talk about People Like Me'*, Stoke-on-Trent: Trentham Books.

Bowman, K. (ed.) (2004) *Equity in Vocational Education and Training: Research Readings*, Adelaide: NCVER.

Bradley, H. (1996) *Fractured Identities: Changing Patterns of Inequality*, Cambridge: Polity Press.

Brah, A. (1992) 'Difference, diversity and differentiation', in J. Donald and A. Rattansi (eds) *'Race', Culture and Difference*, London: Sage.

Brah, A. (1996) *Cartographies of Diaspora: Contesting Identities*, London: Routledge.

Brah, A. (2000) 'Difference, diversity, differentiation: processes of racialisation and gender', in L. Back and J. Solomos (eds) *Theories of Race and Racism: A Reader*, London and New York: Routledge, pp. 431–46.

Brewer, R. M. (1993) 'Theorising race, class and gender: the new scholarship of black feminist intellectuals and black women's labour', in S. M. James and A. P. A. Busia (eds) *Theorising Black Feminisms*. London, Routledge, pp. 13–30.

Brine, J. (1999) *UnderEducating Women: Globalising Inequality*, Buckingham: Open University Press.

Brine, J. (2000) 'TSER and the epistemic community of European social researchers', *Journal of European Social Policy* 10(3): 267–82.

Brine, J. (2002a) 'Further Education participation, European expansion and European erasure', *British Educational Research Journal* 28(1): 21–36.

Brine, J. (2002b) *The European Social Fund and the EU: Flexibility, Growth, Stability*, London: Continuum/Sheffield Academic Press.

British Psychological Society (1999) *Dyslexia, Literacy and Psychological Assessment Report of a Working Party of the Division of Educational and Child Psychology*, Leicester: BPS.

Broadfoot, P. and Pollard, A. (2000) 'The changing discourse of assessment policy: the case of English primary education', in A. Filer (eds) *Assessment: Social Practice and Social Product*, London: RoutledgeFalmer, pp. 11–26.

Burke, P. J. (2002) *Accessing Education Effectively Widening Participation*, Stoke-on-Trent: Trentham Books.

Burke, P. J. and Hermerschmidt, M. (2005) 'Deconstructing academic practices through self-reflexive pedagogies', in B. Street (ed.) *Literacies Across Educational Contexts: Mediating Learning and Teaching*, Philadelphia, PA: Caslon Press.

Bury, M. (1995) 'Ageing, gender and sociological theory', in S. Arber and J. Ginn (eds) *Connecting Gender and Ageing: A Sociological Approach*, Buckingham: Open University Press, pp. 15–29.

Butler, E. (2005) *Getting Real: A Report on Young Women, Girls, Working Futures, VET and VET in Schools*, Security4Women. Available at: http://www.security4women.com.

Butler, J. (1990) *Gender Trouble: Feminism and the Subversion of Identity*, London: Routledge.

Butterwick, S. (2004) 'What outcomes matter? Exploring welfare policy and programs from the perspectives of low-income women', in J. Gaskell, and K. Rubensen (eds) *Educational Outcomes for the Canadian Workplace: New Frameworks for Policy and Research*, Toronto: University of Toronto Press.

Cabinet Office (2001) *Towards Equality and Diversity: Implementing the Employment and Race Directive*, London: Cabinet Office.

Callender, C. and Wilkinson, D. (2003) '2002/03 student income and expenditure survey: students' income, expenditure and debt in 2002/03 and changes since 1998/99', London: Department for Education and Skills.

Campbell, C. (ed.) (2002) *Developing Inclusive Schooling: Perspectives, Policies and Practices*, Buckingham: Open University Press.

Canadian Statistics (2004) 'At a crossroads: first results from the 18–20 year old cohort of the YITS, Ottawa', *Statistics Canada* 2002.

Carby, H. (1997) 'White women listen! Black feminism and the boundaries of sisterhood', in H. S Mirza (ed.) *Black British Feminism*, London: Routledge.

Carter, J., Fenton S. and Modood, T. (1999) *Ethnicity and Employment in HE*, London: Policy Studies Institute.

Casey, K. (1993) *I Answer with my Life: Life Histories of Women Teachers Working for Social Change*, New York: Routledge.

Castells, M. (2004) 'Universities and cities in a world of global networks', Sir Robert Birley lecture, City University, 17 March, Available at: http://www.city.ac.uk/social/birley2004.html

CEC (Commission of the European Communities) (1993) *White Paper: Growth, Competitiveness, Employment: the Challenges and Ways Forward Into the 21st Century*, Luxembourg: Office for Official Publications of the European Commission (OOPEC).

CEC (1995) *White Paper: Education and Training: Teaching and Learning: Towards the Learning Society (COM(95)590)*, Luxembourg: OOPEC.

CEC (1997a) 'Treaty of Amsterdam amending the Treaty on the European Union, the Treaties establishing the European Communities and certain related acts', *Official Journal* 97: 1–144.

CEC (1997b) 'Special Luxembourg European Council on employment', *Bulletin of the European Communities*, 97(11): 7–13.

CEC (1999a) *The 1999 Employment Guidelines: Council Resolution of 22 February 1999*, Luxembourg: OOPEC.

CEC (1999b) 'Regulation (EC) No 1784/1999 of the European Parliament and of the Council of 12 July 1999 on the European Social Fund', *Official Journal*, L213: 13.8.99: 5–8.

CEC (1999c) *The Bologna Declaration on the European Space for Higher Education: a Joint Declaration of the European Ministers of Education*, Luxembourg: OOPEC.

CEC (2000a) Presidency conclusions: Lisbon European Council, 23 and 24 March 2000, http://europe.eu.int/council/off/concl.mar00_en.pdf

CEC (2000b) *Council Decision Establishing Youth Programme 2000–2006*, Luxembourg: OOPEC.

CEC (2000c) *Commission staff Working Paper: A Memorandum on Lifelong Learning*, Brussels: European Commission.

CEC (2000d) *A Memorandum on Lifelong Learning*, Brussels: Directorate General for Education, Training and Youth.

CEC (2001a) *Communication from the Commission: Making a European Area of Lifelong Learning a Reality*, Brussels: European Commission.

CEC (2001b) *White Paper: A New Impetus for European Youth*, Luxembourg: OOPEC.

CEC (2002) Council Resolution of 27 June 2002 on lifelong learning (2002/C 163/01), *Official Journal* C163/1 9.7.2002: 1–3.

CEC (2004a) *Communication from the Commission: Strengthening the Implementation of the European Employment Strategy, Including Proposal for a Council Decision on Guidelines for the Employment Policies of the Member States, and a Recommendation for a Council Recommendation on the Implementation of Member States' Employment Policies, COM(2004)239 FINAL, 7.4.2004*, Brussels: European Commission.

CEC (2004b) *Green Paper: Equality and Non-Discrimination in an Enlarged European Union*, Luxembourg: OOPEC.

CEC (2005a) 'Realising the European Higher Education Area – Achieving the Goals': Conference of European Higher Education Ministers: Contribution of the European Commission, Bergen, 19/20 May 2005, Brussels: European Commission.

CEC (2005b) *Communication to the Spring European Council: Working Together for Growth and Jobs: A New Start for the Lisbon Strategy, COM(2005)24, 2.2.05*, Brussels: European Commission.

CEC (2005c) *Commission Staff Working Paper: Progress towards the Lisbon Objectives in Education and Training, 2005 Report, SEC(2005)419, 22.3.05*, Brussels: European Commission.

CEC (2005d) *Report from the Commission to the Council, the European Parliament, the European Economic and Social Committee and the Committee of the Regions, on Equality between Women and Men, 2005*, Brussels: European Commission.

Chappell, C. and Yates, L. (2004) *Learning Identities*, Sydney: Allen and Unwin.

Clandinin, D. J. and Connelly, F. M. (1995) *Teachers' Professional Knowledge Landscapes*, New York: Teachers' College Press.

Clarke, C. (2004). *Speech to LSDA Summer Conference, 15 June*. London, http://www.dfes.gov.uk/speeches/speech.cfm?SpeechID=127 (accessed 1 August 2005).

Clegg, S. and McNulty, K. (2002) 'The creation of learner identities as part of social inclusion: gender, ethnicity and social space', *International Journal of Lifelong Learning* 21(6): 572–85.

Cockburn, C. (1981) 'The material of male power', *Feminist Review* 9: 41–58.

CoE (Council of Europe) (1973) *The Educational Needs of the 16–19 Age Group: The Janne Report*, Strasbourg: Council of Europe Press.

CoE (1992) *The Unemployment Trap: Long Term Unemployment and Low Educational Attainment in Six Countries*, Strasbourg: Council of Europe Press.

Coffield, F. (1999) 'Breaking the consensus: lifelong learning as social control', *British Education Research Journal* 25(4): 479–99.

Cole, M. (1998) 'Globalization, modernization and competitiveness: a critique of the labour project in education', *International Studies in Sociology of Education* 8(3): 315–32.

Colley, H. (2003) *Mentoring for Social Inclusion: A Critical Approach to Nurturing Mentor Relationships*, London: RoutledgeFalmer.

Colley, H. (2004) 'Learning experiences of adults mentoring socially excluded young people: issues of power and gender', in D. Clover (ed.) *Adult Education for Democracy, Social Justice, and a Culture of Peace*. Proceedings of the Joint International Conference of Adult Education Research Conference and the Canadian Association for the Study of Adult Education, Victoria, BC, Canada, pp. 95–100.

Colley, H. (2006) 'Learning to labour with feeling: class, gender and emotion in childcare education and training', *Contemporary Issues in Early Childhood* 7 (1).

Colley, H. and Hodkinson, P. (2001) 'Problems with *Bridging the Gap*: the reversal of structure and agency in addressing social exclusion', *Critical Social Policy* 21(3): 335–59.

Colley, H., Hodkinson, P. and Malcom, J. (2003) *Informality and Formality in Learning: A Report for the Learning and Skills Research Centre*, London: Learning and Skills Research Centre.

Colley, H., James, D., Tedder, M. and Diment, K. (2003) 'Learning as becoming in vocational education and training: class, gender and the role of vocational habitus', *Journal of Vocational Education and Training* 55(4): 471–96.

Collins, C., Kenway, J. and McLeod, J. (2001) *Factors Influencing the Education Performance of Males and Females in School and Their Initial Destinations After Leaving School*, Canberra: Department of Education, Training and Youth Affairs.

Collins, P. H. (1991) *Black Feminist Thought: Knowledge Consciousness and the Politics of Empowerment*, London: Routledge.

Collins, P. H. (1998) *Fighting Words: Black Women and the Search for Justice*, Minnesota, MN: University of Minnesota Press.

Conlon, G. and Chevalier, A. (2002) *Rates of Return to Qualifications: A Summary of Recent Evidence*, London: Council for Industry and Higher Education.

Connell, R. W. (1989), 'Cool guys, swots and wimps: the interplay of masculinity and education', *Oxford Review of Education* 15: 291–303.

Connell, R. W. (1989) *Gender and Power*, Cambridge: Polity Press.

Connell, R. W. (2000) *Masculinities*, London: Routledge.

Connolly, P. and Neill, J. (2001) 'Boys' underachievement, educational aspirations and constructions of locality: intersections of gender, ethnicity and social class', *International Studies in Sociology of Education* 11(2): 107–30.

Connor, H., Tyers, C., Modood, T. and Hillage, J. (2004) *Why the Difference? A Closer Look at Higher Education Minority Ethnic Students and Graduates*, London: DfES Research Report 552. Available at: www.dfes.gov/research

Corker, M. and Shakespeare, T. (eds) (2002) *Disability/Postmodernism*, London: Continuum.

Crace, J. (2005) 'Status anxiety', *Education Guardian*, 1 March 2005, pp. 2–3.

Crowther, J. (2004) ' "In and against" lifelong learning: flexibility and the corrosion of character', *International Journal of Lifelong Education* 23(2): 125–36.

Dale, A., Fieldhouse, F., Shaheen, N. and Kalra, V. (2002) 'Routes into education and employment for young Pakistani and Bangladeshi women in the UK', *Work, Employment and Society* 16(1): 5–27.

David, M. and Woodward, D. (1998) *Negotiating the Glass Ceiling*, London: Falmer.

Davies, B. (1989) *Frogs and Snails and Feminist Tales*, Sydney: Allen and Unwin.

Davies, B. (2003) 'Death to critique and dissent? The policies and practices of new managerialism and of "evidence-based practice" ', *Gender and Education* 15(1): 91–103.

Davies, B. (1994) *Poststructuralist Theory and Classroom Practice*, Geelong, VIC: Deakin University Press.

Davis, M. (2004) 'Planet of slums: urban involution and the informal proletariat', *New Left Review* 5–34.

Deem, R. and Ozga, J. (1997) 'Woman managing for diversity in a postmodern world', in C. Marshall (ed.) *Feminist Critical Policy Analysis*, vol. 2, London: Falmer Press.

Delors, J. (1996) *Learning; The Treasure Within, Report of the International Commission on Education for the 21st Century*, Paris: OECD.

Delphy, C. and Leonard, D. (1992) *Familiar Exploitation: A New Analysis of Marriage in Contemporary Western Societies*, Cambridge: Polity Press.

Department of Trade and Industry (2004) www.set4women.gov.uk

Department of Victorian Communities (2005) *Community Building Victoria*, http://www.dvc.gov.au

DfEE (1998) *The Learning Age: A Renaissance for a New Britain*, London: The Stationery Office. http://www.dfee.gov.uk/.

DfES (2003a). *21st Century Skills: Realizing Our Potential* (White Paper), London: The Stationery Office.

DfES (2003b) *The Future of Higher Education*, London: DfES.

DfES (2004) *The Level of Highest Qualification Held by Young People and Adults: England 2003*, National Statistics First Release, SRF 03/2004 London: Department for Education and Skills.

du Gay, P. (1996) *Consumption and Identity at Work*, London: Sage.

Dumbrell, T., de Montfort, R. and Finnegan, W. (2004) 'Equity in VET: an overview of the date for designated equity groups', in K. Bowman (ed.) *Equity in Vocational Education and Training: Research Readings*, Adelaide: NCVER.

Dwyer, P. and Wyn, J. (2001) *Youth, Education and Risk: Facing the Future*, London: RoutledgeFalmer.

Eckert, P. and McConnell-Ginet, S. (1999) 'New generalizations and explanations in language and gender research', *Language in Society* 28(2): 185–201.

ECU and JNCHES (2003) *Partnership for Equality: Action for Higher Education*, London: ECU (Equality Challenge Unit) and JNCHES (Joint Negotiating Committee for Higher Education Staff).

Edley, N. and Wetherell, M. (1995) *Men in Perspective: Practice, Power and Identity*, London: Prentice Hall/Harvester Wheatsheaf.

Edwards, R. (1993) *Mature Women Students: Separating or Connecting Family and Education*, London: Taylor and Francis.

Edwards, R. (1997) *Changing Place: Flexibility, Lifelong Learning and a Learning Society*, London: Routledge.

Edwards, R., Ransom, S. and Strain, M. (2002) Reflexivity: towards a theory of lifelong learning, *International Journal of Lifelong Education* 21(6): 525–36.

Elliott, J. (2000) 'The challenge of lifelong learning as a means of extending citizenship for women', *Studies in the Education of Adults* 32(1): 6–21.

Epstein, D., Elwood, J., Hey, V. and Maw, J. (1998) *Failing Boys?*, Buckingham: Open University Press.

Equal Opportunities Commission (2004) *Plugging Britain's Skills Gap: Challenging Gender Segregation in Training and Work*, Manchester: EOC and ESF.

Essed, P. (2000) 'Dilemmas in leadership: women of colour in the academy', *Ethnic and Racial Studies*, Special Issue, Gender and Ethnicity, 23(5): 888–904.

Fanon, F. ([1952] 1986) *Black Skin, White Masks*, London: Pluto Books.

Featherstone, M., Hepworth, M. and Turner, B. S. (eds) (1991) *The Body: Social Process and Cultural Theory*, London: Sage.

Fenwick, T. (2004) 'What happens to the girls? Gender, work and learning in Canada's "new economy" ', *Gender and Education* 16(2): 169–85.

Ferber, M. A. and Nelson, J. A. (eds) (1993) *Beyond Economic Man: Feminist Theory and Economics*, Chicago, IL: University of Chicago Press.

Field, J. (1998) *European Dimensions: Education, Training and the European Union*, London: Jessica Kingsley.

Field, J. (2000a) 'Governing the ungovernable: why lifelong learning policies promise so much yet deliver so little', *Educational Management and Administration* 28(3): 249–332.

Field, J. (2000b) *Lifelong Learning and the New Educational Order*, Stoke-on-Trent: Trentham Books.

Field, J. and Leicester, M. (eds) (2000) *Lifelong Learning: Education Across the Lifespan*, London: RoutledgeFalmer.

Fordham, S. (1996) *Blacked Out: Dilemmas of Race, Identity and Success at Capital High*, Chicago, IL: University of Chicago Press.

Foster, S. A. (2005) *Realising the Potential: A Review of the Future Role of Further Education Colleges*, London: DfES. http://www.dfes.gov.uk/furthereducation/fereview/finalreport.shtml (accessed 1 December 2005).

Foucault, M. (1972) *The Archeology of Knowledge*, London: Tavistock.

Foucault, M. (1973) *The Order of Things: An Archeology of the Human Sciences*, New York: Vintage.

Foucault, M. (1978) *The Will to Knowledge: The History of Sexuality*, vol. 1, Harmonds-worth: Penguin.

Francis, B. (1996) 'Doctor/nurse, teacher/caretaker: children's gendered choice of adult occupation in interviews and role plays', *British Journal of Education and Work* 9: 47–58.

Francis, B. (1998) *Power Plays: Primary School Children's Constructions of Gender, Power and Adult Work*, Stoke-on-Trent: Trentham Books.

Francis, B. (2000) 'The gendered subject: students' subject preferences and discussions of gender and subject ability', *Oxford Review of Education* 26: 35–48.

Francis, B. (2002a) 'Relativism, realism and feminism: an analysis of some theoretical tensions in research on gender identity', *Journal of Gender Studies* 11(1): 39–54.

Francis, B. (2002b) 'Is the future really female? The impact and implications of gender for 14–16 year olds' career choices', *Journal of Education and Work* 15: 75–87.

Francis, B. and Archer, L. (2005) 'British-Chinese pupils' constructions of gender and learning', *Oxford Review of Education* 31(4): 497–515.

Francis, B., Hutchings, M., Archer, L. and Melling, L. (2003) 'Subject choice and occu-pational aspirations among pupils at girls' schools', *Pedagogy, Culture and Society* 11: 423–40.

Francis, B., Osgood, J., Dalgety, J. and Archer, L. (2005) *Gender Equality in Work Experience Placements for Young People*, Manchester: Equal Opportunities Commission.

Francis, B. and Skelton, C. (2005) *Reassessing Gender and Achievement*, London: Routledge.

Fraser, N. (1993) 'Clintonism, welfare and the antisocial wage: the emergence of a neo-liberal political imagery', *Rethinking Marxism* 6: 9–23.

Fraser, N. (1994) 'Rethinking the public sphere: a continuation to the critique of actually existing democracy', in H. A. Giroux and P. McLaren (eds) *Between Borders: Pedagogy and the Politics of Cultural Studies*, New York: Routledge.

Fraser, N. (1997) *Justice Interruptus: Critical Reflections on the Post-Socialist Condition*, London: Routledge.

Fredman, S. (2002) *The Future of Equality in Britain*, Working paper series no. 5 Manchester: Equal Opportunities Commission.

Freire, P. (2004) *Pedagogy of Indignation*, Boulder, CO: Paradigm.

Fryer, R. H. (1997) *Learning for the Twenty-First Century: First Report of the National Advisory Group for Continuing Education and Lifelong Learning*, London: DfEE.

Fuller, A., Beck, V. and Unwin, L. (2005) *Employers, Young People and Gender Segregation*, Manchester: Equal Opportunities Commission.

Fullick, L. (2004) *Adult Learners in a Brave New World: Lifelong Learning Policy and Structural Changes since 1997*, Leicester: NIACE.

Furedi, F. (1997) *A Culture of Fear: Risk Taking and the Morality of Low Expectations*, London: Cassell.

Furedi, F. (2004) *Therapy Culture: Cultivating Vulnerability in an Uncertain Age*, London: Routledge.

Fuss, D. (1989) *Essentially Speaking*, London: Routledge.

Gaskell, J. (1992) *Gender Matters: From School to Work*, Buckingham: Open University Press.

Gaskell, J. and Rubensen, K. (eds) (2004) *Educational Outcomes for the Canadian Workplace: New Frameworks for Policy and Research*, Toronto: University of Toronto Press.

Gee, J., Hull, G. and Lankshear, C. (1996) *The New Work Order: Behind the Language of the New Capitalism*, Sydney: Allen and Unwin.

Gewirtz, S. (2001) 'Cloning the Blairs: New Labour's programme for the re-socialization of working-class parents', *Journal of Educational Policy* 16(4): 365–78.

Gewirtz, S. *et al.* (2005) 'The deployment of social capital theory in educational policy and provision: the case of education action zones in England', *British Educational Research Journal* 31(6): 651–74.

Gibbons. M., Limoges, C. and Nowotny, H. *et al.* (1994) *The New Production of Knowledge: The Dynamics of Science and Research in Contemporary Societies*, London: Sage.

Gilbert, P. (1993) *Gender Stories and the Language Classroom*, Geelong, VIC: Deakin University Press.

Gillborn, D. (2002) *Education and Institutional Racism*, London: Institute of Education, University of London, pp. 1–30.

Gillborn, D. and Mirza, H. (2000) *Educational Inequality: Mapping Race, Class and Gender*, London: HMI.

Gillborn, D. and Youdell, D. (2000) *Rationing Education: Policy, Practice, Reform, and Equity*, Buckingham: Open University Press.

Gilligan, C. (1995) 'Hearing the difference: theorizing connection', *Hypatia* 10(2): 120–7.

Giroux, H. A. and Giroux, S. S. (2004) *Take Back Higher Education: Race, Youth and the Crisis of Democracy in the Post-civil Rights Era*, New York: Palgrave Macmillan.

GLA (2005) *Delivering a Shared Heritage: The Mayor's Commission on African and Asian Heritage*, London: Greater London Authority.

Gleeson, D. and Shain, F. (1999) 'Managing ambiguity: between markets and managerialism – a case study of "middle managers" in further education', *Sociological Review* 47(3): 463–88.

Golding, B. (2004) 'Who is doing the hunting and gathering? An exploration of gender segmentation of adult learning in small and remote communities', in K. Bowman (ed.) *Equity in Vocational Education and Training: Research Readings*, Adelaide: NCVER.

Goodson, I. F. (ed.) (1992) *Studying Teachers' Lives*, London: Routledge.

Goodson, I. F. (1995) 'Studying the teacher's life and work', in J. Smyth (ed.) *Critical Discourses on Teacher Development*, London: Cassell.

Gorman, R. (2005) 'Social exclusion or alienation? An analysis of disability culture as an entry point for understanding disability oppression', paper presented at the Council of Europe and European Commission Youth Research Partnership seminar 'Social inclusion and young people', Budapest, 31 October–2 November.

Gouthro, P. A. (2004) 'Assessing power issues in Canadian and Jamaican women's experiences in learning via distance in higher education', *Teaching in Higher Education* 9(4): 449–61.

Gouthro, P. A. (2005) 'A critical feminist analysis of the homeplace as a learning site: expanding the discourse of lifelong learning to consider adult women learners', *International Journal of Lifelong Education* 24(1): 5–19.

Greed, C. (1991) 'Review symposium', *British Journal of Sociology of Education* 14: 103–7.

Hakim, C. (2002) 'Lifestyle preferences as determinants of women's differentiated labour market careers', *Work and Occupations* 29(4): 428–59.

Hall, S. (1992) 'New ethnicities', in J. Donald and A. Rattansi (eds) *'Race', Culture and Difference*, London: Sage.

Hall, S. (2000) 'The multicultural question', in B. Hesse (ed.) *Un/settled Multiculturalisms*, London: Zed Books.

Halpin, D. (2003) *Hope and Education*, London: RoutledgeFalmer.

Hamilton, M. (1996) 'Adult literacy and basic education', in R. Fieldhouse (ed.) *A History of Modern British Adult Education*, Leicester: NIACE.

Hamilton, M. and Barton, D. (2000) 'The International Adult Literacy Survey: what does it really measure?', *International Review of Education* 46(5): 377–89.

Harding, A. and Greenwall, H. (2002) *Trends in Income and Expenditure Inequality in the 1980s and 1990s: A Re-examination and Further Results*, Canberra: National Centre of Social and Economic Modelling, University of Canberra.

Harding, S. (1991) *Whose Science? Whose Knowledge?*, Buckingham: Open University Press.

Haug, F. (ed.) (1987) *Female Sexualization: A Collective Work of Memory*, London: Verso.

Hayes, D., Mills, M., Christie, P. and Lingard, B. (2006) *Teachers and Schooling: Making a Difference*, Sydney: Allen and Unwin.

HEFCE (2000) *Diversity in Higher Education: HEFCE Policy Statement*, Bristol: HEFCE.

HEFCE (2005) *Young Participation in Higher Education*, Bristol: Higher Education Funding Council for England.

Henry, M., Lingard, B., Rizvi, F. and Taylor, S. (2001) *OECD and Education Policy*, Dordrecht: Kluwer Press.

Henwood, F. (1996) 'WISE Choices? Understanding occupational decision making in a climate of equal opportunities for women in science and technology', *Gender and Education* 8: 199–214.

Henwood, F. and Miller, K. (2001) 'Editorial: Boxed in or coming out? On the treatment of science, technology and gender in educational research', *Gender and Education*, 13(3): 237–242.

Hesford, W. and Kozol, W. (eds) (2005) *Just Advocacy: Women's Human Rights, Transnational Feminisms and the Politics of Representations*, New Brunswick, NJ: Rutgers University Press.

Hesse, B. (2000) *Un/Settled Multiculturalisms: Diasporas, Entanglements, Transruptions*, New York: Zed Books.

Hey, V. (2004) Joining the club?: Academia and working-class femininities', *Gender and Education* 15(3): 319–35.

Hill, D. (2002) 'Global neo-liberalism and the perversion of education', report for University College Northampton, The Institute for Education Policy Studies.

Hochschild, A. R. (1983) *The Managed Heart: Commercialization of Human Feeling*, Berkeley, CA: University of California Press.

Hodkinson, P. and James, D. (2003) 'Introduction: transforming learning cultures in further education', *Journal of Vocational Education and Training* 55(4): 389–406.

Holmes, J. and Meyerhoff, M. (1999) 'The community of practice: theories and methodologies in language and gender research', *Language in Society* 28(2): 173–83.

Hooghe, L. and Marks, G. (2001) *Multi-level Governance and European Integration*, Lanham, MD: Rowman and Littlefield.

hooks, b. (1991) *Yearning: Race, Gender and Cultural Politics*, London: Turnaround Press.

hooks, b. (1994) *Teaching to Transgress*, London: Routledge.

Hope, P. (2005) *Skills for All Programme Research 2001–2004: Policy Implications and Policy Impact*, London: LSE. http://www.dfes.gov.uk/speeches/speech.cfm?SpeechID=226 (accessed 1 August 2005.)

House of Commons Trade and Industry Committee (2005) *Jobs for the Girls: The Effect of Occupational Segregation on the Gender Pay Gap: Sixteenth Report of Session 2004–05*, London: The Stationery Office.

House of Representatives (2002) *Boys: Getting it Right: Report on the Inquiry of Education of Boys*, Canberra: Standing Committee on Education and Training.

Housee, S. (2004) 'Unveiling South Asian female identities post September 11: Asian female students' sense of identity and experiences of higher education', in I. Law, D. Phillips and L. Turney (eds) *Institutional Racism in Higher Education*, Stoke-on-Trent: Trentham Books.

Hughes, C. (2001) 'Developing conceptual literacy in lifelong learning research: a case of responsibility?' *British Educational Research Journal* 27(5): 601–14.

Hutchings, M. (2002) 'A representative profession? Gender issues', in M. Johnson and J. Hallgarten (eds) *From Victims of Change to Agents of Change: The Future of the Teaching Profession*, London: IPPR.

Ivanic, R. (1998) *Writing and Identity: The Discoursal Construction of Identity in Academic Writing*, Amsterdam and Philadelphia, PA: John Benjamins Publishing Company and John Benjamins North America.

Jachtenfuchs, M. (2001) 'The governance approach to European integration', *Journal of Common Market Studies* 39(2): 245–64.

Jackson, S. (2003) 'Lifelong earning: working-class women and lifelong learning', *Gender and Education* 15(4): 365–76.

Jackson, S. (2004a) *Differently Academic? Developing Lifelong Learning for Women in Higher Education*, Dordrecht: Kluwer Academic Publishers.

Jackson, S. (2004b) 'Who's sorry now? Lifelong learning and feminist activism', paper present at SCUTREA 34th Annual Conference, University of Sheffield.

Johnson, R. (1988) 'Really useful knowledge, 1790–1850', in T. Lovett (ed.) *Radical Approaches to Adult Education: A Reader*, London: Routledge.

Jones, L. G. and Jones, L. P. (1989) 'Context, confidence and the able girl', *Educational Research* 31: 189–94.

Josselson, R. (1995) 'Imagining the real: empathy, narrative and the dialogic self', in R. Josselson and A. Lieblich (eds) *Interpreting Experience: The Narrative Study of Lives*, vol. 3, Thousand Oaks, CA: Sage.

Kamler, B. (1999) 'The writing workshop as a space for relocating the personal', in B. Doecke (ed.) *Responding to Students' Writing: Continuing Conversations*, Norwood, SA: Australian Association for the Teaching of English, pp. 287–304.

Kamler, B. (2001a) 'We're not nice little old ladies', *Journal of Adolescent and Adult Literacy* 45(3): 232–5.

Kamler, B. (2001b) *Relocating the Personal: A Critical Writing Pedagogy*, Albany, NY: SUNY Press.

Kamler, B. and Feldman, S. (1995) 'Mirror mirror on the wall: reflections of ageing', *Australian Cultural History: Ageing* 14: 1–22.

Kamler, B. and Threadgold, T. (2003) 'Translating difference: questions of representation in cross-cultural research encounters', *Journal of Intercultural Studies* 24(2): 137–58.

Karmel, T. (2004) *Australia's Approach to Lifelong Learning*, Bonn: UNESCO.

Kelly, A. (1985) 'The construction of masculine science', *British Journal of Sociology of Education* 6: 133–54.

Kemp, D. (1999) 'Preparing youth for the 21st century: the policy lessons from the past two decades', paper presented in Washington, DC, 23–24 February.

Kempinch, B., Butler, E. and Billett, S. (1999) *Irreconcilable Differences? Women in Small Business and VET*, Kensington Park, SA: National Council for Vocational Education Research.

Kilminster, S. (1994) 'Changing working-class women's education: shifting ideologies'. Paper presented at the Annual SCUTREA Conference. Available on Education-line at: http://www.leeds.ac.uk/educol

Kilpatrick, S. and Abbott-Chapman, J. (2003) 'Rural young people's work/study priorities and aspirations; the influence of family social capital', *Australian Educational Researcher* 29(1): 43–63.

Kilpatrick, S., Field, J. and Falk, I. (2003) 'Social capital: an analytical tool for exploring LLL and community development', *British Educational Research Journal* 29(3): 417–33.

Kincheloe, J. (1995) *Toil and Trouble: Good Work, Smart Workers, and the Integration of Academic and Vocational education*, New York: Peter Lang.

Knight, B. (2004) 'Vocational learning in schools as an equity strategy', in K. Bowman (ed.) *Equity in Vocational Education and Training: Research Readings*, Adelaide: NCVER.

Lacey, C. (1977) *The Socialization of Teachers*, London: Methuen.

Lash, C. and Urry, J. (1993) *Economies of Signs and Space*, London: Sage.

Lave, J. and Wenger, E. (1991) *Situated Learning*, Cambridge: Cambridge University Press.

Law, I., Phillips, D. and Turney, L. (eds) (2004) *Institutional Racism in Higher Education*, Stoke-on-Trent: Trentham Books.

Lawler, S. (1999) 'Getting out and getting away: women's narratives of class and mobility', *Feminist Review* 63: 3–23.

Lawrence, K. (2005) *Helping People to Help Themselves: a Study of Training Issues for Aboriginal Women and Their Remote Communities in Central Australia*, Security4Women. Available at: http://www.security4women.com

Laws, G. (1995) 'Understanding ageism: lessons from feminism and postmodernism', *The Gerontologist* 15(1): 112–18.

Lea, M. R. and Street, B. (2000) 'Student writing and staff feedback in higher education: an academic literacies approach' in M. R. Lea and B. Stierer (eds) *Student Writing in Higher Education: New Contexts*, Buckingham: The Society for Research into Higher Education and Open University Press.

Leathwood, C. (2004) 'A critique of institutional inequalities in higher education (or an alternative to hypocrisy for higher educational policy)', *Theory and Research in Education* 2(1): 31–48.

Leathwood, C. (2005a) 'Accessing higher education: policy, practice and equity in widening participation in England', in I. McNay (ed.) *Beyond Mass Higher Education: Building on Experience*, Maidenhead: Open University Press.

Leathwood, C. (2005b) ' "Treat me as a human being – don't look at me as a woman": femininities and professional identities in further education', *Gender and Education* 17(4): 387–409.

Leathwood, C. (2006) 'Gender, equity and the discourse of the independent learner in higher education', *Higher Education*, forthcoming.

Leathwood, C. (2007) 'Gender equity in post-secondary education', in C. Skelton, B. Francis, and L. Smulyan (eds) *Handbook of Gender and Education*, London: Sage.

Leathwood, C. and Hayton, A. (2002) 'Educational inequalities in the United Kingdom: a critical analysis of the discourses and policies of New Labour', *Australian Journal of Education* 46(2): 138–53.

Leathwood, C. and Hutchings, M. (2003) 'Entry routes to higher education: pathways, qualifications and social class', in L. Archer, M. Hutchings, A. Ross, C. Leathwood, R. Gilchrist and D. Phillips (eds) *Higher Education and Social Class: Issues of Exclusion and Inclusion*, London: RoutledgeFalmer.

Leathwood, C. and O'Connell, P. (2003). ' "It's a struggle": the construction of the "new student" in higher education', *Journal of Educational Policy* 18(6): 597–615.

Levitas, R. (1998) *The Inclusive Society? Social Exclusion and New Labour*, Basingstoke: Macmillan Press.

Lewis, I. (2004) 14–19 Stakeholder speech, 9 July, DFES. http://www.dfes.gov.uk/speeches/search_detail.cfm?ID=133 (accessed 1 August 2005).

Lightbody, P. and Durndell, A. (1996) 'Gendered career choice: is sex-stereotyping the cause or the consequence?', *Educational Studies* 22: 133–46.

Lillis, T. (2001) *Student Writing: Access, Regulation, Desire*, London: Routledge.

Lillis, T. M. and Ramsey, M. (1997) 'Student status and the question of choice in academic writing', *Research and Practice in Adult Learning Bulletin* Spring(32): 15–22.

Livingstone, D. (1999a) 'Lifelong learning and underemployment in the knowledge society: a North American perspective', *Comparative Education* 35(2): 163–86.

Livingstone, D. (1999b) *The Education-jobs Gap: Underemployment or Economic Democracy*, Toronto: Garamond Press.

Long, M. and DSF (Dusseldorp Skills Forum) (2004) *How Young People Are Faring: Key Indicators. An Update about the Learning and Work Situation of Young Australians*, Sydney, DSF. http://www.dsf.org.au/papers/169/HYPAF_2004_FINAL_0.pdf (accessed 20 October 2004).

Lopez, G. and Scribner, J. (1999) 'Discourses of involvement: a critical review of parent involvement research', paper presented at AERA Annual Conference, Montreal.

Lopez, I. H. (1993) 'Community ties and law school faculty hiring: the case of professors who don't think white', in B. Thompson and S. Tyagi (eds) *Beyond a Dream Deferred: Multicultural Education and the Politics of Excellence*, Minnesota, MN: University of Minnesota Press.

Lucey, H., Melody, J. and Walkerdine, V. (1996) 'Videodiaries: developing a visual method for youth research', unpublished manuscript.

Lucey, H. and Reay, D. (2002) 'A market in waste: psychic and structural dimensions of school-choice policy in the UK and children's narratives on "demonised" schools', *Discourse* 23: 23–40.

Luttrell, W. (1997) *School-Smart and Mother-Wise: Working Class Women's Identity and Schooling*, London: Routledge.

Lyotard, J-F. (1984) *The Postmodern Condition: A report on Knowledge*, trans. G. Bennington and B. Massumi, Manchester: Manchester University Press.

Mac an Ghaill, M. (1996) 'What about the boys? Schooling, class and crisis of masculinity', *The Sociological Review* 44(3): 381–97.

Mace, J. (1998) *Talking about Literacy*, London: Routledge.

McGivney, V. (1999) *Excluded Men: Men Who Are Missing from Education and Training*, Leicester: National Institute of Adult Continuing Education.

Maclachlan, K. and Tett, L. (2005) 'Diversity, difference and the power to decide in literacies learning', *Proceedings of the SCUTREA Conference*, 2005.

Madden, A. (2004) 'Gendered subject choices', in H. Claire (ed.) *Gender in Education 3–19: A Fresh Approach*, London: ATL.

Mahony, P. and Hextall, I. (2001) 'Performing and conforming', in D. Gleeson and C. Husbands (eds) *The Performing School. Managing, Teaching and Learning in a Performance Culture*, London: RoutledgeFalmer.

Mahony, P. and Zmroczek, C. (eds) (1997) *Class Matters*, London: Taylor and Francis.

Majone, G. (1993) 'The European Community between social policy and social regulation', *Journal of Common Market Studies* 32(2): 153–70.

Malik, K. (1996) *The Meaning of Race: Race History and Culture in Western Society*, London: Macmillan Press.

Malik, K. (2003) 'The dirty D-word', *The Guardian*, 29 October.

Martin, I. (2001) 'Reconstituting the Agora: towards an alternative politics of lifelong learning', *Concept* 11(1): 4–8.

Menon, R. and Bhasin, K. (1998) *Borders and Boundaries: Women in India's Partition*, New Delhi: Kali for Women.

Metcalf, H. and Forth, J. (2000) *Business Benefits of Race Equality: Race Research for the Future*, Research Report no. 177, London: Department for Education and Employment (DfEE).

Miliband, D. (2005) 'Social exclusion: the next steps forward'. Speech at the London School of Economics, 29 November.

Miller, L. and Budd, J. (1999) 'The development of occupational sex-role stereotypes, occupational preferences and academic subject preferences of children aged 8, 12 and 16', *Educational Psychology* 19: 17–35.

Miller, L., Pollard, E., Neathey, F., Hill, D. and Ritchie, H. (2005) *Gender Segregation in Apprenticeships*, Manchester: Equal Opportunities Commission.

Mirza, H. S. (1992) *Young, Female and Black*, London: Routledge.

Mirza, H. S. (1995) 'Black women in higher education: defining a space/finding a place', in L. Morley and V. Walsh (eds) *Feminist Academics: Creative Agents for Change*, London: Taylor and Francis.

Mirza, H. S. (1997a) 'Introduction: mapping a genealogy of black British feminism', in H. S. Mirza (ed.) *Black British Feminism*, London: Routledge.

Mirza, H. S. (1997b) 'Black women in education: a collective movement for social change', in H. S. Mirza (ed.) *Black British Feminism*, London: Routledge.

Mirza, H. S. (2003) ' "All the women are white, all the blacks are men – but some of us are brave": mapping the consequences of invisibility for black and minority ethnic women in Britain', in D. Mason (ed.) *Explaining Ethnic Differences: Changing Patterns of Disadvantage in Britain*, Bristol: Policy Press.

Mirza, H. S. (2005) 'Race, gender and educational desire', inaugural professorial lecture, 17 May, Middlesex University. www.mdx.ac.uk/hssc/research/cres

Mirza, H. S. and Reay, D. (2000) 'Redefining citizenship: black women educators and "the third space" ', in M. Arnot and J. Dillabough (eds) *Challenging Democracy: International Perspectives on Gender*, London: RoutledgeFalmer.

Modood, T. and Acland, T. (eds) (1998) *Race and Higher Education*, London: Policy Studies Institute.

Mohanty, C. T. (1993) 'On race and voice: challenges for liberal education in the 1990s', in B. Thompson and S. Tyagi (eds) *Beyond a Dream Deferred: Multicultural Education and the Politics of Excellence*, Minnesota, MN: University of Minnesota Press.

Mohanty, C. T. (1994) 'On race and voice: challenges for liberal education in the 1990s', in H. Giroux and P. McLaren (eds) *Between Borders: Pedagogy and the Politics of Cultural Studies*, London: Routledge, pp. 145–66.

Mohanty, C. T. (2002) ' "Under Western eyes" revisited: feminist solidarity through anticapitalist struggles', *Signs: Journal of Women in Culture and Society* 28(2): 499–535.

Mojab, S. (1999) 'De-skilling immigrant women', *Canadian Woman Studies Journal* 19(3): 123–7.

Mojab, S. (2000) 'The power of economic globalization: deskilling immigrant women through training', in R. M. Cervero, and A. L. Wilson (eds) *Power in Practice: Adult Education and Struggle for Knowledge and Power in Society*, New York: Jossey-Bass, pp. 23–41.

Mojab, S. and Hassanpour, A. (2004) 'Kurdish diaspora', in I. Skoggard (ed.) *Encyclopedia of Diasporas*, New Haven, CT: Human Relations Area Files, pp. 214–24.

Mojab, S. and McDonald, S. (forthcoming) 'Women, violence and informal learning', in K. Church, N. Bascia, and E. Shragge (eds) *Making Sense of Lived Experience in Turbulent Times: Informal Learning*, Ontario: Wilfrid Laurier Press.

Morgan, D. H. J. (1992) *Discovering Men*, London: Routledge.

Morley, L. (1999) *Organising Feminisms: The Micropolitics of the Academy*, Basingstoke: Macmillan.

Morley, L. (2001) 'Producing new workers: quality, equality and employability in higher education', *Quality in Higher Education* 7(2): 131–8.

Morley, L. (2002) 'Lifelong yearning: feminist pedagogy in the learning society', in

G. Howe and A. Tauchert (eds) *Gender, Teaching and Research in Higher Education: Challenges for the 21st Century*, Aldershot: Ashgate, pp. 86–98.

Morley, L. (2003) *Quality and Power in Higher Education*, Buckingham: Open University Press.

Morris, R. (2001) *Learning Communities: A Review of Literature*, Working paper 01–32, Sydney: UTS Research Centre for Vocational Education and Training.

Morrison, T. (ed.) (1993) *Race-ing Justice, En-gendering Power: Essays on Anita Hill, Clarence Thomas and the Social Construction of Reality*, London: Chatto and Windus.

Moustakas, C. (1990) *Heuristic Research: Design, Methodology, and Applications*, Newbury Park, CA: Sage.

National Audit Office (2002) *Widening Participation in Higher Education in England*, HC 485, session 2001–2002, London: National Audit Office.

NCIHE (1997) *Higher Education in the Learning Society* (The Dearing Report), London: HMSO.

NIACE (National Institute of Adult Continuing Education) (2004) Report on lifelong learning. http://www.niace.org.uk/Information/Lifelong_Learning/Lifelong_learning.htm

NIACE (2005) *I Did it My Way: Journeys of Learning in Europe*, Leicester: NIACE.

Nias, J. (1989) *Primary Teachers Talking*, London: Routledge and Kegan Paul.

Nóvoa, A. and Lawn, M. (eds) (2002) *Fabricating Europe: The Formation of an Education Space*, Dordrecht: Kluwer.

OECD (1996) *Lifelong Learning For All*, Paris: OECD.

OECD (2000) *Literacy in the Information Age: Final Report of the International Adult Literacy Survey*, Paris: OECD.

Office of the Deputy Prime Minister (2004) *Tackling Social Exclusion: Taking Stock and Looking to the Future: Emerging Findings*, London: Social Exclusion Unit.

Oliver, M. (1990) *The Politics of Disablement*, Basingstoke: Macmillan.

Paechter, C. (1998) *Educating the Other: Gender, Power and Schooling*, London: Falmer Press.

Paechter, C. (2000) *Changing School Subjects: Power, Gender and Curriculum*, Buckingham: Open University Press.

Paechter, C. (2004) 'The gendered curriculum', in H. Claire (ed.) *Gender in Education 3–19: A Fresh Approach*, London: ATL.

Pang, M. (1999) 'The employment situation of young Chinese adults in the British labour market', *Personnel Review* 28: 41–57.

Parkes, S. M. (2004) *A Danger to the Men? A History of Women in Trinity College Dublin 1904–2004*, Dublin: Lilliput Press.

Payne, J. (2003) *Vocational Pathways at Age 16–19: An Analysis of the England and Wales Youth Cohort Study*, Nottingham: DfES.

Phillips, A. (1997) 'From inequality to difference: a severe case of displacement', *New Left Review* 224: 143–53.

Phoenix, A. (1996) 'Social constrictions of lone motherhood: a case of competing discourses', in Z. Bortolia Silva (ed.) *Good Enough Mothering?*, London: Routledge.

Pierre, J. (ed.) (2000) *Debating Governance: Authority, Steering and Democracy*, Oxford: Oxford University Press.

Pocock, B. (1998) *Demanding Skills: Women and Technical Education in Australia*, Sydney: Allen and Unwin.

Pocock, B. (2003) *The Work/Life Collision: What Work Is Doing to Australians and What to Do About It*, Sydney: Federation Press.

Pollack, M. A. (1997) 'The Commission as an agent', in N. Nugent (ed.) *At the Heart of the Union: Studies of the European Commission*, Basingstoke: Macmillan.

Pollack, M. A. (2001) 'International relations theory and European integration', *Journal of Common Market Studies* 39(2): 221–44.

Potts, P. (ed.) (2003) *Inclusion in the City. Selection, School and Community*, London: RoutledgeFalmer.

Probert, B. (2001) 'Grateful slaves' or 'self-made women': a matter of choice or policy? Clare Burton Lecture, RMIT, Melbourne.

Pusey, M. (2003) *The Experience of Middle Australia: The Dark Side of Economic Reform*, Sydney: Cambridge University Press.

Puwar, N. (2001) 'The racialised somatic norm and the senior Civil Service', *Sociology* 35(3): 351–70.

Puwar, N. (2004) 'Fish in or out of water: a theoretical framework for race and the space of academia', in I. Law, D. Phillips and L. Turney (eds) *Institutional Racism in Higher Education*, Stoke-on-Trent: Trentham Books.

Quay Connection (2003) *Choice, Participation, Outcomes: Women in VET 2003: Consultation Report*, prepared for ANTA, Canberra, March 2003.

Quinn, J. (2003) *Powerful Subjects: Are Women Really Taking over the University?*, Stoke-on-Trent: Trentham Books.

Ray, R. (1996) 'A postmodern perspective on feminist gerontology', *The Gerontologist* 36(5): 674–80.

Razack, S. (1998) *Looking White People in the Eye: Gender Race and Culture in Courtrooms and Classrooms*, Toronto: University of Toronto Press.

Read, B., Archer, L. and Leathwood, C. (2003) 'Challenging cultures? Student conceptions of "belonging" and "isolation" at a post-1992 university', *Studies in Higher Education* 28(3): 261–77.

Reay, D. (1997) 'The double-bind of the working class feminist academic: the success of failure or the failure of success?', In P. Mahony and C. Zmroczek (eds) *Class Matters*, London: Taylor and Francis.

Reay, D. (2002) 'Class, authenticity and the transition to higher education for mature working-class students', *Sociological Review* 50 (3): 396–416.

Reay, D., David, M. and Ball, S. (2005) *Degrees of Choice: Social Class, Race and Gender in Higher Education*, Stoke-on-Trent: Trentham Books.

Reay, D., Davies, J., David, M. and Ball, S. (2001) 'Choices of degree or degrees of choice? Class, race and the higher education choice process', *Sociology* 34: 855–74.

Reich, R. (1997) 'Why the rich are getting richer and the poor poorer', in A. Halsey, H., Lauder, P. Brown, and A. S. Wells (eds) *Education: Culture, Economy and Society*, Oxford: Oxford University Press, pp. 163–71.

Rhodes, R. (1997) *Understanding Governance: Policy Networks, Governance, Reflexivity and Accountability*, Philadelphia, PA: Open University Press.

Rice, M. and Brooks, G. (2004) *Developmental Dyslexia in Adults: A Research Review*, London: National Research and Development Centre for Adult Literacy and Numeracy.

Richardson, J. (1996) *European Union: Power and Policy-making*, London: Routledge.

Richardson, L. (1998) 'Writing: a method of inquiry', in N. K. Denzin and Y. S. Lincoln (eds) *Collecting and Interpreting Qualitative Materials*, Thousand Oaks, CA: Sage.

Riddell, S. (1992) *Polities and the Gender of the Curriculum*, London: Routledge.

Riddell, S., Brown, S. and Duffield, J. (1994) 'Conflicts of policies and models: the case of specific learning difficulties', in S. Riddell and S. Brown (eds) *Special Educational Needs Policy in the 1990s: Warnock in the Market Place*, London: Routledge.

Riddell, S., Tinklin, T. and Wilson, A. (2005) *Disabled Students in Higher Education: Perspectives on Widening Access and Changing Policy*, London: RoutledgeFalmer.

Riddell, S. and Watson, N. (eds) (2003) *Disability, Culture and Identity*, Harlow: Pearson Prentice Hall.

Rikowski, G. (1999) 'Nietzsche, Marx and mastery: the learning unto death', in P. Ainley and H. Rainbird (eds) *Apprenticeship: Towards a New Paradigm of Learning*, London: Kogan Page Limited.

Rikowski, G. (2001) 'Education for industry: a complex technicism', *Journal of Education and Work* 14(1): 29–49.

Rikowski, G. (2002) 'Fuel for the living fire: labour-power!', in A. C. Dinerstein and M. Neary (eds) *The Labour Debate: An Investigation into the Theory and Reality of Capitalist Work*, Avebury: Ashgate Publishing Limited.

Robertson, D. and Hillman, J. (1997) *Widening Participation in Higher Education for Students from Lower Socio-Economic Groups and Students with Disabilities*, Report 6 for the NCIHE, London: The Stationery Office.

Robson, J. (1998) 'Exploring the professional socialisation of teachers in further education: a case study', *Teacher Development* 2(1): 43–58.

Rolfe, H. (1999) *Gender Equality and the Careers Service*, Manchester: Equal Opportunities Commission.

Rolfe, H. (2005) *Men in Childcare*, Manchester: Equal Opportunities Commission.

Rose, M. (1998) 'The language of exclusion: writing instruction at the university', in V. Zamel and R. Spack (eds) *Negotiating Academic Literacies: Teaching and Learning Across Languages and Cultures*, Mahwah, NJ: Lawrence Erlbaum Associates, pp. 9–30.

Rose, N. (1999) *Powers of Freedom*, Cambridge: Cambridge University Press.

Rubin, B. and Silva, E. (eds) (2003) *Critical Voices in School Reform: Students Living Through Change*, London: RoutledgeFalmer.

Sanghatan, S. S. (1984) *We Were Making History: Women and the Telangana Uprising*, London: Zed Books.

Sanguinetti, J. (1998) 'Within and against performativity: discursive engagement in adult literacy and basic education', unpublished PhD thesis, Deakin University, Geelong, VIC.

Sargant, N. and Aldridge, F. (2003) *Adult Learning and Social Divisions: A Persistent Pattern*, vol. 2, Leicester: NIACE.

Scarr, S. (1998) 'American child care today', *American Psychologist* 53: 95–108.

Schneider-Ross Consultants (2001) *Equality in the University: Setting the New Agenda: A report on Equality Audit for Cambridge University*, Andover: Schneider-Ross Ltd.

Schuller, T. and Field, J. (1998) 'Social capital, human capital and the learning society', *International Journal of University Adult Education*. http://www.lib.unb.ca/Texts/JUAE/Schuller.html

Schwartz, S. (2004) *Fair Admissions to Higher Education: Recommendations for Good Practice*, London: Department for Education and Skills.

Scott, G. (1998) *Feminism and the Politics of Working Women*, London: UCL Press.

Scottish Executive (2000) *Scotland: The Learning Nation*, Edinburgh: The Stationery Office.

Scottish Executive (2001) *Adult Literacy and Numeracy in Scotland*, Edinburgh: The Stationery Office.

Shacklock, G. (2003) 'Networks at work? Embedding interagency working relationships in secondary schools', paper presented at NZARE/AARE Joint Annual Conference, Auckland.

Shacklock, G. (2004) ' "Sociable and employable?": the role of personal and school networks in managing students at risk', paper presented at the Australian Association for Research in Education, University of Melbourne, 28 November–2 December.

Shain, F. and Gleeson, D. (1999) 'Under new management: changing conceptions of teacher professionalism and policy in the further education sector', *Journal of Education Policy* 14(4): 445–62.

Sharpe, S. (1976) *Just Like a Girl*, Harmondsworth: Penguin.

Sharpe, S. (1994) *Just Like a Girl*, 2nd edn, Harmondsworth: Penguin.

Sideris, T. (2001) 'Problems of identity, solidarity and reconciliation', in S. Meintjes, A. Pillay and M. Turshen (eds) *The Aftermath: Women in Post-Conflict Transformation*, London: Zed Books, pp. 46–62.

Sikes, P. (1998) 'Parent teachers: reconciling the roles', *Teacher Development* 2(1): 87–105.

Simmonds, F. (1997) 'My body myself: how does a black woman do sociology?', in H. S. Mirza (ed.) *Black British Feminism*, London: Routledge.

Skeggs, B. (1997) *Formations of Class and Gender: Becoming Respectable*, London: Sage.

Skelton, C. (2001) *Schooling the Boys*, Buckingham: Open University Press.

Skelton, C. and Francis, B. (eds) (2005) *A Feminist Critique of Education*, London: Routledge.

Sklra, L. and Scheurich, J. (2004) *Educational Equity and Accountability: Paradigms, Policies and Politics*, London: RoutledgeFalmer.

Smith, D. (1997) 'From the margins: women's standpoint as a method of inquiry in the social sciences', *Gender, Technology and Development* 1(1): 113–35.

Smith, E. and Keating, J. (2003) *From Training Reform to Training Packages*, Canberra: Social Science Press.

Spender, S. (1982) *Invisible Women*, London: Writers and Readers.

Spivak, G. (1988) 'Can the subaltern speak?', in C. Nelson and L. Grossberg (eds) *Marxism and the Interpretation of Culture*, London: Macmillan.

Spivak, G. (1993) *Outside in the Teaching Machine*, New York: Routledge.

Stalker, J. (2001) 'Misogyny, women, and obstacles to tertiary education: a vile situation', *Adult Education Quarterly* 51(4): 288–305.

Stanworth, M. (1981) *Gender and Schooling*, London: Hutchinson.

Stories of Ageing Project (1999) *We're Not Nice Little Old Ladies*, Melbourne: City of Eira Council.

Strain, M. (2000) 'Schools in a learning society: new purposes and modalities of learning in late modern society', *Educational Management and Administration* 28(3): 281–98.

Street, B. (1984) *Literacy in Theory and Practice*, Cambridge: Cambridge University Press.

Street, B. (2001) 'The New Literacy studies', in E. Cushman, E. R. Kintgen, B. M. Kroll and M. Rose (eds) *Literacy: A Critical Sourcebook*. Boston and New York: Bedford/St Martin's, pp. 430–42.

Street, P. (2005) *Segregated Schools: Educational Apartheid in Post-Civil Rights America*, London: Routledge.

Sudbury, J. (2001) '(Re)constructing multicultural blackness: women's activism, difference and collective identity in Britain', *Ethnic and Racial Studies* 24(1): 29–49.

Summerfield, G. and Aslanbeigui, A. (1998) 'The impact of structural adjustment and economic reform on women', in N. Stromquist (ed.) *Women in the Third World*, New York and London: Garland Publishing.

Swindells, J. (1995) 'Are we not more than half the nation? Women and "the radical tradition" of adult education, 1867–1919', in M. Mayo and J. Thompson (eds) *Adult Learning, Critical Intelligence and Social Change*, Leicester: NIACE.

Taylor, R. (2005) 'Lifelong learning and the Labour governments, 1997–2004', *Oxford Review of Education* 31(1): 101–18.

Teese, R. (2002) *The Cultural Benefits of VET for Early School Leavers*, Melbourne: Educational Outcomes Research Unit, University of Melbourne.

Teese, R. and Polesel, J. (2003) *Undemocratic Schooling*, Sydney: Allen and Unwin.

Tennant, M., Chappel, C., Solomon, N., Yates, L. and Rhodes, C. (2004) *Reconstructing the Lifelong Worker*, London: Routledge.

Tett, L. (2002) *Community Education, Lifelong Learning and Social Exclusion*, Edinburgh: Dunedin Press.

Tett, L. (2003) 'Education and community health: identity, social justice and lifestyle issues in communities', in C. Vincent (ed.) *Social Justice, Education and Identity*, London: RoutledgeFalmer, pp. 83–96.

Tett, L. (2004) 'Literacy, learning and social inclusion', in *Proceedings of the 4th ESREA Research Conference Sections 3–4*, Wroclaw, Poland: ESREA.

Thomas, E. (2001) *Widening Participation in Post-Compulsory Education*, London: Continuum.

Thomas, K. (1990) *Gender and Subject in Higher Education*, Buckingham: Open University Press.

Thompson, J. (1995) 'Feminism and women's education', in M. Mayo and J. Thompson (eds) *Adult Learning, Critical Intelligence and Social Change*, Leicester: NIACE, pp. 124–36.

Thompson, J. (1997) ' "Really useful knowledge": linking theory and practice', in J. Thompson (ed.) *Words in Edgeways: Radical Learning for Social Change*, Leicester: NIACE.

Thompson, J. (2000) 'Life politics and popular learning', in J. Field and M. Leicester, (eds) *Lifelong Learning: Education across the Lifespan*, London: RoutledgeFalmer, pp. 134–45.

Thompson, J. (2001) *Re-rooting Lifelong Learning*, Leicester: NIACE.

Tietze, W., Cryer, D., Bairrao, J., Palacios, J. and Wetzel, G. (1996) 'Comparisons of observed process quality in early child care and education programmes in five countries', *Early Childhood Research Quarterly* 11(4): 447–75.

Times Educational Supplement (2005) 'Women boost student numbers', 'FE Focus', 15 July, p. 1.

Times Higher Education Supplement (2004) 'Distinct lack of ebony in ivory towers', 22 October.

Toynbee, P. (2003) *Hard Work: Life in Low-Pay Britain*, London: Bloomsbury.

Turner, B. (1984) *The Body and Society: Explorations in Social Theory*, Oxford: Basil Blackwell.

Turshen, M. (1998) 'Women's war stories', in M. Turshen and C. Twagiramariya (eds) *What Women Do in Wartime*, London: Zed Books, pp. 1–26.

Usher, R. and Edwards, R. (1998) 'Confessing all? A postmodern guide to the counselling and guidance of adult learners', in R. Edwards, R. Harrison and A. Tait (eds) *Telling Tales: Perspectives on Guidance and Counselling in Learning*, London: Routledge.

Vadgama, K. (2004) Cornelia Sorabji lecture at the seminar, 'Politics and pioneers of South Asian history', Museum of London, 27 March.

Vinson, T. (2004) *Community, Adversity and Resilience*, Sydney: The Ignatius Centre for Social Policy.

Viskovic, A. and Robson, J. (2001) 'Community and identity: experiences and dilemmas of vocational teachers in post-school contexts', *Journal of In-Service Education* 27(2): 221–36.

Visram, R. (2002) *Asians in Britain: 400 Years of history*, London: Pluto Press.

Walby, S. (2005) 'Gendering life-long learning and the knowledge economy', paper presented to the ESRC Seminar Series, Gender and Lifelong Learning, at the University of the West of England, Bristol, March.

Walkerdine, V. (1990) *Schoolgirl Fictions*, London: Verso.

Walkerdine, V. (1992) 'Progressive pedagogy and political struggle', in C. Luke and J. Gore (eds) *Feminisms and Critical Pedagogy*, London: Routledge.

Walkerdine, V. (2003) 'Reclassifying upward mobility: femininity and the neoliberal subject', *Gender and Education* 15: 237–47.

Walkerdine, V. and the Girls and Mathematics Unit (1989) *Counting Girls Out*, London: Virago.

Walkerdine, V., Lucey, H. and Melody, J. (1999) 'Class, attainment and sexuality in late twentieth-century Britain', in C. Zmroczek and P. Mahony (eds) *Women and Social Class: International Feminist Perspectives*, London: UCL Press, pp. 51–67.

Walkerdine, V., Lucey, H. and Melody, J. (2002) *Growing Up Girl*, London: Macmillan.

Waring, M. (1989) *If Women Counted: A New Feminist Economics*, London: Macmillan.

Waslander, S. (1995) 'Choice, competition and segregation: an analysis of a New Zealand secondary school market', *Journal of Education Policy* 16(1): 1–26.

Watson, L. (1999) *Lifelong Learning in Australia: Analysis and Prospects*, Discussion Paper No 1, Canberra: Lifelong Learning Network, University of Canberra.

Watson, N. (2002) ' "Well, I know this is going to sound very strange to you, but I don't see myself as a disabled person": identity and disability', *Disability and Society* 17(5): 509–29.

Weiner, G. (1993) *Feminisms in Education*, Buckingham: Open University Press.

Westwood, S. (1990) 'Racism, black masculinity and the politics of space' in J. Morgan and D. Hearn (eds) *Men, Masculinities and Social Theory*, London: Unwin Hyman.

WEU (2002) *Key Indicators of Women's Position in Britain*. Available at: http://www.womenandequalityunit.gov.uk

Whitehead, J. (1996) 'Sex stereotypes, gender identity and subject choice at "A"-level', *Educational Research* 38: 147–60.

Whitehead, S. and Moodley, R. (eds) (1999) *Transforming Managers. Gendering Change in the Public Sector*, London: UCL Press.

Wikeley, F. and Stables, A. (1999) 'Change in school students' approaches to subject option choices', *Educational Research* 41: 287–99.

Williams, J. (1997) 'The discourse of access: the legitimisation of selectivity', in J. Williams (ed.) *Negotiating Access to Higher Education: The Discourse of Selectivity and Equity*, Buckingham: The Society for Research into Higher Education and the Open University Press.

Williams, P. J. (1991) *The Alchemy of Race and Rights: The Diary of a Law Professor*, Cambridge, MA: Harvard University Press.

Williams, P. J. (1997) *Seeing a Colour-Blind Future: The Paradox of Race*, New York: Noonday Press.

Williams, R. (1961) *Resources for a Journey of Hope*, Harmondsworth: Penguin.

Williams, R. M. (1993) 'Race, deconstruction and the emergent agenda of feminist economic theory', in M. A. Ferber and J. A. Nelson (eds) *Beyond Economic Man: Feminist Theory and Economics*, Chicago, IL: University of Chicago Press, pp. 144–53.

Willis, P. (1977) *Learning to Labour: How Working Class Kids Get Working Class Jobs*, Farnborough: Saxon House.

Yates, L. (2004) 'Creating identities in the new vocationalism: rhetoric, regulation, reproduction and repositioning in Australian schooling', *British Educational Research Association Annual Conference*, Paper presented at University of Manchester, 16–18 September. Available on Education-line at: http://www.leeds.ac.uk/educol.

Yeaxlee, B. A. (1929) *Lifelong Education*, London: Cassell.

Young, I. M. (1990) *Justice and the Politics of Difference*, Princeton, NJ: Princeton University Press.

Young, M. and Spours, K. (1997) 'Unifying academic and vocational learning and the idea of a learning society', *Journal of Education Policy* 12(6): 527–37.

Young, R. (1995) *Colonial Desire: Hybridity in Theory, Culture and Race*, London: Routledge.

Zmroczek, C. (1999) 'Class, gender and ethnicity: snapshots of a mixed heritage', in P. Mahony and C. Zmroczek (eds) *Women and Social Class: International Feminist Perspectives*, London: UCL Press.

Index

Gouthro, P.A. 46
Government Support Training 60
Greed, C. 77
Greenwall, H. 20, 25

Hakim, C. 19
Hall, Stuart 142, 147
Halpin, D. 102
Hamburg Declaration on Adult Learning
   165–6, 175
Hamilton, M. 99, 102
Harding, A. 20, 25
Harding, S. 60
Hassanpour, A. 164, 168
Haug, Frigga 153, 156
Hayes, D. 15
Hayton, A. 42
hegemonic identities 75
Henry, M. 11, 13
Henwood, F. 67
Hermerschmidt, M. 88, 89, 91, 92
Hesford, W. 13
Hesse, B. 76
heterosexual femininity 79
Hextall, I. 13, 21
Hey, V. 78
'high tech' manufacturing industry 37
higher education: classed and masculine
   culture 78; masculinities and non-
   participation 73–6; middle-class
   masculinity and 74–5; non-
   participation and femininities 76–81;
   participation 70–1; undesirable middle-
   class femininities 79–81; working-class
   femininity within educational discourse
   77–8
Higher Education and Social Class study 72
Higher Education Contribution Scheme
   19
Higher Education Funding Council for
   England (HEFCE) 141
Hill, Anita 145
Hill, D. 166
Hillman, J. 70
historic materialism 180
Hochschild, A.R. 116, 117, 118
Hodkinson, P. 110, 166
Holmes, J. 110
home–school discourses 9–10
Hooghe, L. 29
hooks, bell 52, 140, 148–9
hope 102–5

hospitality industry 48
Housee, Shirin 146
Hughes, C. 116, 117
human capital theory 13, 43, 173, 176
human rights infringements 13
Hutchings, M. 50, 61, 66, 72, 81

Identities and Inequalities study 72, 74
identities, teachers' biographies and
   109–10; case study 110–19;
   transforming practice and identity
   117–19
identity 10, 26, 50; social categories and
   122–3
immigrant women, war, diaspora and
   164–75
inclusion 25
independence 47–8
Indian Suffragettes 138–9
individualism 31
industry discourses 9
informal learning 174
information and communication
   technology 31
information society learner 31
International Adult Literacy Survey
   (IALS) 99–100
International Monetary Fund (IMF) 11
Ivanic, R. 89

Jachtenfuchs, M. 28, 29
Jackson, S. 40, 44, 45, 49, 52
James, D. 110
Janne Report (Council of Europe) 27
JIVE 67
Johnson, R. 105
Jones, L.P. 65
Jones, L.G. 65
Josselson, R. 110

Kamler, B. 155, 156, 157, 160
Karmel, T. 9
Keating, J. 16
Kelly, A. 59
Kemp, David 154
Kempinch, B. 25
Kilminster, S. 50–1
Kilpatrick, S. 10, 25, 26
Kincheloe, J. 15
Knight, B. 9
knowledge-based economy 32, 33
knowledge creation 37